The Forgotten Generation

BERG FRENCH STUDIES

General Editor: John E. Flower

ISSN: 1354-3636

The Forgotten Generation
French Women Writers of the Inter-war Period

Jennifer E. Milligan

BERG
Oxford • New York

First published in 1996 by
Berg Publishers Limited
Editorial offices:
150 Cowley Road, Oxford, OX4 1JJ, UK
70 Washington Square South, New York, NY 10012, USA

Berg is the imprint of Oxford International Publishers Ltd.

Library of Congress Cataloging-in-Publication Data

A catalogue record for this book is available from the Library of Congress.

British Library Cataloguing-in-Publication Data

A catalogue record for this book is available from the British Library.

ISBN 1 85973 113 9 (Cloth)
1 85973 118 X (Paper)

Typeset by JS Typesetting, Wellingborough, Northants.
Printed in the United Kingdom by WBC Book Manufacturers, Bridgend,
Mid Glamorgan.

For Mark and Jenny

with love and thanks

Contents

Acknowledgements

I would like to express my gratitude to Elizabeth Fallaize, Jean-Yves Tadié, Christopher Robinson, Mike Holland, Ann Jefferson, David Roe, Adrianne Tooke and Diana Holmes who all played a part in advising me at various stages in this book's development. Christopher's stimulating thoughts on earlier French women writers and Elizabeth's informed and enthusiastic guidance were always much appreciated. It is also a pleasure to acknowledge those who helped me track down primary works: John and Rita Bastin, Claudia Pazos-Alonso, the librarians of the Taylorian Institution in Oxford and of the Bibliothèque Marguerite Durand in Paris, as well as the Left Bank book dealers who are too numerous to mention individually. My very special thanks go to my mother and my husband for their encouragement, support and love, without which this book would have been impossible.

Introduction: A Retrospective Overview

Some books are undeservedly forgotten, none are undeservedly remembered.

W.H. Auden, 'Reading', *The Dyer's Hand* (1968)

In October 1928, in two polemical papers addressed to female students at Newnham College and Girton College, Cambridge on the subject of 'Women and Fiction', Virginia Woolf singled out the rise of the middle-class woman writer at the end of the eighteenth century as a crucial turning point in the history of the *production* of female-authored literature.[1] Some forty years after the publication of *A Room of One's Own* (1929), a similarly momentous change occurred in the *reception* of female-authored literature. Concomitant with the rise of the international women's movement in the late 1960s, a significant number of academics became more fully conscious that women writers had, as Showalter puts it, 'a literature of their own, whose historical, thematic coherence, as well as artistic importance, had been obscured by the patriarchal values that dominate our culture'.[2] This new generation of feminist critics, taking up where Woolf laid off, set themselves the extensive task of redressing the situation. Over the past three decades, while the specific areas investigated have varied considerably, one of the most striking aspects in this general field of critical inquiry has been the large-scale retrieval, re-reading and re-evaluation of female-authored literature from all nations and historical periods. French women's writing in the main has been well served by this process. A considerable amount of serious attention has been, and continues to be, focused on the nineteenth century and the contemporary scene. Anglo-American feminist critics especially have shown a marked interest in the works of recent women writers such as Simone de Beauvoir, Nathalie Sarraute, Marguerite Duras, Françoise Mallet-Joris, Françoise Sagan, Christiane Rochefort, Monique Wittig, Annie Leclerc, Chantal Chawaf, Violette Leduc, Marie Cardinal, Anne Hébert, Claire Etcherelli, Annie Ernaux, Jeanne

Hyvrard and Marie Redonnet.[3] Yet despite the current preoccupation
with reviving neglected generations of women authors, and the keen
interest in feminist advances in the literary environment, many critics
remain somewhat indifferent or oblivious to women's literary endeav-
ours and achievements in France in the first half of the century. This
epoque as a whole, and the 1920s and 1930s in particular, remains
largely uncharted.

One factor which contributes to the continued disregard for this
period is the fact that certain distinguished members of the critical
establishment, most notably Peyre in his influential study *The Contemporary French Novel*, Cixous in her manifesto 'Le Rire de la Méduse'
and more recently Suleiman in *Subversive Intent: Gender, Politics and
the Avant-garde*, affirm that in this earlier period few French women
writers produced literature of sufficient calibre to merit detailed study.
Peyre sums up women's contribution to the French literary scene in
the comment 'France had until lately relatively few women writers
of towering eminence.'[4] Cixous, who throws into question the value
of the entire enterprise of retrospective archival research, similarly
denies the existence of any worthwhile female literary production
prior to the 1970s in the comment:

> After ploughing through literature of different periods, languages and
> cultures, one is always left feeling frightened by this almost pointless
> scouting mission: it is well known that the number of women writers
> (while having grown a very little from the nineteenth century), has always
> been derisory. [This is followed by the footnote:] Flicking through what
> twentieth-century France has allowed to be written, and it is not much
> (have you noticed our infinite poverty in this field? Anglo-Saxon countries
> have clearly had far greater resources), I have only seen female writing
> produced by Colette, Marguerite Duras . . . and Jean Genet.[5]

Suleiman too dismisses early twentieth-century French female writers.
Here again, as in the overview provided by both Peyre and Cixous,
Colette figures as an almost singular anomaly:

> The sad fact is that with the single major exception of Colette (and perhaps
> Anna de Noailles, who never achieved the same degree of recognition),
> there were no outstanding women writers in France in the first half of the
> century, and certainly none who had the tenacity to construct an *œuvre*
> (much less the kind of innovative rule-breaking *œuvre* that can be qualified
> as 'avant-garde' and that requires the self confidence of, say, a Gertrude
> Stein) until Simone de Beauvoir.[6]

Such critics are not in a minority. Many anthologisers, literary historians and critics, even those who are, like Suleiman, explicitly involved in correcting the marginalization of women authors, tend to concur on this portrayal of early twentieth-century French female writers. There is an underlying assumption that quality writing of female authorship only emerged, evolved and reached maturity in the second half of the twentieth century. The first half of the century, in contrast, is habitually portrayed as being stagnant, sterile and silent. This has no doubt dissuaded many would-be scholars in the area.

A second impediment lies in the fact that although our temporal displacement today does provide the advantage of a more panoramic overview, much that went unrecorded in the 1920s and 1930s is lost to us forever. Access to primary material itself is complicated, as female-authored works of the period between the two wars, especially popular romances which were originally produced in relatively inexpensive editions, are not all available from libraries, because the *dépot légal* system was not fully operational in the 1920s. Anne Sauvy cites the specific example of Maryan (not to be confused with Mayran):[7] only three of her ninety-four published novels are kept in the Bibliothèque Nationale, despite its status as a copyright library.[8] A related problem is the widespread use of pseudonyms, which prohibit the establishment of exact statistics on the number of female authors active in the era. Throughout the nineteenth century it was fairly common practice for women to attempt to mask their identities. In the early part of the nineteenth century pen names were chosen to conceal the author's social standing; in the late part of the nineteenth century, as in Great Britain and the United States, pseudonyms were often employed to conceal gender[9] (perhaps to avoid public censure over the pursuit of what was still considered by many an unorthodox female profession, or to circumvent the possibility of publishers' gender bias). This continued well into the Inter-war period when a number of women chose to write under asexual single names[10] and more still opted for explicitly male names.[11] The technical difficulties which result from this may also have discouraged critics from investigating the area.

Yet notwithstanding these deterrents, the recent general upsurge of feminist consciousness has lead to some improvement in the field. Over the last twenty years, a number of publishing houses, including the separatist Editions des Femmes (founded in 1973) and Tierce (founded in 1977), have played an important part in promoting feminist studies, in reissuing out-of-print women-centred texts,[12] and in opening up this area to new generations of readers.[13] There has, for example, been a sharp increase in historical research into the position of women in France during the years between the wars,[14] and, in addition to this, there have emerged an assortment of highly informative studies on individual Inter-war literary figures. Gyp, Lucie Delarue-Mardrus, Rachilde, Gérard d'Houville, Colette, Irène Némirovsky, Catherine Pozzi, Marthe de Bibesco, Elsa Triolet, Clara Malraux, Isabelle Rivière, Marguerite Yourcenar and Louise de Vilmorin have all been the subject of interesting recent monographic biographies.[15] The feature common to a number of these studies is the demand for a critical reappraisal of the author's literary works. Mackinnon describes Elsa Triolet as 'a fascinating figure in her own right, an unduly neglected writer'.[16] Chalon, in the comment 'Louise de Vilmorin is yet to be discovered', suggests that a critical work examining her poetry and fiction is long awaited.[17] Montreynaud reflects that Anna de Noailles 'deserves a rediscovery'.[18] Newman-Gordon notes that 'the corpus of Mardrus's writing awaits fresh evaluation'.[19] Dauphiné, in his study of Rachilde, remarks that she has not been recorded properly in the annals of posterity, claiming that literary histories have done little justice to her works, her sparkling personality, her influence and her impact on the period in which she wrote. In response to this, he demands a reappraisal: 'there too a rediscovery is essential'.[20] These sentiments echo earlier critical studies. Lalou, writing in 1947, refers to the works of Marcelle Sauvageot and Denise Fontaine as having 'prematurely disappeared'.[21] David, presenting Georges de Peyrebrune as 'the current George Sand', comments on 'the total neglect into which her works have fallen'.[22] La Rochefoucauld remarks that Anna de Noailles deserves a greater readership to appreciate her undisputable genius.[23] From the enumeration of demands for reappraisals, it is clear that, although many individual authors do deserve an analytical retrospective (just as many of their works unquestionably merit republication), the problem of women from this period being overlooked is not specific to isolated writers.

In 1929 when the literary historian Larnac published his *Histoire de la littérature féminine en France*, he commented on the need for a comprehensive, well-documented critical and bibliographical overview of the literary achievements of his female peers.[24] To date, no single work has emerged in response to the challenge thrown down by Larnac and these biographers. Even with renewed interest in the period, in the lives and achievements of specific writers, and in the recent reissuing of Inter-war texts, the total redress Larnac demands has not yet been realized. There has been no major endeavour to record and reassess the wide range of female-authored literature of the Inter-war era, no attempt to recapture and preserve the memory of this group of women writers. As a direct result of this, French women's literary contribution in the period continues to be largely ignored by both the critical establishment and the general public; these women writers still remain a 'Forgotten Generation'.

This lacuna in the narrative of literary history gives rise to a peculiar form of canon deformation. In most works covering the period to date, an elite core of writers (habitually comprising Noailles, Colette, Rachilde and Yourcenar) is singled out, sustaining the illusion of the French canon as 'a landscape composed of *isolated monuments* that loom out of an ahistoric past and a social vacuum'.[25] The re-inscription of only these few privileged authors does French literature a major injustice. Not only does it fail to provide an informed, accurate and comprehensive overview of writing in the era, it also effectively undercuts any sense of collective identity or continuity in women's writing in its entirety. As Showalter puts it, 'each generation of women writers has found itself, in a sense without a history, forced to rediscover the past anew, forging again and again the consciousness of their sex.'[26] It follows that one of the major benefits of studying the Forgotten Generation (and juxtaposing prominent canonized and popular writers) is that some of the missing links in the chronicles of literary history will be filled. This should help create a greater sense of cohesion in women's literary heritage, and should facilitate the reshaping of our prevalent perceptions of French women's writing as a whole.

Before embarking on the redress of the adverse effects of canon deformation, before retrieving into prominence authors who have been consigned to the margins of literary history, and before re-reading their neglected works, we first need to understand the precise nature of the historical period in which these women wrote. We need to put their thematic, aesthetic and generic interests in context. We need to investigate the social, political and cultural determinants of their writing, asking what France, and more specifically the position of French women, was like in the Inter-war period. According to popular mythology, the 1920s, known even at the time as the 'Années Folles', was a utopic golden age of opportunity, where everything seemed possible, and fame and fortune appeared to be there for the taking. The literary historian Simon writes that Paris had never been so brilliant, attractive and fertile as in the 1920s.[27] Sachs calls it 'a perpetual 14th of July'.[28] Brody, more recently, continues in the same vein, describing Paris as an 'incredible cultural kaleidoscope', an 'intellectual and artistic Mecca', a 'melting pot that (. . .) offered an ambience and an atmosphere in which musicians, artists and writers flourished in symbiotic relationships'; in short it was 'the cultural centre of Europe in the years between the wars'.[29] This was without question a fascinating period in French cultural history, and Paris did indeed exert an almost magical magnetic attraction in the era, drawing many people from far and wide to its cosmopolitan heart. There followed successive influxes of immigrants from Russia during the Revolution, from Spain at the time of the Civil War, from Germany in the lead-up to the Second World War, and most notably from the United States. Americans had been coming to France in droves since the 1870s, and following the Great War ever-increasing numbers of expatriates converged on Paris. With some relaxation of the sexual code, which now allowed a degree of sexual experimentation at least among the privileged classes,[30] the image of Paris as the capital of tolerance attracted a number of emancipated writers and artists who sought to escape what they considered to be their puritanically restrictive and culturally deprived homeland.[31] The most renowned of these, the body of Anglo-American avant-garde Modernists, who made up the 'Lost Generation', included many celebrated women writers such as Edith Wharton, Gertrude Stein, Anaïs Nin, Mina Loy, Hilda Doolittle, Djuna Barnes, Nathalie Barney, Janet Flanner, Sylvia Beach, Katherine Mansfield from New Zealand, and Jean Rhys of the Dominican Republic. The very names of these writers conjure images of jazz clubs, cocktails, leisure, daring fashion, hedonism and light-hearted gaiety.

Such a picture is not representative of rural or provincial life in the period, nor, for that matter, does it reflect the reality of the experience of the average Parisian. Forbes and Kelly remove the veneer and draw a very different portrait of the French in the aftermath of the Great War: 'beneath the delight in the modern, and the frenetic enjoyment of freedom, there lay a growing melancholy and a sense of emptiness'. It is in this period that the name 'Belle Epoque' was coined for the earlier decades of the century, as people sought to regain a lost sense of security, harmony and prosperity. This nostalgic escapist desire to return to a brighter past, together with the enthusiastic pursuit of excess and self-indulgence in the present, signal an underlying aware-ness that the current situation was far from auspicious, and within a few years of the 1918 armistice it was abundantly clear to most French citizens that there could be no turning back of the clocks. The Great War had irrevocably changed French society, and the ensuing years proved to be some of the most tumultuous in France's political, economic, social and cultural history.[32]

The impact of the war was devastating: 17.5 per cent of the active male population did not return from the trenches, 3 million were wounded, 130,000 mutilated or amputated.[33] This legacy compounded what was perceived to be a demographic crisis. Although Europe's share of the world population had increased steadily from 1800, this growth was not evenly distributed within Europe, which affected the standing of the great powers. Despite the writings of Malthus, military and economic strength were still equated with manpower. In 1800 France had been the most densely populated country in Europe; by 1915 it ranked fifth, well behind Germany.[34] To some extent the problem of the falling birthrate had been masked by the lowering of mortality rates (resulting from medical advances in the treatment of diphtheria, scarlet fever, typhoid and whooping-cough), but the annihilation of the war accentuated the problem as never before. French authorities were haunted by the loss of a generation of young men and by the spectre of depopulation, envisaging it as a threat to national security, and as a severe impediment for industrial recovery. In economic terms the war had been costly to France, and although in the following years the country underwent unparalleled industrial expansion as it asserted its position as an advanced capitalist society and embraced mass-consumerism, technocrats worried about the devalued, unstable franc and escalating inflation. The 'Années Folles' soon became the 'Années Grises de Crises' (the Grey Years of Crisis). By early 1931 bankruptcy drove in epidemic waves through Europe following the Wall Street Crash of 1929, and any remaining illusions of prosperity were shattered as the country plummeted into the worst economic depression of recent times: more than half the French population lived in sprawling cities suffering all the ills of a major housing crisis, 6 per cent of the population were immigrants and unemployment was elevated. Concerns over economic and military weakness intensified in the 1930s, following the accession of Adolf Hitler to the Chancellorship of Germany, and as Forbes and Kelly put it, 'there was a dawning suspicion that the post-war had slipped into another pre-war'.[35]

But it was not just on the economic and military fronts that France was left vulnerable. The war had left a profound imprint too on the nation's political, social and cultural well-being. For the generation of young soldiers returning from the trenches who had witnessed the brutal unremitting carnage, there was a fundamental questioning and reassessment of the very beliefs for which they had gone to war. Some, like the Surrealists André Breton, René Crevel, Benjamin Péret, Paul Eluard, Louis Aragon and Philippe Soupault, in a spirit of bitter, angry, violent rebellion, attempted to sweep clean the past, to eradicate the old values and what they saw as the *ancien régime* of the mind. For some disaffected veterans, the October Revolution, the deposition of the

Tsar and the insurrection of the Russian army symbolized the smashing of yesterday's idols. The foundation of the French Communist Party in 1920, which inspired a sense of idealism in its celebration of the cult of youth, attracted writers such as Paul Nizan, Henri Barbusse and Louis Aragon. Radical political activism flourished too on the right with the continued strength of the pro-fascist Action française, founded by Charles Maurras. This was clearly a time of extremes, and uncertainties; it seemed to many that civilization had gone mad.

Roberts, in her historical survey *Civilization Without Sexes: Reconstructing Gender in Postwar France, 1917–1927*, convincingly argues that gender issues provided a means of allowing the French to conceptualize and discuss the purpose, significance and consequences of the war, and to negotiate and accede to the inevitable political and social reorganization of French society. It is unsurprising that women should have become a focus in this way; their situation in 1918 offered easily assimilated, tangible evidence of change. Although gender roles had already undergone some evolution in the nineteenth and early twentieth centuries, this development had been accelerated with the military and economic exigences of the war. As in Great Britain, the government had encouraged women to play an active part in replacing the soldiers at the front, by working on the land, in the railways, in munitions factories or in reserved jobs on the home front. In the period immediately following the war, although there is no statistical evidence to support any increase in the number of women in the workforce, the type of employment women undertook did alter in a significant way. Working-class women left domestic service for jobs in the tertiary sector and middle-class women moved into the liberal professions. In both cases they became more visible in the public sphere, and the impression this created was intensified by innovations in the world of fashion. For many, the demands of war had meant that less time could be spent on pretty Belle Epoque *haute couture*; clothes had to be off-the-peg, time-saving, practical and non-restrictive (in theory, if not always in practice). The *midinettes* embraced the popular new look of boyish, easy-to-manage, cropped hair and shorter, straighter dresses. This style, which reflected the emergence of women from the domestic sphere and their entry into the workforce, was read by many as an attack on traditional values, as a sign of virilization and as a statement of emancipation. Women were seen to be progressing away from prescriptive nineteenth-century notions of womanhood towards greater independence, autonomy and self-definition.[36]

For writers, journalists, social observers, demographers, legislators, economists and reformers alike, the instability of gender relations became an issue of paramount importance. For instance, much male-authored literature of the early 1920s depicts disillusioned war veterans, unable to cope with the devastating legacy of war and the resultant dislocated patterns of conventional social behaviour. Roberts suggests that for a number of these writers the war had resulted in a direct reversal of the doctrine of the separate spheres. Women in wartime had been released from the cloistered domestic realm; they had become free to engage in work outside the home. Men, in contrast, had had to give up their social and sexual liberties; they had been confined to the trenches and tight army regulations. Newspapers and magazines of the period also showed a preoccupation with debating the issues of female identity. They provided endless commentaries, for example, on the impact of Victor Marguerite's *La Garçonne* (1922), on suffrage, *la crise du foyer* (the problem of working mothers), divorce, adultery, single motherhood, polygamy, abortion, maternal care and the 'problem' of the supposedly legion numbers of single women. The tremendous amount of space given over to the discussion of such topics reflected the growing realization that there had to be a major reassessment of the social organization of gender. This lay at the forefront of political thought in the period, and in parliament three areas in particular proved to be of especial interest: suffrage, the distribution of labour and the redefinition of the family unit.

The first major area of debate in the period concerned political representation for women. Between 1915 and 1922 women in nineteen European countries and the United States received universal suffrage, in many cases as state recognition of their efforts during the war. Great Britain, for example, witnessed in 1918 the establishment of franchise rights for women over thirty and for all women in 1928; in America woman voted as of 1920. In total contrast, French women, on a par with Bulgarians, Italians, Swiss and Yugoslavians, were denied this fundamental right. Suffragette organizations were active in France as in Great Britain, firing the public imagination with open manifestations of their dissatisfaction and unrest in what Albistur and Armogathe record as a profusion of conferences, meetings, parallel election campaigns, petitions, surveys, street demonstrations and leaflet distributions.[37] However, these groups contrast strongly with their British and German counterparts who were expressly struggling for equal rights and opportunities. Their beliefs differ too from the united secular feminism of the more recent French Mouvement pour la Libération de la Femme (MLF) created in 1968, or even the existential feminism advocated by Beauvoir in *Le Deuxième Sexe* in 1949. French Inter-war activists, while fighting under the single banner of feminism, actually adhered to a multiplicity of different associations in which there was no cross-class coalition.[38] The majority of these women

supported the concept of equality in difference, and saw enfran-
chisement and political citizenship as a means to an end – and that end
was often reactionary. For example the Union féminine civique
et sociale (UFCS), founded in March 1925, explicitly followed the
dictates of the Holy See on marital arrangements; women within this
organization wanted a political voice in order to promote regressive
measures such as the return of all married women to the home, and
the repeal of the 1884 divorce laws.[39] So although women campaigned
actively for suffrage in the period, their arguments did little to allay
the fears of legislators. Many anti-clerical politicians believed that a
significant number of women would vote as a block according to the
directives of the Catholic Church, and feared that their united voice
would exert sufficient political pressure to threaten secular republican
values. (The early effects of female suffrage in the United States may
have also have influenced their thinking.[40]) Other equally hostile
critics maintained the old conservative argument that any form of
female emancipation would lead to a denial of the fundamental roles
of wife and mother.

In May 1919 the National Assembly voted by an overwhelming
majority in favour of universal suffrage, but the Senate refused to
consider women's right to vote and defeated the bill in 1922. The
Front populaire, under Léon Blum, offered some appeasement in the
nomination of three women to governmental positions in June 1936:
Irène Joiliot as *secrétaire de la Recherche scientifique*, Suzanne Lacore as
sous-secrétaire de l'Enfance, and Cécile Brunschvicg as *sous-secrétaire de
l'Education nationale*.[41] In 1938 married women were declared legal
majors, but it was only under the de Gaulle government that they
achieved full citizenship. (This was guaranteed in the *Préambule* to the
1946 constitution.) French women were at last granted the franchise
almost one hundred years after their male peers (all men over twenty-
one could vote as of 1848). On 20 April 1945 they voted for the
first time in the municipal elections, and on 21 October 1945 in the
National Assembly elections. Inter-war France remained inequitable
and undemocratic.[42]

The second area which aroused fierce debate concerned the
'proper' position of women in the workforce. In 1804, the Napoleonic Civil Code had set out legislation to solidify bourgeois culture.
At the heart of the Code was the doctrine of the separate spheres,
which posited the 'sexual division of labour, with the husband as bread
winner and the wife as *maîtresse de maison* and mother-educator, raising
the citizens, workers and soldiers of the future'.[43] The ideal bourgeois
woman in this scenario was confined to the domestic realm, her place
was in the home, where her passive dependency served as a guarantor

of respectability, reflecting as it did her husband's affluence and status in the public domain.[44] This binary social structure did not affect the situation of the lower classes. The percentage of working-class women in the labour force (including agriculture) in the early years of the twentieth century was the highest in Western Europe.[45] During the Great war vast numbers of women of all social classes entered employment (often for reduced wages) in a bid to help the war effort, and on the return of demobbed servicemen they were pressurized to return to the traditional realm of home and hearth. Loucheur, the minister for employment, just two days after the armistice on 13 November 1918 asked married women to give up their jobs. One month's severance pay was given to female employees who complied before 5 December 1918. On 5 January 1919 many of those who did not acquiesce suffered mass redundancies. Public opinion, as in Great Britain and the United States, was against those who remained in trades and professions, as Beauman notes: 'after the First World War, women of all classes in paid employment were seen no longer as patriots serving their country but as selfish "limpets" who would not give up their jobs to the men in need of work'.[46] Wage-earning mothers in particular were stigmatized, and in parliament their situation constituted a 'decisive fault line in social policy debates'.[47] Successive conservative legislators throughout the 1920s pledged to restore order through the revision of employment practices, and naturally the debate was revived during the course of the 1930s economic depression. In 1931, for example, 44.3 per cent of married women still earned a living, compared to a mere 10 per cent in England.[48] Faced with such statistics the militant Catholic, Andrée Butillard, founder of the UFCS, set up the Comité du retour des mères au foyer. When she conducted interviews of 30,000 working women she discovered that 80 per cent chose to work from financial necessity; so, under the motto 'Make women autonomous and united', she actively campaigned for legislative measures and monetary incentives which would enable women to return to the home. When the Vichy government came to power, directives were issued to dismiss all married female wage-earners and to provide allowances for single-waged families.

All discussions involving women's employment rights in the Inter-war years were staged against the background of the declining birthrate. From the days of the French Revolution, motherhood had been a major source of conflict between the Catholic Church and republican anti-clericals. In the 1920s and 1930s, given the perceived demographic crisis, the government espoused a pronatalist policy which posited motherhood as being of supreme importance to the country's health and security. For once, legislation on marital arrangements was in harmony with the dictates of the Holy See; for papal views prescriptively spelled out female dependency in marriage, the importance of a home-based family life for women and the veneration of maternity. Throughout the period between the wars women were subject to a two-pronged attack: the government employed a combination of incentives and coercive measures to increase natality figures.

In 1920 there was a strengthening of the already repressive laws prohibiting abortion and contraception under article 317 of the Penal Code. Penalties for pro-abortion propaganda comprised a six-month to a three-year prison sentence and a fine of between 100 and 5,000 francs. Circulating contraceptive advice could result in incarceration for a one- to six-month period, and a fine of between 100 and 3,000 francs.[49] This punitive law, known as the 'loi scélérate', was the 'most oppressive of its kind in Europe'. It did not outlaw the use of prophylactics which remained widely available, but it did appear to seek 'to bring women's sexual practices under legislative control' and 'typified a larger pattern of aggressive state intervention in matters of natality and the family'.[50] Three years later, in March 1923, abortion cases fell under the jurisdiction of the Cour d'assises; judges replaced sympathetic juries and harsher penalties were more rigidly enforced. Pope Pius XI's encyclicals of 1930 and 1931 *Casti Connubii* and *Quadragesimo Anno*, which stated that a woman must procreate or abstain, added further weight to governmental policies. In 1939, when the population of France totalled only 40 million, half that of the united Germany after the *Anschluss* (according to figures provided by the demographer Sauvy), the French government took further action and implemented the *Code de la famille*. Its explicit aim was to tackle depopulation through an increasingly stringent enforcement of anti-abortion legislation.[51] This coercive pronatalism continued throughout the war under the Vichy government. It in turn denounced non-childbearing women, introduced further restrictions on divorce and in the 1942 '300 law' equated terminating a pregnancy with high treason. The 1920s ban on abortions remained in place for over fifty years.[52]

Working in parallel with these repressive measures was a range of maternalist policies, ostensibly focused on improving the welfare of mothers and children. At the pronatalist congresses of 1919 in Nancy, 1920 in Rouen, and 1921 in Bordeaux, 128 affiliated organizations came together to discuss ways of tackling the depopulation problem. They explored issues such as tax incentives and affordable housing for large families, financial help for single mothers, state-funded creches and maternity institutions offering pre- and post-natal care, *primes d'allaitement* to discourage wet-nursing and the teaching of *puériculture* in schools.[53] A number of these ideas came to fruition over the Interwar years in the form of pro-family legislation sponsored by the Conseil supérieur de la natalité. By 1928, for example, there was a development and extension of mandatory maternity leave and benefits. Substantial child and nursing-mother allowances followed in 1932 and 1935. In 1938, when women were declared to be no longer legal minors, the Daladier government established by decree an endowment for mothers who chose to remain at home, equalling 10 per cent of the national average wage. The next year, under the *Code de la famille*, first-birth premiums for all couples who produced offspring within two years of marriage were introduced, as well as appreciable family allowances.[54]

As if to reinforce these laws the vestiges of the previous century's artificial and sentimental respect for motherhood were revived in a popular discourse celebrating the *mère au foyer*. In support of this in 1921 the Premier, Alexandre Millerand, instituted Mothers' Day on which medals were to be annually distributed to mothers of large families: bronze for five living children, silver for eight and gold for ten. Motherhood was presented as a panacea for a wide range of demographic, military, economic and cultural problems, and as a way to re-establish links with an older world of fixed, solid and cherished values. It symbolized continuity and stability in a time of rapid change and disorientation. This played a considerable part in validating traditional life options and in affecting and shaping women's attitudes. Women of all social ranks were encouraged in the belief that motherhood was fully compatible with their personal ambitions and desire for autonomy.

Responses from women to these legislative measures and their underpinning propaganda varied tremendously. At one extreme there was complicity. Andrée Butillard's UFCS saw motherhood as the proper fulfilment of woman's nature, as a remedy for the country's social ills and as a prerequisite for national regeneration. This perspective carried much weight. Holmes draws attention to the fact that in 1935, when *Le Petit Parisien* interviewed women for an article 'Women in Modern Society', all the women surveyed, while accepting that women's position had been revolutionized, said 'that their most cherished ambition was nothing other than one day becoming mothers'.[55] In total contrast, Nelly Roussel, aware of the government's ban on contraception and stringent anti-abortion legislation, believed that for most women, particularly those of the lower classes, motherhood was burdensome. Roussel challenged the government's 1920s legislation, stressing the horror of large families, the physical dangers of pregnancy and the poverty-stricken conditions in which women often gave birth. She argued the case that women should have a greater say in matters of procreation. In *La Voix des Femmes* (6 May 1920) and in speeches given at mass feminist rallies she urged: 'Let's strike, comrades, let's strike with our wombs.' Dr Madeleine Pelletier similarly campaigned for women's reproductive rights and was herself arrested as an abortionist in 1939.

Many feminists, like Pelletier and Roussel, were angered by the fact that, in comparison to their British and American peers, French women played an extremely circumscribed role in devising and implementing pro-family policies.[56] They were incensed by the way in which maternalist rhetoric was employed to deny women's autonomy and equality. After all, women had been refused rights to employment and political representation precisely on the grounds of their maternal capacities. Several feminist organizations did try to use the demographic crisis as a rallying cry for reform, 'as a strategy for claiming political, social and economic rights of mothers and of women generally'.[57] However, because depopulation was deemed a military and economic concern of national importance, pronatalist logic was essentially male-defined, and was often used to conceal diverse hidden agendas. For instance, communists advocated maternity, worrying that the falling birthrate would decimate the working classes. Right-wing groups supported motherhood and pushed for related social reforms, in the belief that giving financial aid to working-class families would defuse employees' potential discontent and militancy. In all of this male officials' real interests did not revolve around the welfare of mothers and infants or the institution and augmentation of women's rights. Pronatalist policies were distinctly reactionary and anti-feminist.

There can be little doubt that the undemocratic, misogynistic nature of patriarchal French society had a profound effect on women writers in the period between the wars. The contextual factors outlined here inevitably influenced female writing in the era – providing women with psychological and political incentives, and often informing their actual choice of genre and subject matter. In the course of this book, then, after exploring the determinants behind the emergence of women's writing in the early twentieth century, we shall examine the critical dialogue established between female authors and the various agencies of the dominant culture. We shall study the tacit criteria underlying literary histories' selection procedures. Given the preferment of certain facets of womanhood in Inter-war society, in an attempt to ascertain whether or not critical judgement has been skewed and distorted by current tastes for reactionary rhetoric extolling ideal femininity, we shall ask if the critical establishment itself has actively encouraged generic and thematic conservatism, and if there has been an attempt to silence more radical writers. Is this the explanation for the absence of so many women from the annals of literary history?

Part two will concentrate on various types of autobiographical self-portraiture as employed by Louise Weiss, Anna de Noailles, Catherine Pozzi, Gyp, Isabelle Rimbaud, Marie Noël, Monique Saint-Hélier, Colette, Jeanne Galzy, Marguerite Audoux, Marthe de Bibesco and Irène Némirovsky. The first aim is to analyse the generic reformulations which result from women's motivation to provide authentic personal testimonies. From this, we shall progress to appraise their reactions to the social roles prescriptively ascribed to women in the period, focusing particularly on responses to pronatalist rhetoric and idealized patriarchal constructions of motherhood. The locus of the third part of this work is popular romantic fiction, with an initial emphasis on works by relatively mainstream, best-selling writers such as Delly, Colette Yver and Raymonde Machard. We shall assess the characteristics, conventions and governing ideology of the genre, asking if it serves as a didactic vehicle for Roman Catholic, patriotic, bourgeois principles, or if instead it subversively espouses the new values of emergent modern women. Widening our focus to include Lucie Delarue-Mardrus, Rachilde, Louise de Vilmorin and several sapphic writers of the period, we shall investigate the varied techniques they employ to disrupt traditional reading practices and their resultant parodic challenge to contemporary male-authored representations of womanhood, their ironic treatment of the cult of heroic masculinity, their attack on the romance's creed of male centrality and their radical reconfiguration of the relationship between the sexes.

In all of this we shall be asking in what ways and to what extent these early twentieth-century writers can be seen as precursors for present-day authors. For although genres are historically relative and mutable through time, we may perceive a shared interest in innovative generic reformulation: a similar concern with breaking down boundaries, challenging hierarchies, blurring the distinctions between autobiography, social criticism, romance, fairy tale, literary satire, fact and fiction. Although French women today are more economically emancipated, sexually liberated and politically empowered than their Inter-war counterparts, there may nonetheless remain basic affinities in their thematic pursuits. Much current female-authored fiction is involved in celebrating the female body and women's autonomy in matters of reproduction. Understanding the psychoanalytic basis of maternal and filial attachments, exploring sexuality, articulating female desire and questing for an 'écriture féminine': these are its staples. Inter-war women played a part in fighting for the freedom which underpins these very projects; so we shall perhaps witness a likeness in earlier writers' exploration of gender construction, their re-evaluation of phallocentricity and their reassessment of the relationship between the sexes.

Whatever our findings, the provision of an accurate analysis of the interests, aims and achievements of this Forgotten Generation of Inter-war women writers should help us to re-establish an overall sense of continuity in women's writing across the century. The retrieval and re-reading of their much-neglected works should help fill some missing lacunae in the narrative of literary history. This work, I hope, will play a part in opening up this fascinating area for further critical investigation and debate, and in so doing encourage and promote the very process of rediscovering the silenced voices from the past.

Notes

1. V. Woolf (1977), *A Room of One's Own*, London, p. 62. Woolf's lectures to the Newnham College Arts Society and the Odtta at Girton, after several alterations and additions, were first published under the title *A Room of One's Own* in 1929 by the Hogarth Press.
2. E. Showalter (1986), 'Introduction: the Feminist Critical Revolution' in E. Showalter (ed.), *The New Feminist Criticism: Essays on Women, Literature and Theory*, 2nd edn, London, pp. 3–17 (p. 6).
3. E. Fallaize (1993), *French Women's Writing: Recent Fiction*, London, provides an overview of female fiction in the cultural context of the 1970s and 1980s together with introductions to some of the more prominent female literary figures on the contemporary scene.
4. H. Peyre (1955), *The Contemporary French Novel*, New York and Oxford, p. 251.
5. With its repeated imperatives challenging and urging women to write, this essay remains firmly focused prospectively. Cixous argues that a retrospective study is of limited value as the works it would bring to light would be so coloured and contorted by the influence of patriarchal society as to be of limited interest. Moreover, such a study would only further reproduce and reinforce the false stereotypical cultural notions of femininity inscribed in these

works. Cixous contends that the future must no longer be determined by the past, and that because women's relationship to the body is analogous to their relationship to writing, women must reclaim the female body, write of and through it, and in so doing, inscribe a new kind of biological (not cultural) femininity. H. Cixous (1975), 'Le Rire de la Méduse', *L'Arc*, no. 61, pp. 39–54 (p. 42). All translations are my own unless otherwise indicated.

6. S.R. Suleiman (1990), *Subversive Intent: Gender, Politics and the Avant-garde*, Cambridge, MA and London, p. 31.

7. A. Sauvy (1986), 'La Littérature et les femmes' in H.J. Martin, R. Chartier and J.P. Vivets (eds), *Histoire de l'édition: le livre concurrencé, 1900–1950*, Paris, vol. 4, pp. 242–55.

8. M. Mayran is the pseudonym of the popular Breton novelist, Mme Albert Deschard. Camille Mayran is the name employed by the Prix Fémina juror and author, Mme Pierre Hepp, née Saint-René-Taillandier.

9. Frappier-Mazur's investigation of this phenomenon reveals that in erotic literature both men and women showed a preference for female pseudonyms. L. Frappier-Mazur (1988), 'Marginal Canons: Rewriting the Erotic' in J. Dejean and N.K. Miller (eds), *The Politics of Tradition: Placing Women in French Literature*, New Haven, CT, pp. 112–28.

10. R. Lalou (1947), *Histoire de la littérature française contemporaine: de 1870 à nos jours*, Paris, vol. 2, p. 830.

11. Male pseudonyms used in the late nineteenth and early twentieth centuries include Pierre Alciette, Antoine Alhix, René d'Anjou, Jean Barancy, Jean Bertheroy, Henry Bister, Guy Chantepleure, Jacques Christophe, André Corthis, Pierre de Coulevain, Jacques Croisé, Michel Davet, Marcel Dhanys, Roger Dombre, Mario Donal, Jean Dornis, Pierre Duchéteau, Victor Féli, Henri Franz, Marion Gilbert, Jules-Philippe Heuzey, Gérard d'Houville, Jean de la Brète, Jean Lander, Maurice le Beaumont, Claude Lemaître, Daniel Lesueur, Camille Marbo, Etienne Marcel, Camille Mauclair, Gilbert Mauge, Camille Mayran, Ely Montclerc, Jacques Morian, Lionel de Movet, Raoul de Navery, Pierre Ninous, Camille Pert, Georges de Peyrebrune, Pierre de Saxel, Claude Silve, René d'Ulmès, Georges du Valon, Jean Vézère, Jacques Vincent, Jacques Vontade, Gaspard de Weede and Guy Witra.

12. Editions de la Différence have republished Catherine Pozzi's novella, poetry and philosophical essay. Albin Michel have reprinted novels by Irène Némirovsky. So too have Grasset et Fasquelle, whose 'cahier rouge' collection also includes two

novels by Marguerite Audoux. The Lausanne-based Editions de l'Aire have republished a selection of novels by Monique Saint-Hélier as well as her memoirs. Mercure de France have shown an interest in more mainstream writers and have reissued Anna de Noailles's autobiography and Rachilde's *La Marquise de Sade*. Other novels by Rachilde, including *Monsieur Vénus*, *La Tour d'amour* and *La Jongleuse*, have also been recently republished by Flammarion, Le Tout sur le Tout and Editions des Femmes respectively. Early works by Elsa Triolet and Louise de Vilmorin are still available in the Gallimard N.R.F. collection, while Yourcenar and Sarraute are soon to take their place with Colette in the Gallimard Pléiade edition's illustrious list.

13. The possible motivations behind this phenomenon are explored in R. Coward (1986), 'Are Women's Novels Feminist Novels?' in E. Showalter (ed.), *The New Feminist Criticism: Essays of Women, Literature and Theory*, London, pp. 225–40.

14. For examples of historical studies see the listing provided in the bibliography. Of especial interest are works by M. Auffret, P. Faveton, M. Higonnet, A. Joffroy and M.L. Roberts.

15. For examples of recent biographies, see the listing provided in the bibliography. Several of these works are of particular note. H. Plat's recent study of Delarue-Mardrus, W.Z. Silverman's work on Gyp and C. Mignot-Ogliasti's biography of Noailles are all very thorough. Gille's study on Némirovsky is unusual in that it takes the form of 'mémoires rêvés', based on personal recollections and readings of her mother's fictional works.

16. L. Mackinnon (1992), *The Lives of Elsa Triolet*, London, p. xii.

17. J. Chalon (1987), *Florence et Louise les magnifiques: Florence Jay-Gould et Louise de Vilmorin*, Monaco, p. 102.

18. F. Montreynaud (1992), *Le XXème siècle des femmes*, Paris, p. 31.

19. P. Newman-Gordon (1994), 'Lucie Delarue-Mardrus' in E.M. Sartori and D.W. Zimmerman (eds), *French Women Writers*, Lincoln and London, pp. 108–20 (p. 109).

20. C. Dauphiné (1985), *Rachilde, femme de lettres 1900*, Périgueux, pp. 145–6 and 52.

21. Lalou, *Histoire de la littérature*, vol. 2, p. 830.

22. A. David (1924), *Rachilde, 'homme' de lettres*, Paris, p. 30.

23. E. de La Rochefoucauld (1956), *Anna de Noailles*, Paris, p. 119.

24. Larnac believed that such a study was sufficiently important to merit an entire volume and announced that his own modest overview of selected contemporary writers did not do the subject proper justice. See J. Larnac (1929), *Histoire de la Littérature féminine en France*, Paris.

25. A.-M. Thiesse and H. Matthieu (1988), 'The Decline of the Classical and Birth of the Classics' in J. Dejean and N.K. Miller (eds), *The Politics of Tradition: Placing Women in French Literature*, New Haven, CT, pp. 208–28 (p. 228).
26. E. Showalter (1982), *A Literature of Their Own*, London, pp. 11–12.
27. P.-H. Simon (1963), *Histoire de la littérature française au XXème siècle, 1900–1950*, 7th edn, Paris, vol. 1, p. 123.
28. M. Sachs (1950), *La Décade de l'illusion*, Paris, p. 17.
29. E. Brody (1988), *Paris the Musical Kaleidoscope, 1870–1925*, London, pp. 112, 15, 135 and 256.
30. Brassaï's photographs of the period reflect changes in social and sexual mores. See Brassaï (1976), *The Secret Paris of the '30s*, translated by R. Miller, London.
31. When France became a republic in this era it appealed to the Americans, who were celebrating their own centennial. The hegira only came to a halt in the early 1930s, a period which marked the end of the halcyon days for many writers who were forced to return home in the wake of the widespread repercussions of the 1929 Wall Street Crash.
32. J. Forbes and M. Kelly (eds), (1995), *French Cultural Studies: an Introduction*, Oxford, p. 69.
33. D. Desanti (1984), *La Femme au temps des années folles*, Paris, p. 22.
34. A. Cova (1991), 'French Feminism and Maternity: Theories and Policies, 1890–1918,' in G. Bock and P. Thane (eds), *Maternity and Gender Policies: Women and the Rise of the European Welfare States, 1880s–1950s*, London and New York, pp. 119–37 (p. 119).
35. Forbes and Kelly, *French Cultural Studies*, p. 70.
36. See Y. Brunhammer (1987), *The Nineteen Twenties Style*, London.
37. M. Albistur and D. Armogathe (1977), *Histoire du féminisme du moyen âge à nos jours*, Paris, p. 383.
38. See Cova, 'French Feminism and Maternity' for an overview of a spectrum of varied feminist positions at the turn of the century.
39. Divorce had been abolished in 1816 and its re-establishment in male favour in 1884 incensed many Catholic feminists. It became available by mutual consent only in 1975.
40. After the Suffrage victory in 1920, American women made the welfare of mothers and children their priority, and, following coordinated intensive lobbying by a broad coalition of women's organizations, they succeeded in influencing the passing of the Sheppard–Towner Maternity and Infancy Act in 1921. Politicians feared 'provoking the wrath of newly enfranchised women voters'

and the bill was passed in the Senate by 63 to 7 votes and in the House of Representatives by 279 to 39 votes. For details see M. Ladd-Taylor (1993), '"My Work Came Out of Agony and Grief": Mothers and the Making of the Sheppard–Towner Act' in S. Koven and S. Michel (eds), *Mothers of a New World: Maternalist Politics and the Origins of Welfare States*, London and New York, pp. 321–42 (p. 328).

41. L. Weiss (1946), *Ce que Femme veut: souvenirs de la IIIème République*, 7th edn, Paris, p. 191. This is presented in an ironically named section 'Three swallows don't make a summer'.

42. For further information see S. Hausse and A. Kenney (1984), *Women's Suffrage and Social Politics in the French Third Republic*, Princeton, NJ.

43. See K. Offen (1991), 'Body Politics: Women, Work and the Politics of Motherhood in France, 1920–1950' in G. Bock and P. Thane (eds), *Maternity and Gender Policies: Women and the Rise of the European Welfare States, 1880s–1950s*, London and New York, pp. 138–59 (p. 142).

44. While this same prescriptive binary rhetoric existed in Britain, in Victorian society women often blurred the distinction of the separate spheres in their voluntary roles as anti-slavery, prison, education and social-welfare reformers. See S. Koven (1993), 'Borderlands: Women, Voluntary Action, and Child Welfare in Britain, 1840–1914' in S. Koven and S. Michel (eds), *Mothers of a New World: Maternalist Politics and the Origins of Welfare States*, London and New York, pp. 94–135 (p. 96).

45. For detailed figures for 1906 see Cova, 'French Feminism and Maternity', p. 125; for Inter-war government statistics see also Offen in Bock and Thane, *Maternity and Gender Policies*, p. 142.

46. N. Beauman (1983), *A Very Great Profession: the Woman's Novel, 1914–39*, London, p. 76.

47. S. Michel (1993), 'The Limits of Maternalism: Policies Toward American Wage-earning Mothers during the Progressive Period' in S. Koven and S. Michel (eds), *Mothers of a New World: Maternalist Politics and the Origins of Welfare States*, London and New York, pp. 277–320 (p. 277).

48. S. Pedersen (1993), 'Catholicism, Feminism, and the Politics of the Family during the Late Third Republic', in S. Koven and S. Michel (eds), *Mothers of a New World: Maternalist Politics and the Origins of Welfare States*, London and New York, pp. 246–76 (p. 257).

49. M.J. Boxer and J.H. Quataert (1987), *Connecting Spheres: Women in the Western World, 1500 to the Present*, Oxford, p. 210.

50. See M.L. Roberts (1994), *Civilization Without Sexes: Reconstructing Gender in Postwar France, 1917–1927*, Chicago and London, pp. 94, 96, 99.
51. The major difference with German pronatalist policy in this period was the German emphasis on eugenics and the sterilization of women who were considered inferior on racial or medical grounds.
52. In 1956 Dr Marie-Andrée Weill-Hallé challenged the law when she set up the French movement for family planning. In 1971 the *Nouvel Observateur* printed the names of some 343 important Frenchwomen who had undergone abortions. In 1973 the Mouvement pour la liberté de l'avortement et pour la contraception (MLAC) was established and in 1974 under the *loi Simone Veil* abortion was legalized. Female contraception soon followed in 1977.
53. See Roberts, *Civilization Without Sexes*, p. 270.
54. See Offen in Bock and Thane, *Maternity and Gender Policies,* p. 149.
55. D. Holmes (1977), 'The Image of Women in Selected French Fiction of the Inter-war Period', unpublished Ph.D. thesis, University of Sussex, p. 42.
56. Sklar offers an interesting comparison with the United States. She argues that decentralization, religious disestablishment (freedom from the aegis of the Church), and greater and earlier dynamic changes in education were key factors in enabling grass-roots civic organizations of middle-class women to function as autonomous political forces with their own gender-specific goals. This meant that women played a major role at every stage in the creation and implementation of maternalist welfare policies. K.K. Sklar (1993), 'The Historical Foundations of Women's Power in the Creation of the American Welfare State, 1830–1930', in S. Koven and S. Michel (eds), *Mothers of a New World: Maternalist Politics and the Origins of Welfare States*, London and New York, pp. 43–94.
57. See Cova, 'French Feminism and Maternity', p. 133.

Part I

But where are the snows of yesteryear?

> François Villon, 'Ballade des dames du temps jadis', *Le Testament*
> (1461–2)

– 1 –

Coming to Writing

The most decisive factor determining the nature of the literary environment in France in the Inter-war period was unquestionably a series of progressive reforms in the French education system dating from the mid-nineteenth century. The first of the new laws, the *loi Falloux* of March 1850, decreed the creation of girls schools in every community of over 800 inhabitants, thus guaranteeing many girls access to elementary formal education. This was extended in 1881 when primary schooling became free, secular and compulsory for all children of both sexes. The Third Republic's higher education system saw similar transformations. As early as 1863 Victor Duruy, the minister for education, had allowed privately financed female secondary schooling to take place, and in December 1880, under the *loi Camille Sée*, the state took the full responsibility for financing universal secondary teaching.[1] Sée's aim was the instruction of future mothers of men and as a result of this certain subjects, namely Greek, Latin, philosophy, mathematics and science, were still considered as unsuitable for girls. By 1924, following an earlier ruling of 1919, Léon Bérard announced that the same *baccalauréat* syllabus, essential for university entrance, should be taught to both sexes, and this greatly facilitated access for women to tertiary education. Already many independent lycées were preparing girls for university, and in the 1880s women began to make a mark on the professions: the first medical degree was issued to a woman, Blanche Edwards, in 1882, the bar was open to women after 1887 and from 1879, under the *loi Paul Bert, écoles normales* had been set up in every region to encourage women to train as teachers. Further legal changes hastened this process; women by this period were entitled to hold a bank account and engage in a career without their husband or father's consent.

While these transformations in the laws governing female education came into action later than reforms in the American system, they nonetheless had far-reaching repercussions.[2] At the most basic level, they resulted in an improvement in literacy figures: while in the Belle

Epoque 194 women in 1,000 could not read, by 1936 this total was reduced to only 48 in 1,000. The number of female pupils in secondary education also improved dramatically, rising from 49,342 in 1930 to 81,004 in 1937. Success rates in the *baccalauréat* examination equally saw a correspondingly marked amelioration. While in 1924 25,000 girls passed the *baccalauréat*, this figure rose to 45,000 thousand in 1938.[3] By as early as 1909 the catalytic effect of universal access to education was already evident, for it was made manifest in a sizeable readership. Allen records that in 1921 almost 37 per cent of adult French people considered themselves active readers.[4] Bertaut bears testimony to large numbers and, as importantly, to the growth of female readers, in his comment that from the early years of the century in France it was women who constituted the real reading public.[5] This is echoed in Nourissier's retrospective survey of the early twentieth century in which he humorously writes: 'What is a reader? One could easily reply – a woman. It is the case that, like money in America, literature in France is in female hands!'[6]

One would expect the escalating growth in successive generations of new women readers to be paralleled by an increase in women writers. Already throughout the nineteenth century, according to a detailed study conducted by Planté, *La Petite Sœur de Balzac: essai sur la femme auteur*, there was a sizeable company of eminent women writers, whose literary contributions demonstrated eclectic interests and diverse talents. In the Fin de Siècle the number of professional French women writers appears to have grown substantially, causing Léautaud, secretary of the *Mercure de France* from 1908 to 1941, to make his infamous comment that there were so many lady writers that it was no longer possible to find any cleaning ladies. Flat in 1909 notes that female authors had ceased to be rare, unique creatures, dependent on a highly specific fusion of particular social and cultural factors. They no longer required a monastic or aristocratic upbringing, for thanks to improved access to schooling, women now were writing *en masse*.[7] Waelti-Walters more recently confirms an increase in 'subversive novels by politically astute and socially conscious women' in the period preceding the Great War.[8]

Certainly, in much of Europe and the United States, as a direct result of feminist advances and improved educational opportunities, this period witnessed a widespread increase in the number of professional woman writers and in their national and international recognition.[9] It is in this era, for instance, that Nobel Prizes (initiated in 1901) for outstanding achievement in the field of literature were first awarded to women authors, namely the Swedish saga writer Selma Lagerlöf (1909), the Italian Grazia Deledda (1926), the Norwegian

Sigred Undset (1928) and Pearl Buck, the American novelist and biographer raised in China (1938). In the history of the Nobel Prize women writers have only ever been recipients on three subsequent occasions: Gabriela Mistral, Nelly Sachs and Nadine Gordimer were laureates in 1945, 1966 and 1991 respectively. An analogous situation may be seen with French-speaking women. In Canada Lucy Maud Montgomery and Mazo de la Roche developed a reputation, while early twentieth-century Belgium saw the emergence many talented writers including Daniel Lesueur (Jeanne Loiseau), Marguerite Duterme, Suzanne Lilar, Hélène Canivet, Felixa Wart-Blondian, Jean Dominique (Marie Closset) and Madeleine Bourdouche. Likewise, in Switzerland the first generation of professional or semi-professional writers, comprising Monique Saint-Hélier, Clarisse Francillon, Dorette Berthoud, Elisabeth Burnod and Noëlle Roger emerged in the 1930s.[10]

The situation in France was no different.[11] Within the Inter-war period itself contemporary male critics demonstrated an awareness of this snowballing female literary movement. In 1929, Larnac affirmed that there had never been such a great number of women writers in France[12] and in 1938 his statement was echoed by Nizan in his review of Elsa Triolet's *Bonsoir Thérèse* in which he confirmed not only the profuse number of women writers but also the prolific nature of their literary output, suggesting that there had never previously appeared so many novels of female authorship, often expressly for and about women.[13] Archival research into various bibliographical sources undertaken for this work goes some way to confirm these findings, and despite the statistical problem caused by the widespread use of pseudonyms, a general overview does suggest a very sizeable body of literature produced by professional French female writers. For instance, the membership of the Société des gens de lettres, an association founded in 1838 by Louis Desnoyers to safeguard the legal rights of authors in matters such as copyright and publication, totalled an astounding 671 women writers in 1937. Like other European, Scandinavian or English-speaking countries, France reaped the rewards of the new education system which had worked positively to promote female literature in Western countries as a whole.

In the 1920s and 1930s French women from all walks of life could now enjoy writing as a pastime, a passion or a profession. Female writers no longer only formed an upper-class intellectual elite based in a great seat of erudition such as Paris. This is evident in the incremental growth in female regional novelists such as Jeanne Galzy (Montpellier), Lucie Delarue-Mardrus (Normandy), Cécile Périn (Brittany), Camille Mayran (Alsace), Raymonde Vincent (Berrichon), Andrée Martignon (the south-west) and Lucienne Fabre (Algeria).

This coincides with a general interest in regionalism in the period in works by Anatole Le Braz, Emile Guillaumin, Gaston Roupnel, Daniel Rops and René Boylesve.[14] It is also apparent in the divergent social status of women writers. Aristocratic writers such as the Princesse Marthe de Bibesco, the Comtesse Elisabeth de Gramont, Gyp, Gérard d'Houville and Michel Davet no longer had a monopoly. Nor was French female literature, unlike its English counterpart of the Inter-war years, in any sense the unique domain of the middle classes either. Critics of the period widely acknowledged the emergence of a major female literary talent from the working classes, Marguerite Audoux, who depicted in novels of a semi-autobiographical nature a life of acute penury in both rural and urban landscapes. While Audoux was undoubtedly not, as critics claimed, the first female proletarian author – Planté in her analysis of the nineteenth century notes the names of two other prominent figures: Antoinette Quarré and Malvina Blanchecotte – she was the first woman from this social class to make such a mark on French literature.[15] In 1910 she was awarded the already esteemed Prix Fémina for her debut novel, *Marie-Claire*, from which the famous women's magazine supposedly took its name. The novel was exceptionally popular, selling in the region of 75,000 copies in early print runs and being translated into nine languages including Japanese; as a point of comparison, Colette's first *Claudine* novel sold around 50,000 copies. *Marie-Claire* and its sequel, *L'Atelier de Marie-Claire* (1920), have both been frequently republished, and today, more than eighty years later, are still in print as part of Grasset's Collection Rouge. Nor was Audoux a unique phenomenon. Her appearance on the literary scene coincides with the more general rise of the proletarian novel, exemplified by writers such as Charles-Louis Philippe, Pierre Hamp, Emile Guillaumin, Jules Romains and Henry Poulaille, and it heralds the emergence in the 1930s of the populist women writers Huguette Garnier, Mme Laurence Algan and Antonine Coulet-Tessier, founder of the Prix du roman populaire.[16]

Just as women writers emerged from varied social milieu, their intellectual pursuits also demonstrated great variety. Paralleling women's progressive participation in the majority of male-dominated professions, outlined in Colette Yver's *Dans le jardin du féminisme* (1922) and more fully documented in *Femmes d'aujourd'hui: enquête sur les nouvelles carrières féminines* (1929), women also became involved in a wide spectrum of eclectic literary activities, from journalism[17] and producing literary biographies,[18] to more intellectual philosophical or psychoanalytical pursuits.[19] That said, it should be acknowledged that in certain circles the stigma attached to the term *femme auteur* had still not completely disappeared and many of the attitudes underlying it remain unchanged well into the Inter-war period and beyond. Taking up writing was often seen by more traditional families as analogous with assuming the type of bohemian lifestyles believed to be lead by Anglo-American New Women. Germaine Beaumont tells an amusing personal anecdote about familial reactions to her own nascent literary ambitions. Not only did she encounter the still widely held opinion that writing was an unsuitable female occupation, she also confronted the firm belief that an interest in certain genres (in her case, poetic works of an innovative or over-ambitious nature) constituted a double transgression. Her earliest creative attempt, perhaps inspired by Elizabeth Barrett Browning's *Aurora Leigh*, took the form of an epic poem. As she explains, her precocity so frightened her family that they dispatched her to a convent and asked the mother superior to prohibit all creative writing. She also explains that, undeterred, she spent the next eight years engrossed in philosophical poetry, and when she did turn to writing as a profession this lent her fictional works an uncommon metaphysical blend of philosophy, supernatural dreams and fantasy, akin to the poetry she so loved.[20] Beaumont's situation draws attention to the fact that in the Inter-war era, women writers were in fact particularly susceptible to external generic manipulation in their coming to writing.

Despite improved access to the literary world, women's activities were to varying degrees circumscribed. As Kolodny suggests: 'what women have so far expressed in literature is what they have been *able to express*, as a result of the complex interplay between innate biological determinants and individual talents and opportunities, and the larger effects of socialization, which, in some cases, may govern the limits of expression or even of perception and experience'.[21] Admittedly, this is not necessarily gender-specific, but the 'effects of socialization' in the type of patriarchal society in force in the early twentieth century did prove to be especially repressive for female writers in terms of the literary genres they could produce. This is most evident in the major literary fields of theatre and poetry.

At first glance, the blossoming of the theatre, cinema, and music-hall in the Années Folles seems to have provided a wealth of opportunities for women. The actress Ida Rubenstein, who made her name with the erotic dance of the seven veils, turned producer and commissioned some of the foremost ballets of the century scored by celebrated international composers including Auric, Debussy, Honegger, Ibert and Stravinsky.[22] Colette's career as a performer is almost as well documented as her written contribution to the theatrical world, while Mme Simone, whose own dramatic works belong to the period after the Second World War, established a reputation as both actress and literary impresario in this earlier period. There were similar openings for writers who chose to turn their skills to reviewing. The journalist Séverine (Caroline Rémy) and the renowned *salonnière* Mme Bulteau produced regular drama columns for the national press. At the instigation of the latter, Gérard d'Houville, under the pseudonym xxx, also wrote critiques for *Le Gaulois, Le Figaro, La République* and *Le Temps*. However, while women were actively involved as comediennes and commentators their place as creators was generally more limited. Literary histories covering the theatre in the late nineteenth and early twentieth centuries note only Rachilde for *Madame la Mort, Le Vendeur de soleil* and the one act *La Voix du sang* (1891), Mme Andrée Méry, the poet Rosemonde Gérard, Marie Lenéru, Marcelle Maurette, Gérard d'Houville for her one play *Je crois que je vous aime* (1927), Colette and Germaine Acremant (née Poulain). This supports Pasquier's epigrammatic assertion:

1. Women love the theatre.
2. The theatre excludes women.[23]

Of the listed dramatists, only Marie Lenéru[24] is singled out as a playwright of talent, and even here there are provisos. Her preoccupation with the spiritual life, her feminist Christianity, and her articulation of the human conflict between the instincts and the intelligence are repeatedly described as being better suited to a different literary genre, namely the traditional female domain of the novel.

Wilwerth offers an explanation for the small number of women successfully involved in writing and producing plays. Unlike novelists, playwrights must be fully integrated into the theatrical world to know the type of drama which works on stage, not just on paper. They must have numerous contacts and real commitment in terms of money, time and energy.[25] Wilwerth suggests that in the Inter-war period women were not sufficiently emancipated either socially or financially to play a full and vital role in mainstream French theatre, and that it was not until after 1960 that dramatists such as Suzanne Lilar, Marguerite Duras, Françoise Sagan and Liliane Wouters had the right conditions to come to the fore. English Showalter, Jr confirms that 'the theater demanded a degree of self-promotion and managerial activity that women could not easily provide' and consequently 'the conclusion is inescapable that social and institutional barriers to staging a play proved a fatal deterrent to women'.[26] To be successful in this area, women still needed active male support. The novelist Germaine Acrement, winner of the Prix Nelly Lieutier in 1921 for *Ces Dames aux chapeaux verts* and the Prix National de littérature in 1927 for *Gai! marions-nous*, despite her literary skill, popular appeal and wide recognition, still required the assistance of her husband, Albert, to adapt her novels for the stage; even Colette, who was both knowledgeable of and well known in this domain, relied on Léopold Marchand with the dramatization of *Chéri*. That said, the theatrical world did continue to promote one sub-genre popularized by two women writers of the eighteenth century, Félicité de Genlis and Françoise de Graffigny: the morally educative play for children. Showalter explains that this sub-genre was tolerated and even encouraged by the establishment because women traditionally enjoyed exercising limited authority in the domestic situation as 'moral guide, teacher, or governess'. The embodiment of this role in literature seemed proper, appropriate and chiefly unthreatening, while providing an outlet for women frustrated and thwarted by 'the mainstream theater and the larger society it represented'.[27] The most prolific early twentieth-century writer of these educative plays was Henriette Bezançon, whose works were rarely performed, and who receives virtually no attention, far less acclaim, in either anthologies or literary histories.

Access to poetry in the Inter-war years was equally restricted, albeit mainly for aesthetic rather than pragmatic reasons. The dominant schools in the early twentieth century were largely inimical to women. Marinetti's Futurist movement (founded in Italy in 1909) held as part of its central doctrine contempt for women, an active combat of feminism, and a destruction of nostalgia, romance and sentimentality. Guillaume Apollinaire, writing until 1918, despite his claimed attempt to diminish the barriers between masculine and feminine, depicted human eroticism as a form of war, rape or hunting in which the woman is consistently the victim. In the Inter-war period, Surrealism, under André Breton, was equally misogynistic. The Surrealists chose to mythify and glorify woman as a muse, or source of poetic inspiration, through the juxtaposition of the spiritual and carnal in her. Women, however, were not valued as creators in their own right, and the objectification inherent in this process, which implicitly denied female autonomy, alienated many women writers. Indeed, during the movement's most dynamic period in the late 1920s, not a single woman was included as an official member of the all-male elite central core. A few women (often wives or lovers) were active on the periphery. Suleiman records the contribution made by Fanny Beznos, Madame Savitsky and Valentine Penrose, all involved in the review *La Révolution surréaliste*, and Nadejda Kroupskaia, Gala Eluard, Marie-Berthe Ernst and Valentine Hugo, who contributed to the *Surréalisme au service de la révolution* review. To this list one might add Lise

Deharme, Leonora Carrington, Yanette Deletang-Tardif, Antoinette d'Harcourt, the Dadaist Céline Arnauld and Breton's protégé, the prepubescent poet/muse, Gisèle Prassinos. Surrealism only opened its doors more fully to women in the mid-1930s when the movement needed new blood, and female Surrealism reached its apex after the Second World War when the central party was largely dispersed and Breton lost his dominant hold. Even in this era most female Surrealists, such as Joyce Mansour, Jacqueline Lamba Breton, Nelly Kaplan, Rita Kernn-Larsen, Dora Maas, Marie-Louise Mayoux, Frida Kahlo, Dorothea Tanning, Alice Rahon Paalen, Méret Oppenheim, Kay Sage, Lee Miller, Léonor Fini, Eileen Agar, Marie Cerminová Toyen, Nusch Eluard, and Annie Le Brun, were considerably younger than their male counterparts, most were of foreign extraction, and many were involved in the visual arts rather than writing. Paul Valéry's poetry, in contrast to Surrealism which revered the free, unfettered imagination, sought to celebrate the intellect with its heavy reliance on classical techniques, allusions and philosophy. Given the fact that female secondary schooling was still in its infancy, and that girls were just beginning to embark on the same syllabuses as their male peers, it is unsurprising that few French women were engaged in Valérian poetic ventures. As with the theatre, in the early twentieth century one poetic domain was favoured by most established *femmes de lettres*: the simple, elegiac, lyric poem. Characterized by narcissism, sentimentality and the old Romantic credo of the servitude of love, like the educative play, it offered no challenge to stereotypical female roles, and was considered to be ideologically conservative, a harmless vent for female creativity. According to Moulin, within the Inter-war era the form changed little and witnessed no real stylistic or thematic innovation until the eve of World War Two when many works became increasingly abstract and universal.[28]

Given the gender-specific restrictions evident in both the realm of poetry and theatre, many female writers directed themselves towards the more open and accessible fictional genres, especially the perennially popular novel. This was an area in which numerous women had already successfully secured a reputation. It required no special training, and it was a domain too which offered the possibility of both sound financial remuneration, and in the specific case of the *feuilletons* linked to daily newspapers, lengthy employment and a regular income. Most importantly perhaps it was the genre which reached the largest number of readers in the period,[29] and which allowed the greatest freedom to communicate on the subject of the contemporary representation of gender relations. This was a major incentive for many women coming to writing in the first instance. Showalter's overview of the history of female-authored fiction in *A Literature of Their Own*, Gilbert and Gubar's *No Man's Land: The Place of the Woman Writer in the Twentieth Century* and Dudovitz's study of the development of the popular novel, *The Myth of Superwoman: Women's Bestsellers in France and the United States*, all suggest that women systematically take up writing fiction at times of major social upheavals when gender itself becomes, to borrow Gilbert and Gubar's terminology, a battleground. As we saw in the introduction, in the turbulent 1920s and 1930s, in the aftermath of the social and political transformations wrought by the Great War, there existed fundamental 'contradictions between the ways women were perceived by the larger society and how they perceived themselves'.[30] Pronatalist legislators, journalists and propagandists ruthlessly promoted female subordination to the cherished, conservative image of the married mother confined 'to the narrow circle of the family, in the landscape of the husband's stew pot and the children's chamber pot', as Jeanne Rougé so aptly puts it.[31] While women, in a very visible way, demonstrated their dissatisfaction with this role through their adoption of the latest fashions and through more conspicuous political action, with no right to suffrage, no access to the major forum for political redress, they found that their successes in challenging authoritarian prescriptions of their social role were somewhat circumscribed. Yet, they urgently wanted the autonomy and the power to redefine themselves. So, like their female ancestors in the time of the Revolution and the establishment of the Empire, women took decisive action and followed what had become for them the only viable path to freedom: they turned to the novel and endeavoured to create a literature of their own.

Although by the Inter-war period women now were guaranteed the right to education, financial liberty and a degree of personal independence, and although restrictive social factors provided a strong psychological motivating force, the act of coming to writing itself, for many women, was still fraught with difficulties on both the domestic and the public front. In the private sphere, for a number of women, the discouragement they faced proved especially abstruse, insidious and destructive. This is the subject of Louise de Vilmorin's deeply ironic first novel *Sainte-Unefois* (1934) and it is also evident in numerous personal testimonies.[32] For example, in the most recent biographical study on Elsa Triolet, Mackinnon records Triolet's claim that her husband, Louis Aragon, was unsupportive, took little or no interest in her career as an author, and in the early days of their relationship actually tried to dissuade her from writing,[33] preferring to consider her a passive, inspirational poetic muse, and immortalizing her as a symbol of the French spirit in his resistance poems.[34] With André Malraux and his wife Clara Goldschmidt the situation was not so very different. He too firmly believed that their shared life should be his unique material, his own artistic property. So, not only did he show little enthusiasm for Clara's articles for *L'Indochine*, or her unpublished plays *Impermanence, Le Jeu, Le Silence* and *Le Vieux Cheval*, he found her more ostensibly autobiographical works *Livre de Compte* (1933) and *Le Portrait de Grisélidis* (1945) quite unacceptable. For her part Clara bitterly resented her husband's mythomania, the way in which he reinterpreted events to gain public approval (in particular his version of their attempted theft of the Khmer statues printed in the *Chicago Tribune*) and the way in which he wrote her out of the novels that detailed their Asian adventure. It was only when their divorce came through in January 1942 that Clara began to overcome the destructive effects of marital discouragement through writing her multi-volume autobiography which earned her wide recognition.[35] The same pattern also recurs with Malraux's lovers. Chantal, who charts the relationship between Malraux and Josette Clotis, attributes Clotis's abrupt relinquishment of her literary career,[36] specifically her failure to complete the manuscript of *La Clé des champs*, to Malraux's discouragement, his criticism and his rigorous correcting of her drafts to conform to his conception of art.[37] Louise de Vilmorin suffered an analogous fate with Malraux. She too maintained to her biographer, Chalon, that during their second liaison her literary production stopped because her fascination with witty linguistic games and toying with varied levels of reality were quite alien to Malraux's more prosaic, ordered outlook, and, as with Clotis, it was his vision which dominated.[38]

These personal testimonies, although highlighting the overt discouragement certain women writers experienced, do not paint the full picture, because the personal discouragement and generic manipulation faced by many French women novelists during the 1920s and 1930s were often but a prelude to the more tangible resistance they encountered in the public arena, where the hegemony of power remained in male hands. This situation is portrayed in a profusion of novels from the Inter-war period. Of particular note is Suzanne Normand's *Cinq femmes sur une galère* (1926) which tells of five young girls, all driven by utopic visions of independence, who experience bitter disillusionment as they encounter gender-based opposition in the male-dominated literary world. Régine, a translator, and Laure, a professional journalist, both experience the whims of editorial boards when their respective commissions (for an anthology of eighteenth-century female poets, and news articles on the social predicament of single mothers) are withdrawn. Gilberte, a publisher, is paid half the salary of her male counterparts, has limited promotion prospects, is never granted access to the all-male executive committees, and so has no real editorial power to promote the numerous female-authored manuscripts she reads. Normand's novel openly challenges the unjust sex discrimination at play in the literary realm. Another interesting fictional example is provided by Lucie Delarue-Mardrus's *L'Ange et les Pervers* (1930). Here the central protagonist is a hermaphrodite writer, Marion Valdeclare, who frequents the lesbian circle of Laurette Wells and the male homosexual gatherings of Ginette Labrée. As (s)he moves between these two worlds (s)he switches gender, and experiences the quite different degrees of encouragement given to men and women by various factions within the literary establishment. What is perhaps most interesting about Delarue-Mardrus's novel is that Marion's experience is based on the real-life problems faced by Pauline Mary Tarn who received acclaim prior to 1902 when her love poetry was produced under the masculinized pseudonym René Vivien, but who received public censure when her true identity was revealed, and when the lesbian context of her works was made explicit.[39]

There is a considerable body of factual documentation on the Inter-war literary world which also highlights the difficulties experienced by women writers in the period. Peyre, for example, is among the first to admit that 'the position of a woman of letters is especially arduous. She enters a world fashioned by man, and has to meet standards set by him. She has to live imaginatively in an artistic and literary universe created by man'.[40] Penetrating the Inter-war literary world, far less flourishing in it, was by no means straightforward, as at every stage in the process of promoting, producing and distributing fiction, the role played by women was restricted. Anne Sauvy, in her comprehensive study of the Inter-war world of editing and publishing, notes that in this particular area women held an intelligent but limited role.[41] France saw no equivalent of Virginia Woolf's private Hogarth Press, and the only ostensibly female publishing group, Cent femmes amies des livres, unlike the more recent separatist Editions des femmes, was neither feminist nor innovative, given its limited focus on re-editing already acclaimed works by well-established writers. The promotion and distribution of female fiction was equally male-dominated. In England in the Inter-war period Boots lending library monitored an extensive network of readers.[42] In France the situation was quite different. The public reading rooms, *cabinets de lecture,* which had worked to promote the popular novel in the nineteenth century, were now in disrepute and decline, and a modern extensive library system had still not evolved to replace them. Nor was the substantial growth in the number of readers met by a parallel increase in book shops, although a wider range of distribution points did gradually come into use.[43] Whereas English women had a significant influence on their reading material – their opinions, preferences and exigences were relayed to the publishers, who could then more efficiently tailor their material to suit changes in demand – in France, editors of large publishing firms and editors of the many popular magazines which promoted and advertised current literary works had much more freedom to impose their tastes on the reading public.

An additional difficulty experienced by a number of women writers in the early twentieth century was the male-dominated critical establishment's failure to provide due or adequate recognition. Frappier-Mazur argues that 'starting with Scudéry, women's novels, when first published, were often attributed to male authorship or collaboration' and she cites three early twentieth-century examples: Rachilde, Colette and Liane de Pougy.[44] We are today perhaps most familiar with Colette's situation and the tale of Willy coercing his young wife to ghost write some six best-selling novels: *Claudine à l'école* (1900), *Claudine à Paris* (1901), *Claudine en ménage* (1902), *Claudine s'en va* (1903), *Minne* (1904) and *Les Egarrements de Minne* (1905). But this is not a unique example; more names could be added to Frappier-Mazur's list. Marguerite Audoux's debut work, a semi-autobiographical novel, was attributed to its promoter in the *Grande Revue*, Giraudoux, as people simply presumed the name Audoux to be an abbreviated pseudonym. Less innocent and certainly more debilitating is the case of Catherine Pozzi who, following advice from her clandestine lover Paul Valéry, published her first autobiographical novella, *Agnès* (1927), anonymously. The critics naturally tried to decipher the identity of the author; some considered Adrienne Monnier[45] who sold a special edition of the work produced at the author's expense in her Parisian bookshop-cum-library; others favoured the artist Marie Laurencin;[46] others still Valéry's daughter Agathe. When Crémieux suggested that the author was none other than Valéry himself, claiming to recognize the same cryptic style of *Lettre de Mme Emilie Teste* (published anonymously a few years previously in 1924), Valéry, fearing that a denial of authorship would compromise his marital relationship, refused to clarify the situation.[47] Pozzi, who was already much aggrieved by what she considered Valéry's plagiarism of her as yet unpublished philosophical notes, felt doubly betrayed.

These examples show the vulnerability of young women confronting the publishing world. However, it is not simply a question of appropriation. This is only one aspect of a more extensive problem women writers have always faced: the fact that their literary achievements have throughout history often been undervalued and at times unacknowledged. Here one might consider the reception of the highly prolific Gyp (Sybille Gabrielle Marie-Antoinette de Riquetti de Mirabeau, Comtesse de Martel de Jonville), who wrote from 1885 to 1933. Most critics are content to acknowledge varied aspects of Gyp's work: her representation of the tomboy and the flirt; her 'bright and spirited, pleasantly satirical and witty irony';[48] her ability to 'shake the yoke of fashion, caste and clan and to escape the influence of both milieu and professional deformation';[49] her great psychological analysis;[50] and most often her anti-semitism and her virulent attacks on the *Action française*, which peak in *Le Chambard* (1928). Gyp's greatest contribution, her innovative revival and adaptation of the novel in dialogue form, passes largely unremarked. While both Thième, in 1933 in an entry on Gyp in the *Bibliographie de la littérature française de 1800 à 1930*, and more recently Mylne acknowledge Gyp's role as originator of the modern *roman dialogué*, most literary histories persist in attributing the emergence of this sub-genre to Roger Martin du Gard. He himself did not admit his indebtedness to Gyp, for as Mylne states: 'how could he conceivably admit that he was indebted to such a writer? To acknowledge admiration of Tolstoi or Ibsen is one thing, but Gyp – the author of books about children, and one who avowedly wrote only to make money, who found politics more interesting than literature, and who was a woman. . .'[51] A similar situation occurred with the late nineteenth-century poet Marie Krysinska.[52] In *L'Observateur français* on 16 November 1890 Maurras does acknowledge her contribution to the evolution of modern poetic form, stating: 'Mme Marie Krysinska used free verse eight years ago, at a time when not one of our contemporary poets had yet thought of it. She has therefore almost invented an art form.' Yet, despite Krysinska's cardinal role, it is the name of Gustave Kahn which is most closely associated with the genre.

Clearly the hegemony of power lay so solidly in male hands that coming to writing was no easy matter for the early twentieth-century French female author. What women required to overcome these multiple difficulties in both the private and public spheres was their own major support networks. To a certain extent this was provided by the literary salon, as here women had a history of exerting considerable authority, power and influence, and this continued throughout the Belle Epoque and Inter-war era. One might recall the important *salonnières* Mme Claude Ferval, Mme Bulteau, Mme Arman de Caillavet, Mme d'Aubernon, Mme de Peyrebrune, Laure Hayman,

Princesse Mathilde, Comtesse Greffuhle, Duchesse de Rohan, Comtesse d'Haussonville, Princesse de Polignac (Willametta Singer), Comtesse Emmanuela Potocka, Mme Strauss, Nathalie Barney, Rachilde and Juliette Adam (founder of *La Nouvelle Revue*). The Inter-war literary salon, under the auspices of these women, served several indispensable purposes, supplying venues to bring a wide range of writers together, acting as a non-intimidating forum for debate and giving the opportunity to women to share the reading of their latest works. They played a part in the discovery of hidden talents (Rachilde, during the course of her Tuesday salons, was the first to realize that Colette was the real author of the *Claudine* series) and they also fostered and promoted the work of lesser-known authors (as was the case with Mme Bulteau's encouragement of Catherine Pozzi). They created the possibility of sustained female nurturance, even providing patronage in certain cases.

A further organization helped unite women writers in their pro-fessional capacities, and worked to promote female fiction as a whole: the Prix Fémina. It was created in 1904, by Mme C. de Broutelles, founder of the *Vie heureuse* magazine, to rival the major French literary award, the Goncourt (itself initiated four years previously), which was considered as having slighted female fiction. In 1904 Huysmans had withdrawn his nomination of Myriam Harry's *La Conquête de Jérusalem* in favour of Léon Frapié's *La Maternelle*, for what he stated were purely gender-related reasons, announcing in *La Fronde* on 1 February 1905 that the author was a woman and that the committee did not want to create such an annoying precedent. This well-documented, overt misogyny was not unique to Huysmans, but seems to have char-acterized the Goncourt jury as a whole. In 1917, on the death of Mirbeau, when the single female member, Judith Gautier, had a last-minute change of mind in casting her vote, Descaves publicly declared that they would be well advised in future never to elect any women. On Gautier's death, a month later, this was put into effect in the rejection of the nominations of Colette, Séverine, Mme Alphonse Daudet, Aurel and Rachilde. Colette did in fact become the next female juror, but this was not until twenty-eight years later in 1945, the year after the committee made its first award to a woman, Elsa Triolet, for *Le Premier Accroc coûte deux cent francs (1944)*.[53]

The Prix Fémina, in a direct response to this masculine solidarity, had a solely female jury, and throughout its history brought together a spectrum of critics, poets, dramatists, journalists, socialites and novelists as diverse as Colette Yver, Jeanne Galzy, Mme Simone, Rosemonde Gérard, Anna de Noailles, Lucie Delarue-Mardrus, Séverine, Germaine Beaumont, Marcelle Tinayre, Rachilde and

Daniel Lesueur. The majority of the jurors, like the Parisian *salonnières*, belonged to the leisured class, and it was they who each personally contributed an annual sum of 200 francs in prize money, until the publishers Hachette took over the provision of the annual financial remunerations. This made another marked contrast with the Goncourt award where the 5,000 francs prize came solely from a trust fund. The creation of the Prix Fémina, then, served as a major cultural and political landmark, for it publicly highlighted the sexual discrimination at play in French society as a whole and in the Parisian Parnassus in particular. Furthermore, it encouraged women in the belief that gender-specific oppression in the literary world could be opposed and indeed surmounted. It helped hearten and motivate aspiring female authors to such an extent that, notwithstanding the multiple practical and psychological difficulties to be faced, they turned in considerable numbers to writing.

Why, then, from such a substantial body of copious, widely read, Inter-war women writers do only a handful of names remain well known to us today? For the majority of writers, the heart of the problem does not lie in their contemporary reception, because the reputations of many female authors in the Inter-war years were actually well established. Numerous women were extensively honoured in their own lifetimes. In 1933, for example, while the Prix Goncourt was conferred on a male author – André Malraux for *La Condition humaine* – some 16.5 per cent of France's literary prizes went to women.[54] In the period as a whole, one-third of the recipients of the Prix Fémina awards were female, the laureates comprising Jeanne Galzy for *Les Allongés* (1923), Marie Le Franc for *Grand Louis, l'innocent* (1927), Dominique Dunois for *Georgette Garou* (1928), Geneviève Fauconnier for *Claude* (1933), Claude Silve for *Bénédiction* (1935), Louise Hervif for *Sangs* (1936) and Raymonde Vincent for *Campagne* (1937).[55] In 1930, Germaine Beaumont, with *Piège* (1930), won the Prix Renaudot, a most prestigious award which in its history has only been given to women on five subsequent occasions, in 1953, 1962, 1973, 1984 and 1985.[56] Yvonne Brisson, the feminist polemicist Louise Weiss, Colette, Anna de Noailles, Louise de Vilmorin and Marguerite Yourcenar all took their allotted place in the legion of honour lists. Even the Académie française honoured female writers when in 1918 it awarded Gérard d'Houville the Grand Prix de Littérature for her corpus as a whole, and in 1980 when it opened its doors to its first female member in over 300 years as Marguerite Yourcenar took up her prestigious chair and joined the elite ranks of the forty 'Immortals'. The Académie Royale de Belgique similarly conferred membership on Anna de Noailles in 1921, Colette in 1935, the Belgian author Marie Gevers in 1938 and Yourcenar in 1970.

Much as in the rest of Europe and America, numerous French female writers in the 1920s and 1930s undoubtedly made a striking impact on the literary scene, and were both commercially successful and widely acclaimed by contemporary critics. There is evidently a major discrepancy in the way in which these authors were viewed by their peers and how they are now conventionally perceived, as despite public renown in the Inter-war era, many of these women writers now constitute little more than a 'Forgotten Generation', and, as Bernikow has pointed out, 'when women writers were lost *someone lost them*'.[57] An overview of the reception process experienced by these authors is revealing. The neglect of some writers may be related to the change in tastes and exigences of the reading public in the period following the Second World War. Individuals such as Gyp or Elisabeth de Gramont, whose studies of contemporary mores are suffused with nostalgia for the Belle Epoque, may quite simply have been considered dated. Moreover, in the early years of the Fourth Republic, France experienced severe paper shortages which meant that publishers re-edited or reprinted only a restricted number of Inter-war works. Great efforts were expended on up-and-coming authors, on new literary schools, and on works adhering to the latest demands for political commitment or radical narrative experimentation. Inter-war and indeed post-war women did not form a cohesive school or movement with clear-cut aesthetic principles or political aims in the way that the popular existentialists now did. Because of this, their works were considered harder to market, so women's fiction as a whole saw severe cut-backs throughout the 1940s and early 1950s.

A further element in the general marginalization of French Inter-war female writers may lie in the reception accorded to their Anglo-American peers. The diverse activities of the bohemian Modernists of the Parisian Left Bank – Shakespeare and Co.'s publication of Joyce's banned *Ulysses* (1922), Josephine Baker's wild dancing to jazz improvisations, Nin's erotic fiction, Barney's overt lesbian relationships, Radclyffe Hall and Romaine Brooks' cross-dressing – fired the popular imagination. The extrovert, demonstrative nature of the Lost Generation's challenge to the restrictive behavioural norms of their country of origin served to guarantee their renown and render them immortal. Thus it is that Suleiman's study of the Inter-war era singles out Gertrude Stein as an exemplary woman writer, and Henri Peyre, writing for an American readership, comments that 'even George Sand and Colette pale when ranked beside the dozen women novelists who have contributed to English fiction since Jane Austen. French Fiction of 1910–30 does not seem to boast the equivalent of Willa Cather, or Virginia Woolf, or even Rosamund Lehmann'.[58] Even Shari Benstock's *Women of the Left Bank: Paris, 1900–1940*, which provides fascinating insights into the Parisian literary world, contains only limited reference to a few French women writers moving in Anglo-American circles, such as Colette, Lucie Delarue-Mardrus, Anna de Noailles, Georgette Leblanc and Elisabeth de Gramont. In the annals of literary history, the Lost Generation of Anglo-American modernist writers are retrospectively considered to have dominated the Parisian literary scene of the 1920s and 1930s, and this has lead to their overshadowing, indeed eclipsing, their French counterparts.

This, however, is not the complete picture, and a more polemic explanation suggests itself. Our major source of information on any previous generation's literary production is the critical anthology or literary history. Such encyclopedic works, in the apparently simple acts of condemning, commending or even simply classifying, have the greatest say in determining a work's value and establishing or ensuring an author's lasting reputation and renown. The woman author's fate rests largely in their hands. So, if we are to examine and explain the process through which French Inter-war female writers have, with the passing of time, been accorded such a marginal place in the country's literary history as to be virtually consigned to oblivion, if we are to redress their marginalization effectively, then we must analyse the highly subjective, perhaps even prejudicial, nature of canon formation through an investigation of the interplay of conscious and subconscious aesthetic tastes and political ideologies governing its underlying selection procedures. We must turn our attention to the canon compilers.

Notes

1. N. Bensadon (1980), *Les Droits de la femme des origines à nos jours*, Paris, p. 58.
2. The American government encouraged women in their pursuit of education to an unprecedented scale throughout the nineteenth century. By 1880 (when secondary schools were first open to French women) there were already 40,000 women in higher education in the United States, and one-third of all graduates were

female. Ten years later, the number of women in universities rose to 56,000, and the establishment of elite women's colleges – Vassar (1865), Smith (1875), Wellesley (1875) – added visibility to this trend. This situation was due in part to the fact that many female teachers did not stay in the profession after marriage so there was a constant demand for women to take their places, and partly because women needed greater access to education if they were to play a full part in the esteemed social settlement movement. For more details see K.K. Sklar (1993), 'The Historical Foundations of Women's Power in the Creation of the American Welfare State, 1830–1930' in S. Koven and S. Michel (eds), *Mothers of a New World: Maternalist Politics and the Origins of Welfare States*, London and New York, pp. 43–93 (pp. 62–3).

3. It was not until 1965 that equal numbers of men and women were successful in this examination. For a more detailed study of French women in education see E. Charrier (1931), *L'Evolution intellectuelle féminine*, Geneva.

4. See J.S. Allen (1991), *In the Public Eye: a History of Reading in Modern France, 1800–1940*, Princeton, NJ, pp. 61–7. He gives literacy figures for over fourteen-year-olds in 1921 as 99.1 per cent men and 98.4 per cent women.

5. J. Bertaut [1909], *La Littérature féminine d'aujourd'hui*, Paris, pp. 5–6.

6. F. Nourissier (1960), 'Le Monde du livre' in B. Pingaud (ed.), *Ecrivains d'aujourd'hui, 1940–1960*, Paris, p. 41.

7. P. Flat (1909), *Nos Femmes de lettres*, Paris, p. i.

8. J. Waelti-Walters (1990), *Feminist Novelists of the Belle Epoque: Love as a Lifestyle*, Bloomington and Indianapolis, p. 1.

9. Many English-speaking women forged a solid long-standing reputation, most notably in America Ellen Glasgow, Flannery O'Connor and Marjorie Rawlings (winner of the Pulitzer prize); in England Dorothy Richardson, Margaret Kennedy, Mary Webb, Virginia Woolf, Agatha Christie, Dorothy L. Sayers, Rosamund Lehmann, Ivy Compton-Burnett and Vita Sackville West; in Scotland Willa Muir, Catherine Carswell and Nan Shephard; in the Republic of Ireland Elizabeth Bowen. Throughout Europe many women achieved widespread recognition: in Turkey Halidé Edip Adivar; in Czechoslovakia Teréza Navakova; in Hungary Anna Lesznai and Marit Kaffka; in Poland Zofia Nalkowski, Maria Dabrowski, Zofia Korsak, Helena Boguszewska, Ewa Szelburg-Zarembina, Maria Kuncewiczowa, Maria Kasterka, Pola Gojawyczyńska, Wanda Walsilewska and Halina Gorska; in Germany Margaret zur Bentlage, Vicki Baum, Anna Seghers, Gertrude von le Fort, Gabrielle Reuter

and Ina Seidel; in Italy Amalia Guglielminetti, Matilde Serao, Ada Negri and Sibilla Aleramo; in Spain Emilia Pardo Bazan; in Portugal Florbella Espanca, Fernanda de Castro, Virginia Vitorino and Judite Teixeira; and in Russia Lidia Seifoulina, Anna Akhmatova, Lydis Tchoukovshaïa, Marina Ivanovna Tsvetaïeva and Alexendra Kollontaï. The same is true of the Scandinavian countries, which saw the emergence of Sigrid Boo in Norway; Karin Boye and Ahnes von Krusenstjerna in Sweden; in the Netherlands Ina Boudier-Bakker; in Finland Aïno Kallas, Lempi Jaas Kelainin, Maila Talvio, Edith Sodergran and Maria Jotuni; not to mention the appearance of the ever-popular Danish author Karen Blixen (better known as Isak Dinesen). This phenomenon is not totally unique to European countries as the South African Ethelreda Lewis, the Brazilian Rachel de Queiroz, the Uruguayan Juana de Ibarbourou, the Chilean Gabriela Mistral, the Argentinean Alfonsina Storni all achieved international eminence.

10. See C. Makward and O. Cazenave (1988), 'The Others' Others: Francophone Women's Writing' in J. Dejean and N.K. Miller (eds), *The Politics of Tradition: Placing Women in French Literature*, New Haven, CT, pp. 190–207 (p. 201).

11. Several non-nationals also wrote in French in the era, most notably the sapphists Nathalie Barney and Renée Vivien; the Surrealist Leonora Carrington; the Dutch realist author Neel Doff who depicted the hardship of the working classes; Russian-born Irène Némirovsky, author of some nineteen psychological novels; and the journalist Zinaïda Alexeïevna Chakhovskaïa Schakovskoy (whose fictional works appeared under the pseudonym Jacques Croisé) who produced a gamut of lyric impressionistic poetry, novels, criticism and historical studies, all in the Inter-war period.

12. J. Larnac (1929), *Histoire de la littérature féminine en France*, 2nd edn, Paris, p. 223.

13. See M. Atack and P. Powrie (eds), (1990), *Contemporary French Fiction by Women: Feminist Perspectives*, Manchester, p. 2.

14. See P.-H. Simon (1963), *Histoire de la littérature française au XXème siècle, 1900–1950*, 7th edn, Paris, vol. 1, p. 69.

15. C. Planté (1989), *La Petite Sœur de Balzac: essai sur la femme auteur*, Paris, p. 47.

16. Audoux's appearance predates the formation of the populist literary school of 1929 under Léon Lemonnier and André Thérive which, although not expressly political, aimed to present the working classes in the most favourable light possible.

17. Journalism attracted many women writers including Rachilde, Louise Weiss and Maryse Choisy.

18. Female authors involved in this area are Georgette Leblanc Irène Némirovsky, Isabelle Rivière, Denise Le-Blond Zola, Marthe de Bibesco, Marie-Louise Pailleron and Myriam Harry.
19. This is evident in the works of Marie Bonaparte, Catherine Pozzi, Jeanne Galzy and Simone Weil.
20. See entry on Germaine Beaumont (1954) in *Le Prix Fémina: ancien Prix Vie heureuse, Album du cinquantenaire, 1904–1954*, Paris.
21. A. Kolodny (1978), 'Some Notes on Defining a "Feminist Literary Criticism"' in C.L. Brown and K. Olson (eds), *Feminist Criticism*, London, pp. 37–55 (p. 39).
22. E. Brody (1988), *Paris the Musical Kaleidoscope, 1870–1925*, 2nd edn, London, p. 224.
23. M.-C. Pasquier (1984), '"Mon nom est Persona": les femmes et le théâtre' in M.-C. Pasquier (ed.), *Stratégies des femmes*, Paris, pp. 259–73.
24. Marie Lenéru's first work (promoted by Léon Blum and Fernand Gregh), *Les Affranchis* (1911), was performed at the Odéon in that year and at the Comédie-Française in 1927. Presentations of *Le Redoutable* based on the Dreyfus affair (1912) and *La Triomphatrice* (1913) were also given at the Odéon, while *La Paix, Le Bonheur des autres* and *La Maison sur le roc* were produced posthumously in 1922, 1925 and 1927 respectively. Her career is detailed in E. de La Rochefoucauld (1969), *Femmes d'hier et d'aujourd'hui*, Paris, pp. 145–53.
25. E. Wilwerth (1986), *Visages de la littérature féminine*, Brussels, p. 224.
26. English Showalter, Jr. (1988), 'Writing off the Stage: Women Authors and Eighteenth Century Theater' in J. Dejean and N.K. Miller (eds), *The Politics of Tradition: Placing Women in French Literature*, New Haven, CT, pp. 95–111 (pp. 111 and 97).
27. Ibid., p. 111.
28. J. Moulin (1963), *La Poésie féminine de Marie de France à Marie Noël, époque moderne*, Paris, p. 16.
29. In terms of the number of copies produced and sold, literature far surpassed any other type of book in the period. See Allen, *In the Public Eye*, pp. 50–70.
30. R.L. Dudovitz (1990), *The Myth of Superwoman: Women's Bestsellers in France and the United States*, London and New York, p. 5.
31. Jeanne Rougé's comment of 1933 is recorded in S. Pedersen (1993), 'Catholicism, Feminism, and the Politics of the Family during the Late Third Republic' in S. Koven and S. Michel (eds), *Mothers of a New World: Maternalist Politics and the Origins of Welfare States*, London and New York, pp. 246–76 (p. 265).

32. This situation is not unique to French writers of the period. Zelda Fitzgerald, for instance, suffered a similar fate. Following the publication of her autobiographical novel *Save me this Waltz* (1932), she was confined by her husband to a series of American 'rest cure' institutions, where writing was forbidden. She died in 1948 leaving her last work incomplete.

33. Early works by Elsa Triolet include *A Tahiti* (1925), *Fraise-desbois* (1925), *Camouflage* (1928) and *Colliers* (written in Russian in 1931 and published in 1973), and *Bonsoir Thérèse* (1938) written in French.

34. See L. Mackinnon (1992), *The Lives of Elsa Triolet*, London, pp. 150 and 96–7.

35. For more information see three biographical studies: C. de Bartillat (1985), *Clara Malraux: le regard d'une femme sur son siècle, biographie – témoignage*, Paris, especially pp. 21, 65, and 184; A. Madsen (1989), *Silkroads: the Asian Adventures of Clara and André Malraux*, New York, pp. 17 and 198; and I. de Courtivron (1992), *Clara Malraux, une femme dans le siècle*, Paris, pp. 54, 93, 199 and 215.

36. Prior to meeting Malraux, Clotis had produced three fictional works, *Le Temps vert* (1932), *Une Mesure pour rien* (1934) and *Le Vannier* (1946 posth.), which had been praised by Pourrat, Drieu la Rochelle and Montherlant.

37. Numerous examples of Malraux's discouragement are provided by S. Chantal (1976), *Le Cœur battant: Josette Clotis, André Malraux*, Paris.

38. For further details and examples of this see J. Chalon (1987), *Florence at Louise les magnifiques: Florence Jay-Gould et Louise de Vilmorin*, Monaco, pp. 104 and 151–2.

39. She withheld her later works from the critics. Five volumes of poetry appeared posthumously under the name Renée Vivien: *Dans un coin de violettes* (1909), *Le Vent des vaisseaux* (1909), *Haillons* (1910), her prose poems *Vagabondages* (1917), and a collected edition of poems, *Poésies complètes* (1923–4).

40. H. Peyre (1955), *The Contemporary French Novel*, New York and Oxford, p. 256.

41. A. Sauvy (1986), 'La Littérature et les femmes' in H.J. Martin, R. Chartier and J.P. Vivets (eds), *Histoire de l'édition française: le livre concurrencé, 1900–1950*, Paris, vol. 4, pp. 242–55 (p. 255).

42. In 1925 Boots circulated 25 million volumes and this figure rose to 35 million in 1939, according to statistics provided by N. Beauman (1983), *A Very Great Profession: the Woman's Novel, 1914–39*, London, pp. 10–11.

43. See A.-M. Thiesse (1984), *Le Roman quotidien: lecteurs et lectures populaires à la Belle Epoque*, Paris, p. 30.
44. L. Frappier-Mazur (1988), 'Marginal Canons: Rewriting the Erotic' in J. Dejean and N.K. Miller (eds), *The Politics of Tradition: Placing Women in French Literature*, New Haven, CT, pp. 112–28 (p. 118).
45. Adrienne Monnier produced two volumes of anti-conformist poetry, *La Figure* (1923) and *Les Vertus* (1928), and under the pseudonym J.M. Sollier, *Fableaux* (1932). These were re-edited, with additional hitherto unpublished poems and fables, in the early 1960s.
46. Marie Laurencin produced one collection of poetry, *Carnet des nuits* (1942), which was re-edited posthumously with additional poems in 1956.
47. On 9 May 1927 Henri Fourgassié gave Catherine a copy of *L'Echo* where it was written 'on assure que Paul Valéry a collaboré'. See Catherine Pozzi, *Journal 1913–1934*, Paris, pp. 370–2.
48. H. Lemaître (1985), *Dictionnaire Bordas de littérature française*, Paris, p. 361.
49. Michel Missoffe (1932), *Gyp et ses amis*, Paris, p. x.
50. Nietzsche, in *Ecce homo*, in a chapter entitled 'Why I'm so cunning' ('Pourquoi je suis si malin'), assumes Gyp is a male author and presents her in a highly laudatory fashion as one of the greatest contemporary French psychological novelists.
51. V. Mylne (Spring 1991), 'Martin du Gard, the *Roman dialogué*, and Gyp', *French Studies Bulletin*, no. 38, pp. 3–5 (p. 4).
52. Marie Krysinska published a range of poems in *Chronique parisienne*, *Le Chat noir* and *La Libre Revue*, before producing three poetry collections: *Rythmes pittoresques* (1890), *Joies errantes* (1894) and *Intermèdes* (1904).
53. For additional details see R. Gouze (1973), *Les Bêtes à Goncourt: un demi-siècle de batailles littéraires*, Paris.
54. The particular awards were as follows: de l'Académie belge (2), de l'Alsace littéraire, des Amis de la Fontaine, Amyot, Fémina, Minerva, Paul Linter, du Premier Roman, du Roman d'aventures, Séverine, de la Société des gens de lettres (3: du Conseil municipal, Barratin and Léon Durauchel) and Verhaeren. For information on all aspects of French literary awards see *Guide des Prix littéraires* (1955), 2nd edn, Paris.
55. Previous female winners include Myriam Harry in 1904 for *La Petite Fille de Jérusalem*, André Corthis in 1906 for *Gemmes et moires*, Colette Yver in 1907 for *Princesses de science*, Marguerite Audoux in 1910 for *Marie-Claire* and Camille Marbo in 1913 for

La Statue voilée. No award was made during the First and Second World Wars. The impressive roll of female names continues throughout the 1940s and 1950s with A.M. Monnet, Gabrielle Roy, Maria Le Hardouin, Anne de Tourville and Dominique Rollin.

56. The value of such awards should not be underrated. According to figures provided by François Nourissier the winner of the Goncourt could expect to sell some 100,000–350,000 books, the Fémina 60,000–150,000, and the Renaudot and Iterallié around 75,000. As the author was entitled to between 10 and 15 per cent of the publishing rights, a major award signified several years' financial security.

57. L. Bernikow (1980), *Among Women*, New York, p. 34.

58. Peyre, *The Contemporary French Novel*, p. 251.

- 2 -

'Miss'-Representations

In early eighteenth-century France there coexisted two distinct forms
of literary guide: what Dejean terms 'the worldly anthology' and 'the
pedagogical anthology'.[1] The former, the more long-standing of the
two, was targeted at an already educated, non-gender-specific, adult
readership who wanted to keep abreast of the literary scene. Much
like a present-day books-in-print catalogue, it offered a wide display
of available reading material. In contrast, the pedagogical anthology
emerged in this period in the aftermath of the late seventeenth-century
Querelle des Anciens et des Modernes. As the curriculum in educational
institutions changed and contemporary French texts took their place
alongside works of classical literature, it was assumed that school-
masters would require guidance on what constituted suitable reading
material for the socially elevated French schoolboy. Educators, theorists and critics endeavoured to select literature deemed worthy of
detailed scholarly analysis (both works amenable to Batteux's increasingly popular *explication de texte* methodology, and works deemed
ideologically sound by critics such as Gouget), and to inscribe these
great French classics in the new form of highly selective compilation.[2]
In this way the modern canon, as it is known today, came into being.[3]
   While the specific nature of the canon of works promoted by
literary histories and anthologies has often been, and continues to be,
a subject of much controversy, the overall power and authority of
these compilations is undisputed. Several factors contribute to this:
most obviously the weight of the printed word and the particular
closed form of these works, which are unaccountable and provide
no opportunity for redress. The firmly established bond with the
educational process is equally responsible, as even today these works
continue to play an important role as school and university textbooks,
as is indicated in the preface to Castex and Surer's *Manuel des études
littéraires françaises* which explains that the guide is intended for students
at all levels – in *collèges, lycées,* universities and teacher-training colleges.
Their authors, too, are frequently involved in education and this

was especially so in the period immediately preceding the Great War, between 1890 and 1914, when literary critics, historians and anthologizers, almost without exception, formed part of the academic establishment. Most importantly, the considerable influence of canonical compilations stems naturally from the hierarchical power structure of the teacher-student relationship.

This power became especially problematic in the early twentieth century when canonical works underwent a further metamorphosis. Literary appreciation, which had traditionally come to form their mainstay, was replaced by a form of criticism which was more avowedly neutral. This reflected the growing credence accorded to scientific documentation, which had already exerted an influence in the literary world where empirical verifiable evidence had proved most fashionable with the late nineteenth-century Naturalist school. In the realm of literary analysis it was Gustave Lanson who stressed the primordial importance of an objective methodology, and his theories proved highly influential until the late 1960s.[4] For Lanson, criticism had to be based on objective facts, comprising primary and secondary bibliographical information and detailed studies of changes made by writers to their manuscripts.[5] Through such analyses critics could come to have a balanced and fair understanding of the development within an author's works and consequently could establish just what determines the specificity of any given writer. Lanson's claimed objectivity was related to only two inter-connected phases of the critics' task: the *explanation* and *classification* of literature. However, as already indicated, since the mid-eighteenth century, when the link with literary guides and education was first forged, the critics' major role had notably altered: their work had become primarily the *selection* of great authors who would constitute the canon. This aspect of the critical process is highly subjective; here the critics have the greatest recourse to personal opinions. As Moi puts it: 'aesthetic judgements are historically relative and deeply imbricated in value judgements', that is to say that all literary choices are coloured by socio-cultural conditions, and objectivity in this area is impossible.[6] This creates a particularly interesting problem: Lansonian objectivity may all too easily be misconstrued. The intended reader – the school child, university student, or trainee teacher, already in a subservient position in academic hierarchies – may be misled into accepting as valid not just the supposedly objective way in which a writer is represented, but also the very selection procedure employed to determine which writers should form part of a pedagogical anthology or educational syllabus. The privileges entailed by this combination of a very real authority and an appearance of objectivity are all too clearly open to abuse.

In recent years, feminist critics and theorists have become more fully conscious of the extent to which women have been overlooked in canonical works.[7] There are indeed many illustrations of this marginalization. Lanson's own overview of French literature from medieval times to the 1950s, *Histoire de la littérature française*, is a case in point. Despite his faith in objective methodology and claimed impartiality, Lanson fails significantly to recognize female achievement or give it adequate analysis. One need only consider the percentage coverage given to women writers to see an example of this gendered bias. Of 1,601 writers discussed only 97 are female (6.06 per cent), and in the Inter-war period, when female fiction was so prevalent, this drops to a mere 1.88 per cent.[8] In this acute under-representation of women writers Lanson is not in any sense unique.

Canonical compilations covering the Inter-war period may be separated into two different categories. In works belonging to the first of these groupings, only a limited number of writers feature, as the purpose is to create or reinforce a canonical model through an exceedingly severe process of elimination. In the most extreme cases a number of these works notably ignore female fiction in its entirety. Raimond's *Le Roman contemporain* is a fairly typical example in that it aims to give an overview of the French novel by focusing on modern classics, yet it finds only seven men worthy of attention and no women. The 1926 Sagittaire *Anthologie de la nouvelle prose française* proposes a selection of writers whom the reading public consider representative of the period as a whole.[9] When one considers the high percentage of women readers who constitute this discerning public, it is surprising that the twenty-five selected modern French prose writers are all men. Most frequently, though, a very limited number of women are mentioned, as table 2.1 indicates.[10] Although on occasion the proportion of pages dedicated to Inter-war women writers in these works may go as high as 4.60 per cent (Lagarde et Michard) the total number covered never goes above 3.03 per cent (Brée) and, more importantly, it is without fail the same limited selection of women who repeatedly feature. In sections depicting the pre-war period reference is made to two writers. The first of these is Anna de Noailles (née de Bibesco-Branconvan) who produced fourteen volumes of lyric poetry including her prose poems *Exactitudes* (1930) and three posthumous collections, an autobiography *Le Livre de ma vie* (1932), three novels – *La Nouvelle Espérance* (1903), *Le Visage émerveillé* (1904) and *La Domination* (1905) – and a considerable number of articles, prefaces and essays.[11] The second author from this early period is Rachilde (Mme Alfred Valette, née Marguerite Eymery), who wrote from 1877 to 1942. In the Inter-war era the single author

Table 2.1

Date	Author	Period	% pages	Women: men
1949	Picon	1900–49	0.28	10:354
1950	McMillan	1919–49	2.02	1:55
1951	Lanson (Tuffrau)	1919–39	1.18	1:52
1953	Castex et Surer	1900–19	1.45	1:61
		1919–39	1.61	1:68
1956	Cazamian	1900–55	0.00	0:53
1960	Pingaud	1940–60	–	6:53
1962	Brée	1900–60	3.17	1:32
1962	Lagarde et Michard	1900–14	0.46	1:35
		1914–39	4.60	1:47
		1939–62	4.30	5:49
1970	Chassang and Senninger	1900–19	1.58	1:25
		1919–39	1.60	1:70
		1939–70	8.47	5:54

featured is Colette. In the post-war period homage is paid to three writers whose literary careers started in the Inter-war years: Nathalie Sarraute whose prose poems *Tropismes* were first published in 1939, Simone Weil whose works were written before 1943 though published posthumously, and Marguerite Yourcenar.[12] Thus some six women who produced literary works in the 1920s and 1930s feature. When one recalls that not six, but over six *hundred* women authors registered in 1928 as members of the Société des gens de lettres, this minimal representation in scholarly works is disturbing.

Not all literary manuals are so severe in their selection procedure. A comparatively small body of works do, in fact, provide a more extensive coverage of women writers. This second type of encyclopedic manual gives a more panoramic overview of particular periods and in so doing depicts a wider range of heterogeneous writers in a variety of diverse fields. As may be seen in table 2.2, the number of women writers included in these compilations is significantly increased. Instead of some six Inter-war women featuring, the figure now reaches 14 at worst (Abry and Audic) and 239 at best (Bethléem). These numbers may be somewhat deceptive if seen in isolation. While a larger number of women do appear, they still constitute a fairly small part of the overall number of writers. Again Bethléem's overview is most favourable with a female:male ratio of just under 1:8. Most importantly, though, women are given a considerably lower percentage page coverage than their male counterparts. Here it is impossible

Table 2.2

Date	Author	Period	Women	% of total no. authors
1932	Bethléem	1851–1932	239	13.3
1940	Clouard vol i	1885–1914	44	5.2
	vol ii	1914–1940	10	6.5
1942	Abry and Audic	1900–1942	14	3.7
1947	Lalou	1870–1947	97	6.3
1955	Peyre	1910–1955	71	8.2
1962	Clouard	1915–1960	120	8.4
1963	Simon	1900–1950	34	4.8
1982	Daspre and Décaudin	1913–1976	131	6.4

to give exact figures as all too frequently female writers receive scant mention, often having only a few lines, not pages, dedicated to their work and lives. This in part results from the fact that, like the anthological compilations, these expansive historical overviews are also attempting to create or reinforce an already accepted canon. From a wide general survey they highlight the classics by contextualizing them, implicitly contrasting them with works deemed of lesser interest which receive a correspondingly small coverage. In this there is often a marked polarization of 'high' and 'low' literature and many popular and indeed best-selling writers of both sexes find themselves cast out to the fringes. In a number of these works, populist male writers too, such as Lucien Jean, Charles Louis-Philippe, Elie Faure, Jean-Richard Bloch, Pierre Hamp, Jean Guéhenno, Emile Guillaumin, Léon Lemonnier, André Thérive, Eugène Dabit, Henri Troyat, Henry Poulaille, André Sevry and Henri Pollès, suffer a similar fate. In the main, though, it is women writers who are most systematically reduced to serving only the secondary role of constituting a general framework, and in the majority of these manuals, while a few sporadic names appear in the main body of the text, or in footnotes, women are segregated and classified together as a homogeneous entity. So even when women's writing in these works is recognized the literary historians accord it an inferior place. What we see, as Evans notes, is 'an impure, convoluted form of negative inclusion', 'a trivialized and distorted presence'.[13] This physical position on the periphery, then, reflects the critics' ideological marginalization of women writers.

Although the narrow anthological and broad historical overviews of Inter-war literature have quite a different format, their underrepresentation of women writers is essentially uniform and their failure to valorize women writers adequately is problematic. According to Parker and Pollock, the canon presents talented women writers as 'a strange phenomenon, an exception (. . .) often transformed into a legend (. . .) and the existence of the larger community of women artists to which she belonged is obliterated by the mystifying notion of individual genius. With such an ideology artists become exceptional beings and women artists exceptions.'[14] The implications are obvious. Not only is there a tendency towards tokenism in the representation of women writers who successfully penetrate these male preserves, but the establishment also transforms women writers into opponents vying for the same limited space, such that, as Heilbrun argues, exceptional women become 'the chief imprisoners of non-exceptional women, simultaneously proving that any woman could do it and assuring, in their uniqueness among men, that no other woman will'.[15] This effectively isolates women, undermining possibilities of solidarity and mutual support. Most importantly, though, canonical under-representation dismantles any sense of a strong female tradition and denies future generations of women writers full access to their specific literary heritage.

The limited recognition of women writers is rarely acknowledged, far less explained or justified, by literary historians and anthologizers. Indeed, canon compilers themselves seldom offer any account of the selection procedures they employ. A notable exception is Bethléem, the critic featured in the earlier tables who most favourably represents female fiction in terms of both numbers and percentage page coverage. Bethléem does in fact submit certain criteria for his selection procedure, and his study is of interest as it helps illuminate the general selection principles more commonly in use. His unique work *Romans à lire et romans à proscrire* has much in common with a books-in-print catalogue in that it claims not to be a literary, critical or scholarly work, nor indeed a philosophical or historical study of the major novels of the period. It sets itself apart from the pedagogical manual, for the works selected and classified in it are judged in relation to religious and moral law. Its six general categories include novels banned by the Roman Catholic Church as heretical or pornographic literature whose readers are punishable by excommunication; works which depict and justify challenges to familial and marital relationships; works which are suitable only for readers of mature age and judgement; *romans honnêtes*; Catholic novels aimed specifically at an adolescent reader; and finally tales for children. In distinguishing his work from the mainstream, Bethléem suggests that aesthetic taste is the basis of most canonical selection, a point supported by several further literary historians. Castex and Surer inform their readers that Lanson's ardent followers

admire 'his scientific authority, his intellectual honesty and his literary
taste'. They continue in the same vein with their assertion in relation
to Thibaudet that criticism is 'first and foremost the art of developing
a *taste* for fine works'.[16] Selection is presented not so much a personal,
subjective choice, but rather as the direct result of adhering to a universally accepted standard of what constitutes good taste: established
critics appear, quite intuitively, to recognize taste, and almost all
women writers fail to meet its demands! While canon compilers shy
from openly admitting the ideological basis of their judgements,
gender (like race, creed, religion and political persuasion) evidently
plays a covert, highly complex part. If the under-representation and
resultant misrepresentation of women writers are to be fully understood and corrected, we must now unearth and assess these canonical
assumptions concerning gender through a detailed examination of the
general terminology employed to discuss canonized writers and a study
of the actual way in which successful women are portrayed in literary
histories.

An analysis of two typical critical works helps illuminate the situation.
Germaine Brée and Margaret Guiton's *The French Novel from Gide to
Camus* is a classic example of a literary history which under-represents
women writers. Of the twenty-one authors it discusses in full, not one
is female. The single selection criterion employed is indicated in the
introduction:

> To the question, What should the *man of letters* be in our time? Allen Tate
> has answered: '*He* must re-create for *his* age the image of *man*, and *he* must
> propagate standards by which *other men* may test that image, and distinguish
> the false from the true.'
>   This definition explains the particular prestige of the French novel of the
> period between the two wars. If the names of Gide, Proust, Bernanos,
> Saint-Exupéry, Malraux, Sartre and Camus have become familiar to so
> wide a reading public in so many different countries it is because these
> novelists effectively created *a new image of man* for their age.[17] (my italics)

It is this prioritizing of masculinity as much as literary innovation
which dominates Brée and Guiton's choice of authors, as their chapter
titles, 'The Masters' and 'Returns to Man', equally attest. The gender
discrimination implicit in their terminology, which persists throughout
the anthology, reinforces stereotypical assumptions about the natural
inferiority of women, assumptions stressed by Peyre in *The Contemporary French Novel*. Peyre openly acknowledges that women authors
are in 'exile from a vast section of literature' because of the male-

dominated nature of the publishing world; yet, he still holds that women are personally responsible for their own canonical omission and takes it upon himself to chastise and instruct budding female authors – women novelists will continue to be excluded until they 'universalize their experience in powerful works of fiction'. They must 'hold the mirror up to men, creating male characters in whom men are forced to recognize themselves'.[18] This echoes the attitude of many nineteenth-century critics, who, according to Planté, hold that only male writers can successfully produce works of universal interest.[19] Peyre then cites several successful post-war women writers as an example: Marguerite Duras has vigour, Denise Fontaine has produced 'among the most serious and virile attempts by a woman writer of her generation', while Simone de Beauvoir and Béatrice Beck have created 'some fiercely "masculine" and thoughtful works'.[20]

Femininity, for Peyre, Brée and Guiton, is of secondary and consequently lesser interest, at best a failed Woolfian dream of androgyny. In Brée and Guiton's work, while no reference is made to female Inter-war fiction, the post-war 'feminine novel' does receive brief mention in contradistinction to a dominant male tradition as: 'another reaction against the conscious "virility" of the novel of commitment'.[21] Women are repeatedly represented as being distanced from the major male intellectual and cultural debates of the day. There is no awareness of women writers' concern over the traumatic legacy of the war, of the current economic problems of inflation, the devaluation of the franc and soaring national debt, or indeed the political issues of depopulation, the emergence of mass consumerism, unparalleled industrial expansion, escalating class tension, the rise of the Soviet state in the 1920s and of Nationalist Socialism in Germany in the 1930s. There is no appreciation of their interest in contemporary aesthetic preoccupations with complex generic experimentation or with the novel's representational crisis, and there is no recognition of their philosophical interest in the sway of phenomenological thought. Nor for that matter is there even any real acknowledgement of their endeavour to create a new means of expressing and understanding the nature of being female in the period – a theme, which as we have seen in the introduction, preoccupied legislators, journalists, industrialists and demographers alike. In short, while these issues may concern actual French women in their daily lives, they are deemed too important, too 'masculine' to form any major part of female-authored literature, and for many canon compilers, it is this single concept of masculinity, often under the guise of universality, which is the standard of excellence against which writers are to be judged. This is their highest form of approval and acclaim. Atwood's analysis of present-day literary reviews sees the same code of values in action, for while men are not commended for transcending their gender, 'it is the height of approbation to describe a woman as *unrepresentative* of her sex'.[22] It is particularly interesting, then, that of the six celebrated female authors who appear in canonical anthologies covering 1918 to 1939 two are explicitly accepted because of supposedly masculine qualities in their fiction: Rachilde and Marguerite Yourcenar.[23]

Of these writers, Rachilde was the first to make her mark on the literary world, and almost at once contemporary male critics keenly appropriated her fiction to a male realm. David is perhaps the best example of this, for even the title of his critical monograph on Rachilde highlights his interest, *Rachilde, 'homme' de lettres*. His work is structured around a series of journal articles and unpublished letters from male writers and admirers which share a common feature of focusing on Rachilde's virility. David and the critics he cites persistently place Rachilde in an exclusively male ongoing tradition. Barrès, for example, refers to her affectionately as 'Mademoiselle Baudelaire', while Maeterlinck sees in her works the influence of Rimbaud, Whitman and Lautréamont. A further facet of male appropriation, omnipresent in David's work, rests on a sharp distinction being drawn between Rachilde and her female peers. From the opening paragraphs, David highlights Rachilde's uniqueness: he transforms the standard metaphor of woman as flower by describing Rachilde in terms of a giant, purple, elaborate, sharp cactus. He cites Huysmans who sees Rachilde as 'the only *femme de lettres* who was a real author'. He includes Rémy de Gourmont who in an unpublished letter of 1895 wrote to Rachilde 'you cannot literally be a woman, for if you were you would be the worst kind of monster'.[24] This treatment of Rachilde is not unique to the critics selected by David. Bertaut also holds that Rachilde is 'less female than her female peers',[25] while Tailhade in *Le Français* (21 February 1901), placing her name in an illustrious list of male writers alongside Hoffman, Poe, Sade and Crébillon *fils*, compares her style most favourably with that of earlier bluestockings, an opinion reiterated by Retté in *La Meuse* (13 February 1905).

That Rachilde approved this emasculation, there can be little doubt. Like her male biographers, she perpetuates the myth of her innate masculinity, in terms of her life story. In *Pourquoi je ne suis pas féministe* (1928) she shows no admiration for, or attachment to, any of the female members of her family, even going so far as to deny having any maternal feelings for her daughter Gabrielle. Largely self-taught, she acknowledges no maternal instruction. Rather, she attributes her literary tastes and education to her grandfather's 3,000-volume library. Her espousal of masculine values continues in her choice of pseud-onyms, Jean de Childra and Rachilde, which, as she explains in *Quand j'étais jeune* (1947), she pretended in her early adolescence was the name of a medieval Swedish gentleman whom she had contacted in spiritualist seances. The most obvious instance of her virilized self-portrait is her decision in the 1880s to refer to herself in the masculine and to wear male clothing, for which she required a special dispen-sation from the *préfecture de police*, granted on the grounds that male attire would facilitate her work as a journalist. Rachilde took this privilege to its logical extreme by having printed 'Rachilde, *homme de lettres*' on her professional calling cards (hence the title of David's study).

Moreover, in her critical works, particularly in her literary column in the *Mercure de France*, Rachilde clearly demonstrates a single-minded valorization of the masculine. Only a few women writers of the era receive any degree of approval, and these all conform to her concept of a masculine model. She says admiringly of Séverine 'she is not a woman of letters, she is a man of action',[26] and in her review of *La Retraite sentimentale*, she talks of Colette's Claudine as though both the author and heroine were male.[27] Conversely, authors she considers 'feminine' are lauded only if they are unthreatening: the dramatist Marie Lenéru and Aurel (Auvélie de Faucamberge) who was refused a position on the Goncourt jury. As a result of Rachilde's desire to be seen as exceptional, her overall attitude to women writers was deprecatively dismissive, such that, as Dauphiné suggests, Rachilde comes across as a traitor, a renegade, who, having secured an enviable degree of power and renown, refuses all solidarity with her peers and joins the male camp.[28] While it should not be forgotten that Rachilde's intense ambitiousness and desire to distinguish herself from the mass of female writers does result, in part at least, from her attachment to the elitist Romantic image of the artist being separate and superior, and, of course, from the literary environment in which she wrote, where the male-dominated establishment encouraged competitiveness by its minimal recognition of female talent, it is nonetheless the case that her vitriolic attack on her female peers was frequently excessive, as is evident in her overview of women writers: 'All these *femmes de lettres*, generally speaking, have come out of their intimate settings in order to display themselves on the literary stage dressed up as gossip columnists.'[29] For the literary stars of the period she expressed mainly contempt. In particular, Anna de Noailles aroused fierce jealousy, because her literary achievements were so widely eulogized and Rachilde bitterly commented on this public recognition to Léautaud, saying: 'The *légion d'honneur* is a fine thing, given all the prostitutes who are recipients.'[30] Noailles was seen as an imitator, who mimicked the intellectual snobbery of a Proustian environment, and as a writer whose talent was akin to that of Francis Jammes. Renée Vivien, similarly, was accused of exploiting the period's taste for both sapphism and decadence, while Marcelle Tinayre and Colette Yver (Antoinette de Bergevin) came under attack for the mediocrity of their style, their deficient imaginative powers and their supposedly feminist rewritings of ultra-conventional scenes.[31] For Rachilde, feminism was little more than a fashionable pose, as her ironic *Pourquoi je ne suis pas féministe* all too clearly indicates. Some recent criticism on Rachilde's own literary contribution (which will be discussed at length in chapter six) suggests that here too she colluded with, and was not simply subject to, the masculinization process. Birkett, for example, notes that Rachilde 'found a market and packaged herself for it', as far from being a feminist, as certain critics have suggested, Rachilde was more than willing 'to play and play up to the decadent stereotypes'. For Birkett, her fiction is an act of 'self-castration' in which the creative imagination is at the service of male masochistic fantasies: 'From the beginning, she accepts dependency on men as the price of existence, and writes to extend dependency, glamorizing submission and painting the pleasures of self-delusion.'[32] Her close relationship with the masculine held fast throughout her writing career, and in this she was not alone.

Marguerite Yourcenar underwent a remarkably similar process. Her biographical details show strong links to traditional male realms of experience – her mother died when she was just ten years old and she spent her adolescence travelling with her father and voraciously reading works of philosophy, history, art and literature under the guidance of a private tutor. As with Rachilde, her choice pseudonym shows an attachment to the notion of a male authorial persona as 'Yourcenar' is a near anagram of her paternal surname 'Crayencour'. But the attribution of masculinity is most evident in terms of her reception. After twenty-five years of writing, she reached an expansive reading public and received great critical acclaim with the publication of *Mémoires d'Hadrien* in 1951 (a subject also treated by Rachilde in her play 'La mort d'Antinoüs'[33]), and from this date onwards literary historians and scholars have systematically stressed the masculine nature of her writings. Interestingly enough, Yourcenar supports this reading as she in turn dismisses her early works which did not secure her place in the male-dominated canon. She retrospectively considered her writing career in three stages: 1922 to 1934, 1934 to 1948, and post-1948, her most successful period.[34] Much of the literature produced in the 1920s and 1930s, the first two phases of her career – she wrote twelve works and planned what were seen to be her major contributions to literature: *Mémoirs d'Hadrien* (1951), *L'Œuvre au noir* (1968) and *Archives du nord* (1977) – she denounces outright in her interview with Galey. She rejects her earliest poetry collections, *Le Jardin des Chimères* (1921) and *Les Dieux sont pas morts* (1922), despite the fact that their themes furnished material for the later *Les Charités d'Alcippe* (1956). Her fourth work, *La Nouvelle Eurydice* (1931), she attacks for its weak and artificial construction, not to mention its traditional dependence on romance and scenic beauty. *Pindare* (1932) too she berates as a weak work produced when she was still 'an adolescent who knew virtually nothing'.[35] Even her early drafts of *Mémoires d'Hadrien*, the novel which secured her renown as a 'masculine writer', written between 1924 and 1926, that is, between the age of twenty and twenty-three, Yourcenar disparagingly undermines: 'All these manuscripts have been deservedly destroyed.'[36]

For the critics, three aspects of Yourcenar's writings merit the masculine label: her limited depiction of women, her distinctive voice or style and her thematic preferences. Yourcenar holds that women have played a minimal part in making history, limited as they have been to the private sphere. Consequently, while female characters may well appear in *Feux* (1936), share the stage in *Denier du rêve* (1934) and *Nouvelles orientales* (1938), and feature more prominently in the case of Sophie in *Le Coup de grâce* (1939) and Plotina in *Mémoires d'Hadrien*, by and large their roles are circumscribed or ineffectual. With the exception of 'Anna Soror' relationships between women, especially mother–daughter rapports which flourish in most female-authored fiction, are strikingly absent. In the main, Yourcenar's protagonists, with whom critics feel she strongly identifies, are male and their frequent homosexual preference further relegates women to a position of minor interest. This lack of well-defined, vibrant, active female characters is reflected in the paralleled absence of a dominant female voice. King, writing on the gendered voice, highlights many aspects of Yourcenar's fiction which she believes resemble a more masculine form of discourse: 'Her style, with its use of maxims, abstractions, technical vocabulary, detailed descriptions, bears little resemblance to most definitions of women's style. Her syntax is controlled, clearly articulated, never obscure; she uses a great number of complex sentences, with many subordinate clauses.'[37] To this, one could easily add Kramarae's description: 'forceful', 'efficient', 'blunt', 'authoritative', 'serious', 'sparring' and 'masterful'.[38] King also notes Yourcenar's tendency to employ a tone which is 'pedagogical', 'explanatory' and 'hypothesizing', and 'a deliberately authoritative, perhaps extremely "aristocratic" voice, that attempts to be more "manly" than most men'.[39] Critics too find Yourcenar's relatively impersonal subject matter masculine. Her novels are characterized by a well-delineated and distanced geographical and historical framework. Her fiction covers a temporal and spatial terrain as diverse as classical Greece (*Feux*), Ancient Rome (*Mémoires d'Hadrien*), medieval Belgium (*L'Œuvre au noir*), the Orient (*Nouvelles orientales*), Austro-Hungary before the Great War (*Le Coup de grâce*), Elizabethan times (*Une Belle matinée*), eleventh-century Italy (*Denier du rêve*) and seventeenth-century Holland (*D'après Rembrandt*). Critics seize on this as evidence of masculinity. Peyre, for example, in an analysis of the French novel aimed at American students, suggests that Yourcenar stands in contrast with the female talent preceding her in his list as she brings to literature an 'immense and solid culture'.[40] Peyre considers a wide-developed cultural knowledge as specific to men. However, in this he fails to place Yourcenar in the social context of the Inter-war period which saw women travelling extensively and writing about their voyages. Here one might consider the exemplary explorer and writer Alexandra David-Neel who toured China and who was the first woman to enter the forbidden territories of Tibet, and the novelists Myriam Harry, sent by the government on many diplomatic missions, and Lucie Delarue-Mardrus who travelled extensively in both North Africa and the Middle East. Robinson, more recently, offers a much more convincing analysis of Yourcenar's attempts to 'arrogate to herself some of the freedom of the "ruling class"'. He argues that her conflation of power with male rather than female homosexuality allows her to distance herself from inimical contemporary, patriarchal, heterocratic norms and to transpose her own values (which he aligns with a 'continuum' approach to lesbianism) onto male images – this being analogous to the Modernist taste for cross-dressing. Robinson writes: 'what Yourcenar seems to be doing is to focus on the philosophical issues of identity and personal liberty, laying claim to equal status with male writers by inserting herself into a *male* homosexual writing tradition (Gidean) and by taking on what would traditionally be defined as a 'male' (i.e. abstract) approach'.[41]

An overview of Yourcenar's attitudes to other writers confirms this reading. Like Rachilde she read widely and admitted to being greatly interested and influenced by a range of writers (a number of whom are homosexual, as Robinson suggests). She acknowledged having studied the classics, Shakespeare, the Metaphysical poets, Yeats, Swinburne, Russian works by Merezhkovski and Tolstoy; and while she only came to French writers in her late adolescence she succeeded in reading Barrès, Proust, Rimbaud, Apollinaire, Rilke, Gide, Racine,

La Fontaine, Péguy and, much later, Baudelaire, Cioran, Roger Caillois, Ionesco, Nietzsche, Schopenhauer and Mann. What is particularly striking in this wide spectrum of acknowledged learned writers is the absence of other women. In her reception speech at the Académie Royale de Belgique in March 1971 she recognizes no female predecessors. In her reception speech at the Académie française ten years later, in January 1981, she briefly mentions three: – Mme de Staël, George Sand and Colette. In each case, rather than stress the authors' literary skills, she indicates reasons for their exclusion, concluding somewhat ironically that the Academy, far from being misogynistic, revered femininity too much.[42]

In her interview with Galey she cites only six women writers worthy of acclaim. The female author receiving her fullest commendation she hails as a Japanese Proust: 'When I am asked the woman writer I most admire the name Murasaki Shikibu springs to mind, as I have for her a great respect and extraordinary reverence.' Selma Lagerlöf, winner of the Nobel Prize for Literature, who features in *Sous bénéfice d'inventaire* (1962), receives muted praise. She is introduced as her father's favourite and described as 'a very great writer who is, in addition, female', where her gender is clearly incidental. Lagerlöf is of interest to Yourcenar solely because of her shared fascination with mythology, not because of her excellent analysis of childhood which Yourcenar wholeheartedly condemned. Virginia Woolf, who also features in *Sous bénéfice d'inventaire*, is reduced to an unusual personality, with Yourcenar focusing on her physical frailty and trivializing her work. When it comes to female writers nearer to home Yourcenar becomes increasingly volatile and dismissive. The most notable example of this is her attack on France's most popular children's fiction writer: 'I must say that I have always loathed the works of the Comtesse de Ségur. The Bibliothèque Rose series still fills me with horror when I see a copy: those children annoyed me, as they seemed unrealistic and spoiled by conventions through which I saw all too easily.' Simone Weil is named in passing as a great writer but Yourcenar is quick to inform us that she is part of no tradition, beyond any scale of judgement and hence comparison. Indeed, the only French woman to be honoured in any way is Renée Montlaur,[43] who is depicted as 'a forgotten writer who is quite unknown today'.[44] What one sees here are three traits: firstly an acknowledgement only of unknown, inaccessible writers (distanced both geographically and through language – Shikibu is Japanese, Lagerlöf is Scandinavian); secondly, a belittling of any female literary endeavour which differs from her own; and thirdly, a suppression of rivals, which, as we have seen, is not uncommon among successful women writers.

This analysis of the critical works by Peyre, Brée and Guiton, and the case-studies of Rachilde and Yourcenar, would seem to suggest that the severe under-representation of women in canonical anthologies is related to gender, as both male critics and women schooled in their way of thought, particularly those who benefit from the existing system, deem the attribution of masculinity as the highest form of compliment. This raises a simple question: if highly valorized masculinity lies at the heart of canonical selections, what part is played by femininity, its antithesis, in the under-representation of Inter-war women writers?

Contrary to what one might expect, femininity does not necessarily result in canonical exclusion. Indeed, of the six most acclaimed French Inter-war women writers appearing in critical compilations, both Anna de Noailles and Colette are ubiquitously eulogized for what critics see as their literary embodiment of the feminine. However, this commendation of femininity is often little more than feigned praise and the way in which Noailles, Colette and many under-represented 'feminine' authors are portrayed in canonical works differs in significant respects from the treatment accorded to their 'masculine' counterparts. The most startling aspect of the entries on most 'feminine' writers in literary historical overviews is the way in which they are consistently and persistently presented chiefly in terms of their individual biographies. As Didier puts it: 'from the start – even in the most favourable cases – we see this tendency amongst critics, when judging a novel of female authorship, to identify the echoes of the writer's personal life. The critics take a markedly lesser interest in the private lives of male authors.'[45] While the average Frenchman may not be familiar with Noailles's literary corpus, he cannot fail to be aware of her Cretan origins, her much-extolled exotic beauty, her fashionable entourage, her magnificent aristocratic home and her glittering social life. Similarly, Colette's renown rests to a considerable degree on her adopted roles as 'serious writer, popular writer, vaudeville artist, trapeze then theater artist, make-up artist; *enfant terrible*, and at the end *grande dame* of French letters; cook, gardener, cyclist, journalist, traveller, hostess, pin-up girl, three times wife; lesbian mistress, lover, a daughter, a mother'[46] and her well-documented, liberated, bohemian lifestyle which continues to this day to furnish material for multiple biographical studies. In the Inter-war years, the Parisian publishing world only exacerbated the problem of the prioritizing of biography over literary analysis. Nourissier stresses that editors, faced with an avalanche of manuscripts, selected works for publicity reasons, only choosing to promote writers whose picturesque lives would in some way provide suitable material for a successful launch.[47] Many writers, in order to have a novel published, had to be willing to reveal certain details of their private lives, had to indulge in self-dramatization, or at least be prepared to be a party to it. While this procedure is not unique to women – after all, who can forget Grasset's huge publicity campaign to promote the vulnerable seventeen-year-old Raymond Radiguet's *Le Diable au corps* (1923) – it is much more commonplace with relatively inexperienced female authors. Examples of this abound, such as that of Rachilde, who achieved recognition in the wake of the much-publicized Belgian courts' decision on *Monsieur Vénus* (1884), which was deemed indecent and resulted in Rachilde receiving a sentence to serve two years' imprisonment and a heavy fine. Irène Némirovsky's name became well known in the capital when Grasset asked Parisian newspapers to help track down this prodigious new writer who had supposedly submitted the manuscript of *David Golder* (1929) without giving her contact address. In contrast, Zénaïde Fleuriot, Bethléem laments, did not achieve fame precisely because she chose not to create a stir with her personal life. He suggests that had she been immoral like George Sand, she would have been feted as a genius; however, as a good Christian woman, she received no publicity.[48] Marguerite Audoux, after the success of her debut novel, resented the way in which her personal life had been manipulated by editorial boards and critics, and as a consequence of this, as Daspre and Décaudin record, she refused to exploit her success, gave few interviews, did not frequent literary salons and so never became a *femme de lettres*.[49] Audoux perhaps suffered for this as the remaining three of her four books were not so well reviewed or received by the public. However, the effect of complying with editors and surrendering one's life as material for marketing techniques proves, in the main, to be equally if not more adverse, as the case of Louise de Vilmorin illustrates:

> Her peals of laughter, her exciting companions, did not alleviate the melancholy Louise experienced when she was refused recognition as a 'proper' writer, always being unfairly classified as a writer of and for the upper classes.
> Louise de Vilmorin has suffered the same misfortune as Anna de Noailles earlier, and, more recently, Jean Cocteau: their bright personalities have thrown their works into shadow.[50]

For Vilmorin, being part of the Parisian intelligentsia or *glitterati* resulted in her works being eclipsed and not taken seriously. This has dire consequences reaching far beyond the lives of individual writers.

The most fundamental problem with this preoccupation with biography is the way in which the writer's literary contribution is repeatedly underplayed; when the criteria for canonical selection move from the literary to the libidinal, and emphasis falls on the anecdotal rather than the analytical, the nation's whole perception of its female literary tradition risks becoming alarmingly distorted.

Given the prevalence of this recourse to biography in its varied forms, literary histories seem not just to *under-represent* non-canonized women writers, but to *mis-represent* them, indeed one might say *'miss'- represent* them, as their entries are repeatedly governed by prescriptive ill-informed understandings of the female sex. This pejorative attribution of a certain notion of femininity to all women is a well-documented, omnipresent phenomenon in the art world and in the realm of the Anglo-American novel where, as Miles notes: 'For the last hundred years or so the awareness of a woman writer's sex has been so important as to form the basis of any committed critical observation.'[51] With Inter-war French women writers the situation is no different: because if critics do go beyond discussing the writer's life and her relationships, if they turn to her work, the attribution of abstract notions of femininity persist. The term 'féminin' itself is frequently employed, despite the fact that critics are often reluctant to offer any clear definitions of it. While Bertaut, for example, may categorically state 'the woman of letters is first and foremost a woman, that is to say, a being with a certain sensitivity, a certain intelligence, a certain taste and a certain temperament', he actually seems *uncertain* or unwilling to specify just what characteristics do, in fact, constitute the female gender.[52] The situation is further complicated by the fact that while the adjective used to describe a woman in English has two distinct forms: 'female', which is most often used to denote a biological category, and 'feminine', which refers to the social, historical, cultural construct woman, in the French language only one adjectival form exists: 'féminin'. By definition it simply means 'of woman' and has no innate connotations of the concept of femininity. However, a study of the way in which the term is employed reveals that for the majority of critics 'féminin' does indeed come to mean 'feminine', not 'female' and that it carries with it a whole baggage of cultural overtones.

The Inter-war female author, by and large, despite the major social and political changes in her actual situation, is still classified by critics as though she were a passive, subaltern mid-nineteenth-century creature confined to the domestic sphere, writing for personal pleasure and not as a profession. This outdated, inaccurate concept of womanhood extends into the critics' analysis of the style, themes and generic choices made by female authors. Femininity, presented as the antithetical opposite of masculinity, in its evocation of a woman's delicate physical form, implies that female-authored literature is of a correspondingly slight intellectual weight and lacks authoritative strength and command. Abry, for instance, introduces his section on women writers with the comment: 'Feminine delicacy finds its place in the analytical novel. Many women writers have demonstrated their talent in this domain.'[53] This notion recurs in the *Le Petit Echo de la mode*'s monograph on Mathilde Alanic which refers to her 'feminine frailty'.[54] Lalou sees the populist writer, Huguette Garnier, as a typical woman 'impregnated with sensitivity',[55] while Peyre holds that Vilmorin 'maintains the light, graceful, and mundane tradition of the feminine novel'.[56]

This representation of the French Inter-war female author as subordinate, dependent and ancillary, as an object displayed for the pleasure of the voyeuristic male gaze, is most evident in the critics' insistence on presenting women writers in terms of their familial or sentimental relationships. Marie de Régnier (née de Heredia), who wrote mainly under the pseudonym Gérard d'Houville, is an especially interesting example of this. In her lifetime she was widely acclaimed by critics and the public alike. In 1910 when *L'Intransigeant* asked its reader to select the top three women writers deemed worthy to be members of the Académie française, they placed d'Houville in top position before Anna de Noailles and Colette. Eight years later her literary works were recognized by the critical establishment when she became the first woman to receive the Grand Prix de littérature de l'Académie française. Throughout the Inter-war years she was increasingly prolific, as Fleury, her most recent biographer, stresses: 'Marie's literary output suddenly accelerated. Between 1925 and 1930 successive novels, short stories, newspaper columns, articles and prefaces appeared at a quite uncommon pace.'[57] By 1958 she had been doubly crowned by France's major literary body, as in this year she received the Grand Prix de poésie de l'Académie française, and she remains to date the only woman honoured in this way. Around this time she was also awarded the Grand Prix de la Société des poètes français, was made a commander of the legion of honour and was elected president of the Académie Mallarmé. Despite her obvious achievements and popularity, Gérard d'Houville, unlike Colette and Anna de Noailles, is not fully accepted by the establishment. When her name does appear in literary histories covering the era, her literary contribution is overlooked and her life becomes the focus of the critic's attention. It is repeatedly presented through a series of relationships with men. Critics are at pains to inform the reader that her father is José-Maria de Hérédia and they attribute d'Houville's decision to write to her filial love. They discuss at length her romantic rapports with Henri de Régnier, Pierre Louÿs, Tinan, Vaudroyer, Bernstein, D'Annunzio and Chaumeix, attributing her switch from poetry to fiction to her definitive break with Pierre Louÿs.

The presentation of the female writer through her dependent relationship with men is extensive. The most prominent relational roles to appear in literary histories are those of wife and mother. Mme Colomb (née Joséphine-Blanche Bouchet), is introduced by Bethléem as the daughter of a doctor and wife of a teacher, while Camille Marbo (Mme Marguerite Appell) is presented as the daughter of the vice-rector of the University of Paris and wife of Emile Borel, the professor of its science faculty.[58] Bethléem omits to inform the reader that Camille Marbo collaborated with her husband, who founded the *Revue des mois*. Even Rachilde suffers this treatment as much attention falls on her husband Vallette, with whom she jointly launched the *Mercure de France*.[59] Peyre portrays Elsa Triolet as 'the Russian-born wife of Aragon, of whom he sang rapturously in his wartime poems'.[60] Similarly, almost every entry on Lucie Delarue-Mardrus informs the reader that she is the wife of the Norman doctor who translated *Les Mille et une nuits*. Delarue-Mardrus was only married for fourteen years and in this time wrote seven works (from 1900 to 1914); her career continued until the year of her death 1945 and during this more prolific period she produced a further forty-six works. Yet despite these statistics she is still defined in relation to her husband. Even the commemorative publication on the Prix Fémina fails to introduce its more active members as authors in their own right. Yvonne Sarcey's entry is the most extreme example. It reads: 'The daughter of the renowned critic Francisque Sarcey, the widow of Adolphe Brisson (the founder of *Annales*) and the mother of Pierre Brisson (the director of *Le Figaro*), she was born in 1869.'[61] Moulin also notes this role of mother of sons when she attributes Cécile Sauvage's poetic inspiration to 'the concern of her cultured father, the love of her husband Pierre Messiaen (who translated Shakespeare and Emily Dickinson), the affection of her sons Olivier and Alain'.[62]

While the condition of being married and being a mother may well affect a writer's output and interests, exposing the particular difficulties women face does not seem to be the critics' primary purpose. Rather, the prioritizing of this type of information serves two purposes. In each of these cases, the writer's destiny is shown to be her marital or maternal state rather than her own literary talent, and it follows that her professional status is somewhat undercut, her literature is rendered insignificant and she is effectively thrust unceremoniously back into the domestic sphere.[63] This emphasis on household obligations is stressed in many literary histories and contemporary reviews. The *Petit Echo de la mode*'s article on Mathilde Alanic, for example, metaphorically likens the writer to a mother in an enclosed personal realm: 'We all love to think of Mathilde Alanic surrounded by the children of her thoughts and heart, in this light, beautiful garden perfumed with flowers and softened by peaceful shade – the garden of her literary works.'[64] When Bethléem says of Mme Julie Lavergne (née Ozanaux) 'while carrying out her domestic chores with admirable zeal she allowed herself the pleasure of writing', it is unquestionably the home, not the writing, which is given the prominent position.[65]

The second interesting aspect of this insistence on women writers as relational beings is that they are, almost without exception, never placed in relation to other women. There is no information concerning whether they have daughters or dependent elderly aunts to care for, or what their mother's social position might have been! In certain entries in literary histories this lack of information is notable. Bethléem introduces Claude Chauvière as the daughter of 'a former *député* of the fourteenth district of Paris who is well known for his stance against the Church', before informing the reader that she is Colette's secretary and biographer. Rosemonde Gérard's marriage to Edmond Rostand is repeatedly mentioned, but her maternal ancestry, which features Mme de Genlis, generally passes unremarked. At the other extreme, many of the male-centred relational roles highlighted by the critics are somewhat tenuous. Clouard is not content to tell the reader that Camille Mayran is the wife of Pierre Hepp (writer and director of the *Revue de Paris* until the 1914 war); he places her in relation to her great-uncle Taine.[66] Simon insists on the importance of the fact that Geneviève Fauconnier is Alain-Fournier's sister.[67] Bethléem explains that Marcelle Adam is the granddaughter of Adolphe Adam,[68] and Peyre presents Béatrice Beck as 'the daughter of one of Gide's friends'.[69] Linking women's names to the names of male writers carries with it the implication that these women have achieved a degree of recognition or greatness because of the link rather than because of the quality of their own work, which is discussed only in second place. This technique quite clearly recalls the nineteenth-century critic Sainte-Beuve's belief that a woman's literary production is determined by her patron, tutor, father or sexual partner. Moreover, in emphasizing the vital importance of paternal lineage as a gauge of social position or respectability, critics appear unwilling to accept the social changes effected by the Inter-war years. They do not adequately recognize that women had full access to both schooling and the professional world in this era, that they could publish what they wanted freely, without recourse to parental permission, and that their class or status was related now to their own work or education. This insistence on male-centred relational roles, then, is among the worst forms of 'miss'-representation as it so completely undermines female autonomy.

When literary historians do focus on the actual works produced by women writers this same reductive concept of femininity persists and is most obviously related to the author's thematic interest. In studies of the canonized 'feminine' authors Anna de Noailles and Colette two central features are stressed: the depiction of romantic love and a pantheistic affinity with the natural world, what Lemaître sees in respect of Noailles as 'the communion between heart and nature'[70] – and here there is a sharp distinction with the innovations and intellectualism of Symbolist and Parnassian verse. The representation of Colette is similarly coloured by reference to sensuality and a love of the natural world. Castex and Surer, for example, conflate these two traditional facets of femininity in their anthology entry on Colette, when they introduce an excerpt from *Les Vrilles de la vigne* (1908) concerning the countryside, with the statement: 'Here Colette describes the raptures and the torments of the female soul.'[71] These same themes filter down to readings of non-canonized writers. Flat, for example, notes that Lucie Delarue-Mardrus depicts nature with a sincere and perfect attention to detail;[72] while Bertaut states that Mme Catulle Mendès glorifies nature, Gabrielle Reval (née Logerot) describes Parisian parks and Mme Marguerite Burnat-Provins delineates the changing seasons.[73]

This results in two further misrepresentations of women writers. Firstly, it implies that as women supposedly share the same thematic interest, their works are homogeneous. Colette's reception speech at the Académie Royale de Belgique, when she succeeded Anna de Noailles, refutes this implication. Focusing precisely on these two thematic interests, she demonstrates the differences and not the similarities in her work and Noailles's. Colette opens with the insinuation that her nomination as Anna de Noailles's successor results from this illustrious organization's desire to continue to pay homage to a woman writer involved in the 'cult of nature'; and as critics have supposed and demonstrated that the same 'wild and pagan feeling towards the natural world' is shared by Noailles and Colette they have assumed, erroneously, that she is a suitable replacement. Colette goes on to differentiate herself from Noailles by indicating the dissimilar character of their working methods, styles and perspectives. She suggests that while she herself records memories and detailed studies of actual natural phenomena, Noailles is more idealistic than realistic, preferring to invent and improvise. Following on from this, Noailles tends towards high lyricism whilst she, in contrast, gives a more 'prudent exaltation controlled by prose'. This colours their treatment of love as Noailles is motivated by an abstract desire for 'glory' whereas Colette claims to prefer 'love of more mortal dimensions'. Colette is at pains to stress that love of nature has many guises and is not in any sense unique to them or indeed to women as a whole. Nature is 'everything under the sky which, without human volition, can breathe, flourish, renew itself, resist change, decline and die'; as such, it is a vast and profound source of literary inspiration, so it is unsurprising that it should captivate many writers, including women.[74] For Colette, the inherent bond between gender and the realms of love and nature is spurious, as the themes designated by the critics as feminine are, in fact, of universal significance.

Secondly, the critics' persistent conflation of 'feminine' writing with nature and love recalls the way in which women were represented in the nineteenth-century art world. For Ruskin in the mid-nineteenth century, the ideal bourgeois woman, like a perfect lily, exemplified fragility, grace, beauty and passivity. In the period from 1880 to 1914, although women were no longer considered such ideal creatures, their portrayal as naiad or woodland nymphs remained a staple of the Paris salon exhibitions because in this representation women were still not an active threat to men.[75] Fusing modern women's writing with outmoded notions of womanhood and in particular the reductive imagery of the natural world enabled the critics to imply an inferiority in both women themselves and their literary production.

From such critical evaluations it is evident that the canon does set up binary divisions according to the prescriptive nineteenth-century bourgeois concept of separate spheres, in which the public active realm of experience considered unique to men is enshrined, and in which women's experience, based on circumscribed notions of ideal womanhood, is correspondingly denigrated. Feminist critics, from the Inter-war years on, have noted this gender bias, this double standard. Virginia Woolf commented widely on the way in which the canon refuses to recognize the value of women's source material: 'it is the masculine values that prevail (. . .) And these values are inevitably transferred from life to fiction. This is an important book, because it deals with war. This is an insignificant book because it deals with the feelings of women in a drawing room.'[76] However, it is not simply a question of subjects deemed germane to cultural representations of masculinity receiving special canonical appreciation. Canon compilers extrapolate from hierarchical thematic categories, with all their connotations of alterity and inferiority, to suggest that women writers' preference for certain types of literature conforms to the selfsame pattern. This raises the crucial question: what is responsible for canonical exclusion – a woman's supposed femininity or the form she employs; her gender or her choice of genre?

Literary historians would have one believe that their governing criteria are related more to genre than to gender. When Thiesse and Mathieu conducted a detailed investigation of the selection process for the *agrégation* syllabus this was the very explanation they received for the de-selection of already established women writers.[77] Ostensibly, Mme de Sévigné and George Sand were eliminated from the course as the epistolary novel and the idealist novel, the genres they respectively preferred, were said to be dated. Schor's independent research confirmed this justification: 'It is not because Sand was a woman, rather because (like so many other women authors) she is associated with a discredited and disregarded representational mode that she is no longer ranked among the canonic authors.'[78] Here, Schor suggests that 'many' women suffer because of the genres they employ, that canonical exclusion on these grounds is common practice.

An overview of entries on Inter-war female writers in literary histories reveals that the notion of femininity, whether it be attributed ironically, disapprovingly or as a term of admiration, is consistently twinned with one of two literary genres: the autobiography or the romance. Bertaut, for instance, talks of never-ending autobiographies, suggesting that all literature for the woman writer is 'a form of secular confession in which she admits her disillusionments, her misfortunes great and small, where she murmurs her hopes, where she unburdens her overflowing soul'.[79] The same occurs with romantic fiction. According to Clouard, for example, a woman's essence is inextricably linked to her romantic life and its fictional representation. In his first literary history, guided by his belief that female-authored studies of love have proliferated since the 1930s, he introduces the romance with the words: 'If one were to segregate all those writers who investigate love then women's names would head the list.'[80] This attitude filters through to his depiction of individuals. Gérard d'Houville, Anna de Noailles and Lucie Delarue-Mardrus are discussed in a subsection referred to as 'this court of love'. He suggest that Camille Mayran is a romantic writer fired by passion, while Mme George-Day is characterized by her dreams of sentimental escapism. This insistence on the bond between women writers and romantic subjects is maintained in his revised edition published over twenty years later in which he stresses that women's dominant role in this domain is only to be expected. Clouard is not alone in this form of criticism. Simon describes Geneviève Fauconnier as 'a novelist of the female heart',[81] while in a speech to the Académie française on 28 November 1918, Lamy described Gérard d'Houville as a romantic novelist in whose works love reigns absolute.[82]

The most problematic aspect of this type of criticism is the all too common logical slip from descriptively recording the existence of a link between women and certain literary genres (in terms of both authorship and readership) to asserting in a more prescriptive fashion that this bond is innate, natural and unavoidable. Many influential critics are not content just to detect details of an individual author's personal or romantic life in her work; instead, they effectively reduce and homogenize women's literary production, as they progress in their analysis to maintain that women *can* do nothing other than transpose and transcribe their own lives. However, in promoting this claim that women's preference for the romance and the autobiography is pre-ordained and uniquely determined by gender, the critics deny the element of women's free choice, effectively negating the dynamic nature of the relationship between women and writing. Additionally, they mask the part played by patriarchal social conventions, peer pressure, current editorial tastes, the promise of monetary gain, the gender-specific financial and political difficulties inherent in the realm of poetry and theatre – in short, the external forces, often emanating from the literary establishment itself, which may have conspired to encourage women to devote their time and talent to these two literary forms.

Just as the thematic interests attributed to women are downgraded in canonical binary divisions, so too are their supposed generic preferences repudiated. This is particularly evident in the case of autobiographical works. In her interviews with Galey, for instance, Yourcenar argues that autobiography (be it recollections of childhood or adult outpourings of confidences), now at a far remove from Rousseau's *Confessions* (1781), is quite jaded and hackneyed. She considers the genre offensive, seeing in it an inherent degree of falsity and a supreme demonstration of narcissistic egoism. She says of her contemporaries: 'What nevertheless strikes me about the bulk of French poems and novels I read is the extent to which they remain so narrowly subjective, immured in dreams, nightmares, often pulpy fantasies, or even arid personal deserts.'[83] Yourcenar's own contrasting reserve is evident not just in her most celebrated work on Hadrian (she describes it as 'a work in which I deliberately attempted to efface myself'[84]), but more surprisingly in her own 'autobiographical' project. Her plan of 1923 to produce a family history, which saw fruition in the three-volume *Le Labyrinthe du monde*, is at a far remove from the traditional autobiography.[85] *Archives du nord*, the second volume, for example, provides a fictional representation of her ancestors and ends with the last twenty-five years of her father's life. Yourcenar herself is strikingly absent from the first two volumes. As with all her novels, there is, as King rightly notes, 'a very conscious distancing of the author from the material recounted, almost the opposite of the outpouring of personal emotion often seen as the epitome of a woman's mode of expression'.[86]

Similarly, Rachilde, again as part of an attempt to distinguish herself from her peers, and to achieve full and equal recognition from the male-dominated establishment, rejects autobiographical works as insular and narrow, labelling mediocre any writer 'who contemplates his own navel and only writes about himself'. Regarding her own fiction she states: 'I don't like speaking about myself. Perhaps I have the opposite fault of most *femmes de lettres* who begin by focusing on themselves rather than studying the world around them or reaching for the stars. We who are novelists, historians and narrators are not made to exist only in and for ourselves.'[87] Women's writing, for Rachilde, is parochial, not universal. Moreover, its standard subject matter is held to be of limited interest. Assuming that women are confined to the domestic, private sphere, and that consequently their lives lack diversity, autonomy and value, many critics, like Rachilde, repeatedly denigrate women's source material. When depicted from without, by male writers, a woman's life may achieve social significance; when women paint it from within its value is greatly reduced. There is a simple reason for this: it is generally considered that women's autobiographical novels lack intellectual weight. Perhaps because women until 1924 did not have the advantages of formal schooling in classical literature, in metaphysics and logic, it has generally been assumed *a priori* that their work is simplistic. Even established female authors suffer from this imputation. Colette, who initially benefited from autobiographical readings of the Claudine series – *Claudine à l'école* (1900), *Claudine à Paris* (1901), *Claudine en ménage* (1903) and *Claudine s'en va* (1903) – soon found that her fiction came under heavy censure precisely because of her choice of genre. Lalou describes her as 'the least intellectual of writers'.[88] D. and G. McMillan see her 'lacking in moralizing or intellectual preoccupations'.[89] In the case of minor writers, these charges of egocentricity, parochialism, limited vision and absence of sustaining interest, fall thick and fast. Indeed, the same terms noted by Atwood in her analysis of the representation of women's autobiographical work in Anglo-American literary reviews – 'vague, weak, tremulous, pastel', 'subjective', 'confessional', 'personal', 'neurotic' and 'narcissistic'[90] – regularly appear in entries on women writers in French literary histories as does the additional word 'simple', which Simon, Clouard and Lemaître, for instance, all apply to Marguerite Audoux's corpus. Because women's impulse towards autobiography is presented as natural, naive and simplistic (a representation of womanhood at odds with the actual evolving socio-political situation of women in the Inter-war era), the critics do not credit them with original aesthetic or philosophical interests. From an overview of critical studies covering the period it is clear that the autobiographical genre as a whole is not subject to incursive censure, but that autobiographical works of female authorship are sharply distinguished from autobiographies produced by male writers (such as those by André Gide, François Mauriac, Julien Green, Marcel Jouhandeau and Michel Leiris which are seen as embodying great insight and lucidity as well as offering exciting generic experimentation), and that the former alone come under attack. The concept of gender becomes twinned with that of genre in such a way that it helps bring about the canonical exclusion of woman writers.

The reception of romances is no different, as these are consistently and cynically presented as over-sentimental, simplistic, trivial or limited: Lalou dismisses romances because of their 'feminine' domestic setting where the major subjects, he feels, are preening and endless cups of tea;[91] Clouard finds the romance plot lacking in virile action; and Simon, who argues that all women want is to recount love stories and vindicate the rights of passion against the wider interests of society as a whole, suggests that Marcelle Tinayre and her peers' intellectual skills are negligible, their judgement askew and their political values uninformed.[92] The critical reception of women writers, then, appears to be governed by three dominant principles: – women are feminine, the genres they use are linked to their femininity and these genres are of second-rate importance in literary hierarchies. By implication, as Parker and Pollock note, 'institutionally constructed segregation is represented as evidence of an innate inequality of talent',[93] 'feminine' writers are deemed to be of minor value, and, as a result of this, women as a whole are marginalized in canonical works. These interdependent principles which underlie canon formation play a significant role in confining lesser-known writers, writers perhaps of considerable talent and insight, to the realms of literary oblivion. In consequence they bring about a major impoverishment of French literature as a whole and women's part in it in particular.

In recent years, the heavily gender-based representations of canonized women writers has undergone a degree of reassessment. Holmes, for instance, in her monographic study on Colette, highlights the reductive presentations given by conventional critics. She counters the accepted perception of Colette in both France and Great Britain as

'a writer of charming animal tales and rather spicy fiction' with a very
different Colette who, intellectually distanced and distinct from the
narrator, is toying with artificially imposed binary gender divisions and
their conventional signifiers.[94] Similarly, King in *French Women Novelists: Defining a Female Style* argues a case for reinterpreting Sarraute
and Yourcenar. Sarraute's *Tropismes* (1939), she holds, serves as a
classic Chodorovian example of a woman's undefined ego boundaries.
Yourcenar, despite her overtly masculine style, is, King claims, also
recuperable. In *Alexis ou le traité du vain combat* (1929) Alexis's linguistic
hesitations are seen to resemble 'a feminist commentary on the inade-
quacies of the language of society'.[95] King sees Yourcenar's interest
in heroes who are outsiders, or as she puts it 'social misfits', as being
partly attributable to her own position as a woman:

> In the final analysis [her writings] show precisely a woman's reaction to
> her experience of being considered part of the inferior social group, by
> seeking in some way to enter the dominant group through the values
> and perspective of her work. Yourcenar is a woman whose particular
> experience produces a pro-male perspective but one that is nevertheless
> essentially the perspective of a woman.[96]

While these re-readings still assume the existence of an essential femininity, they move away from prescriptive narrow traditional definitions
and take more into account the actual condition of being a woman
in this particular era. Most significantly, they demonstrate that feminist
critics are at last working to re-establish a female literary tradition
which includes some of France's most widely acknowledged women
writers.

That said, little work has been carried out to date on those women
writers whose brief appearance in historical overviews is at odds with
the acclaim they received in their own lifetime, women who remain
subject to the adverse effects of canon deformation. In an attempt
to redress their under-representation and 'miss'-representation, the
following chapters offer a re-reading of a range of works categorized
by the critics as autobiographies and romances, illuminating the
specific way in which women writers themselves understand these
forms together with their varied responses to cultural constructions
of femininity and masculinity. They explore more fully the real nature
of the fascinating relationship between genre and gender in Inter-war
French female-authored literature.

Notes

1. There is an analysis of the evolution of French literary compilations in the final chapter of J. Dejean (1991), *Tender Geographies: Women and the Origins of the Novel in France*, New York, pp. 159–99.
2. Gouget's eighteen volume *Histoire de la littérature française* (1740), which according to Dejean sought to 'police the reading habits of the "Honnête Homme" and thereby shape both his taste and his national prejudices', was targeted at pedagogues and explicitly aimed to bring about the transformation of their male students into 'good Christians . . . useful to society'. Ibid., p. 188.
3. The term 'canon', whose etymological roots denote a simple system of rules and codification, was first used in France in the seventeenth century to demarcate a collection of divinely inspired works meeting papal approval.
4. Gustave Lanson taught in several lycées, lectured at the Sorbonne, and from 1920 to 1927 was director of the Ecole normale supérieure.
5. Lanson's methodology is outlined in A. Lagarde and L. Michard (1962), *XXème siècle*, Paris, p. 668.
6. T. Moi (1985), *Sexual/Textual Politics*, London and New York, p. 85.
7. Dejean's analysis of the eighteenth-century canonical works demonstrates that from their inception, critical school manuals have been particularly hostile towards fiction produced by women, and that following their early exclusion, female writers have been increasingly written out of literary history.
8. 1.88 per cent is the percentage of women covered; the space they are allocated in the work is 1.18 per cent as in table 2.1.
9. *Anthologie de la nouvelle prose française* (1926), Paris, pp. 1, 3 and 4.
10. Table 2.1 displays the authors and date of publication of the anthologies/histories; it shows the period the work covers; the penultimate column indicates the percentage coverage given to women; and the final column registers the proportional ratio of women to men and here, for clarity, the exact figures are given.
11. See J. Larnac (1931), *Comtesse de Noailles: sa vie, son œuvre*, Paris, for a listing of over 300 critical articles and reviews covering the thirty years of Noailles's career.
12. For brief biographies, thematic overviews, surveys of criticism, together with primary and secondary bibliographies for all six canonized authors of the period see E.M. Sartori and D.W.

Zimmerman (eds), (1994), *French Women Writers*, Lincoln and London, pp. 78–89, 335–45, 346–56, 513–23 and 535–48.

13. M.N. Evans (1987), *Masks of Tradition: Women and the Politics of Writing in Twentieth-century France*, Ithaca, NY and London, p. 13.

14. R. Parker and G. Pollock (1987), *Old Mistresses: Women, Art and Ideology*, London, pp. 26 and 29.

15. C.G. Heilbrun (1989), *Writing a Woman's Life*, London, p. 81.

16. P.-G. Castex and P. Surer (1953), *Manuel des études littéraires françaises, XXème siècle*, Paris, pp. 60 and 134.

17. G. Brée and M. Guiton (1962), *The French Novel from Gide to Camus*, New York, p. 3.

18. H. Peyre (1955), *The Contemporary French Novel*, New York and Oxford, p. 283.

19. C. Planté (1989), *La Petite Sœur de Balzac*, Paris, p. 82.

20. Peyre, *Contemporary French Novel,* pp. 314, 315 and 285.

21. Brée and Guiton, *French Novel*, p. 236.

22. M. Atwood (1986), 'Paradoxes and Dilemmas; The Woman as Writer' in M. Eagleton (ed.), *Feminist Literary Theory*, Oxford, pp. 74–6 (p. 75).

23. Neither Simone Weil nor Nathalie Sarraute is overtly described in terms of gender in canonical compilations. Critics emphasize the unique status of Weil's literature which recounts her spiritual and intellectual development. With Sarraute the emphasis falls on her part in the male–dominated *nouveau roman* movement. Colette and Anna de Noailles are both consistently portrayed as feminine and this will be discussed in the second half of this chapter.

24. A. David (1924), *Rachilde 'homme' de lettres,* Paris, pp. 61, 44, 42 and 49.

25. J. Bertaut [1909], *La Littérature féminine d'aujourd'hui*, Paris, p. 222.

26. Rachilde (1 July 1917), 'Revue de la Quinzaine', *Mercure de France*, vol. 122, no. 457, pp. 127–31 (p. 128).

27. Rachilde (1 March 1907), 'Revue de la Quinzaine', *Mercure de France*, vol. 66, no. 233, pp. 112–17 (p. 13).

28. C. Dauphiné (1985), *Rachilde, femme de lettres 1900*, Périgueux, p. 125.

29. Rachilde (16 February 1912), 'Revue de la Quinzaine', *Mercure de France*, vol. 95, no. 352, pp. 813–17 (p. 813).

30. Rachilde's comment is recorded in P. Léautaud (1929), *Journal littéraire*, Paris, vol. 3, p. 324. Rachilde accepted the award herself in 1924, having refused it two years previously.

31. For further details see Dauphiné, *Rachilde,* pp. 66–74.

32. J. Birkett (1986), *The Sins of the Fathers: Decadence in France 1870–1914*, London, pp. 159, 160 and 189.

33. Rachilde (September 1898), 'La Mort d'Antinoüs', *Mercure de France*, vol. 27, no. 105, pp. 638–46.
34. The middle period saw the publication of the original *Denier du rêve* (1934) and *Feux* (1936), Yourcenar's renunciation of writing in 1939 when she emigrated to the United States, and her work scripting plays and translating negro spirituals.
35. M. Yourcenar (1980), *Les Yeux ouverts: entretiens avec Matthieu Galey*, Paris, pp. 38, 46, 52 and 53.
36. M. Yourcenar (1974), 'Carnet de notes de *Mémoires d'Hadrien*', in *Mémoires d'Hadrien*, Paris, p. 307.
37. A. King (1989), *French Women Novelists: Defining a Female Style*, London, p. 133.
38. C. Kramarae (April/June 1977), 'Perceptions of Female and Male Speech', *Language and Speech*, vol. 20, no. 2, pp. 151–61.
39. King, *French Women Novelists*, pp. 133 and 114.
40. Peyre, *Contemporary French Novel*, p. 334.
41. C. Robinson (1995), *Scandal in the Ink: Male and Female Homosexuality in Twentieth-century French Literature*, London, pp. 226–30.
42. Yourcenar sardonically notes that Mme de Staël could not become a member of the French Academy as she was Swiss by birth and Swedish by nationality; George Sand was too feminine, 'une femme si admirablement femme'; while in the case of Colette membership is not even raised as an issue. The Ancien Régime *salonnières*, as a group, are praised as patrons of male academicians.
43. Renée Montlaur, normally spelled Monlaur, is the pseudonym of Mlle Reynès, who also wrote under the combined name M. Reynès-Monlaur. She was born in Montpellier in 1870. The date of her death is unrecorded. The work which most appealed to Yourcenar, no doubt, and which inspired her descriptions of the Nile, *Après la neuvième heure*, describes the influence of Jesus's love on the first Christians. Her other writings are all of a religious nature and cover the lives of the abbess Angélique Arnauld and Saint Geneviève, the coming of Christianity to Brittany and Greece, diverse conversions, religious persecution evident in Belgian sisterhoods and the more general dissolution of the monasteries.
44. Yourcenar, *Les Yeux ouverts*, pp. 117, 13, 19–20, 45.
45. B. Didier (1982), *L'Ecriture femme*, Paris, p. 136.
46. C. Portuges and N.W. Jouve (1994), 'Colette' in E.M. Sartori and D.W. Zimmerman, *French Women Writers*, Lincoln and London, pp. 78–89, p. 78.
47. F. Nourissier (1960), 'Le Monde du livre' in B. Pingaud (ed.), *Ecrivains d'aujourd'hui, 1940–1960*, Paris, pp. 29–39 (p. 30).

48. Abbé L. Bethléem (1932), *Romans à lire et romans à proscrire*, 11th edn, Paris, p. 454.
49. A. Daspre and M. Décaudin (1982), *Manuel d'histoire littéraire de la France de 1913 à nos jours*, Paris, vol. 6, p. 304.
50. J. Chalon (1987), *Florence et Louise les magnifiques: Florence Jay-Gould et Louise de Vilmorin*, Monaco, p. 119.
51. R. Miles (1987), *The Female Form: Women Writers and the Conquest of the Novel*, London and New York, p. 5.
52. Bertaut, *La Littérature féminine*, p. 16.
53. E. Abry, P. Crouzet and C. Audic (1942), *Histoire illustrée de la littérature française*, Paris, p. 805.
54. *Le Petit Echo de la mode*, 21 September, 1924, no. 38.
55. R. Lalou (1947), *Histoire de la littérature française contemporaine: de 1870 à nos jours*, Paris, vol. 2, p. 786.
56. Peyre, *Contemporary French Novel*, p. 334.
57. R. Fleury (1990), *Marie de Regnier: l'inconstante*, Paris, pp. 192 and 256.
58. Bethléem, *Romans à lire*, pp. 258 and 531.
59. It was Rachilde's already considerable literary standing which secured the journal's early prestige, and her short stories, serialized novels and reviews, which ran regularly until 1914 and period-ically until 1925 when Charpentier took over, which played a major role in maintaining the journal's continued success and reputation.
60. Peyre, *Contemporary French Novel*, p. 332.
61. *Le Prix Fémina: ancien Prix Vie heureuse, Album du cinquantenaire, 1904–1954*, (1954), Paris, p. 56.
62. J. Moulin (1963), *La Poésie féminine de Marie de France à Marie Noël, époque moderne*, Paris, p. 169.
63. Birkett comments ironically on this gendered division of the public and the private realm: 'indeed, public life is such *because* women are removed from it. Women do not simply *exist within* the private sphere; they *are* the private sphere.' J. Birkett (1991), 'Whistling like a Woman: the Novels of Alice Walker' in J. Birkett and E. Harvey (eds), *Determined Women: Studies in the Construction of the Female Subject, 1900–1990*, London, p. 202.
64. *Le Petit Echo de la mode* (21 September 1924), no. 38.
65. Bethléem, *Romans à lire*, p. 556.
66. H. Clouard (1947), *Histoire de la littérature française du symbolisme à nos jours*, Paris, vol. 2, p. 332.
67. P.-H. Simon (1963), *Histoire de la littérature française au XXème siècle, 1900–1950*, 7th edn, Paris, vol. 1, p. 56, and vol. 2, p. 94.
68. Bethléem, *Romans à lire*, p. 86.

69. Peyre, *Contemporary French Novel*, p. 312.
70. H. Lemaître (1985), *Dictionnaire Bordas de littérature française*, Paris, p. 560.
71. Castex and Surer, *Manuel des études*, p. 77.
72. P. Flat (1909), *Nos Femmes de lettres*, Paris, p. 65.
73. Bertaut, *La Littérature féminine*, pp. 156–65.
74. Colette (1963), 'Discours de réception de Madame Colette à l'Académie Royale de Belgique' in J. Cocteau (ed.), *La Comtesse de Noailles oui et non*, Paris, pp. 195–211 (pp. 202–3).
75. See B. Dijkstra (1986), *Idols of Perversity: Fantasies of Evil in Fin-de-siècle Culture*, Oxford.
76. V. Woolf (1977), *A Room of One's Own*, London, p. 70.
77. A.-M. Thiesse and H. Mathieu (1988), 'The Decline of the Classical and Birth of the Classics' in J. Dejean and N.K. Miller (eds), *The Politics of Tradition: Placing Women in French Literature*, New Haven, CT, pp. 208–29.
78. N. Schor, 'Idealism in the Novel: Recanonizing Sand' in J. Dejean and N.K. Miller (eds), *The Politics of Tradition: Placing Women in French Literature*, New Haven, CT, pp. 56–77 (p. 61).
79. Bertaut, *La Littérature féminine*, pp. 120 and 286.
80. Clouard (1947), *Histoire de la littérature française*, vol. 1, pp. 341, 342, 590, 372 and 179.
81. Simon, *Histoire de la littérature française*, vol. 1, p. 56.
82. E. Lamy's discourse is reproduced in part in Bethléem, *Romans à lire*, pp. 135–6.
83. Yourcenar, *Les Yeux ouverts*, p. 253 and 228–9.
84. Yourcenar, 'Carnet de notes', p. 329.
85. This autobiography comprises *Souvenirs pieux* (1974), *Archives du nord* (1977) and *Quoi? L'Eternité* (1988 posth.).
86. King, *French Women Novelists*, p. 109.
87. Rachilde (1947), *Quand j'étais jeune*, Paris, p. 32.
88. Lalou, *Histoire de la littérature française*, vol. 2, p. 601.
89. D. and G. McMillan (1950), *An Anthology of the Contemporary French Novel, 1919–1949*, London, p. 73.
90. Atwood, 'Paradoxes and Dilemmas', p. 75.
91. Lalou, *Histoire de la littérature française*, vol. 2, pp. 834 and 605.
92. Simon, *Histoire de la littérature française*, vol. 1, p. 72.
93. Parker and Pollock, *Old Mistresses*, p. 35.
94. D. Holmes (1991), *Colette*, London, p. 3.
95. King, *French Women Novelists*, p. 111.
96. Ibid., p. 108.

Part II

There is no such thing as autobiography, there's only art and lies.

Jeannette Winterson, *Art and Lies* (1995)

– 3 –

Autobiographical Fallacies

If one takes the standard, literalist, purist definition of the post-1770s European autobiography as a 'real person's retrospective prose account of his/her own individual life, in which the main emphasis is placed on the development of his/her personality',[1] then contrary to the expectations raised by literary histories, fully-fledged traditional autobiographies by French Inter-war women writers are a very rare commodity indeed. Despite the critics' suggestion that there is nothing more natural for a woman than to sift through her experiences, to trace her developmental pattern, to wish to record her life for posterity, the number of published female-authored autobiographies is severely limited compared to the extensive number of female-authored novels. Why this discrepancy? What motivations and objectives governed women's generic choice and usage? Catherine Pozzi stands out for her illuminating analysis of the complex difficulties inherent in the supposedly innate and easy bond between women and autobiography. Her multi-volume *Journal 1913–1934*, although not in itself an autobiography *per se*, is of especial interest, for it provides both a conscious and subconscious testimony to the intellectual, emotional and psychological adversities she, as a female author, faced in writing about her personal identity, and as importantly, it serves as a forum in which Pozzi is able to posit and test, with varying degrees of success, a range of diverse strategies to overcome these problems.

One of the most interesting aspects of Pozzi's journal is her investigation of the dearth of female-authored journals, diaries, memoirs or autobiographies, placed under public scrutiny on the printed page. She suggests that when an autobiography is for private perusal then, generally speaking, it is quite innocuous and can be therapeutic, allowing a woman to explore, review and evaluate her inner life; when it is intentionally produced for a wider readership, Pozzi feels that the writer's relationship with her work changes fundamentally. We see this experience in her own journal, especially in the final volumes where, becoming increasingly preoccupied with her imminent death, she charts an oscillating attraction and repulsion for the move to print. Pozzi suggests that there is a single comprehensive explanation for this widespread situation: when women contemplate having their works published they are automatically influenced either subconsciously or consciously by what they consider to be their potential audience's assumptions and demands. She outlines in some detail three specific elements of audience expectations which she herself found disturbing, with the implication that these precise areas are also problematic for female autobiographers in general.

The major aspect of readerly exigences which Pozzi finds unfavourable concerns the conventional subject matter of published autobiographical works. Throughout history many renowned male writers have produced works which, no doubt because of the traditional relationship between lettered men and the public sphere, share a common theme: the documentation of personal interactions with great people and momentous events.[2] Faced with the weight of printed works reinforcing and enshrining this precedent, Catherine Pozzi senses a discrepancy in her own aims or interests and those deemed 'proper' to the genre. In the last few years of her life, when she looks back on her work and the subject it privileges, her comments are particularly revealing. In 1931 she writes: 'I ought to make *this* diary into *a* diary, I have known so many people', 'Je devrais faire de *ce* journal *un* journal, j'ai connu tant de gens' (p. 582). She feels that in terms of the genre's standard preoccupations, her own contribution is inadequate because she has not depicted the renowned people in whose circles she moved – the great scientists, thinkers, writers and socialites of her day, specifically her close friends Mme Bulteau (Toche), Nathalie Barney, Colette, Anna de Noailles, Marie Bonaparte, Edmée de La Rochefoucauld and Gérard d'Houville. A little later, in her diary entry for 24 March 1934, she continues in the same vein when she writes: 'I don't know who killed Stavisky. Doubtless these pages will be of no interest whatsoever because they won't even have mentioned such things'(p. 644).[3] Pozzi recognizes that she has not provided solid documentation of the historic events through which she has lived, that she has effectively rejected the public for the private, the physical for the reflective. However, despite a temporary tendency to rectify this problem by the inclusion of increased references to current affairs, Pozzi finally decides to put forward a case championing the autobiographer's prerogative to prioritize the personal rather than the public. She defends her right to focus exclusively on her intellectual and spiritual growth, even if this does mean that she inverts traditional hierarchies and that her work contradicts fundamental readerly expectation of autobiographical works.

This very privileging of the personal leads to a second major problem registered by Pozzi. For the vast majority of the reading public, autobiography was conceived as a mimetically realistic, plausible and verifiable account of the author's life.[4] This, together with editors' modern marketing strategies which cultivated and incited a taste for scandalous revelatory gossip, led to readerly expectations of authentic highly personal insights, tastes reinforced by Rousseau's problematic legacy in the genre. Pozzi resents this situation on two counts. Her diary demonstrates her total horror at the prospect of seeing her own emotional life set out in print as a market commodity, and in places Pozzi quite explicitly condemns contemporary editorial trends for the exposure of the intimate details of new writers' lives, when she talks of her horror of externally enforced universal self-exhibitionism (pp. 362 and 489). Moreover, like both Sand and later Beauvoir, she wants to resist inculpating her lovers. Despite her confused feelings for Paul Valéry, she refuses to heed intrusive readerly expectations and exigences, and decides against using her diary as a kind of redress or revenge. She insists on preserving her own privacy and suggests that this dilemma may have led to many women deciding against publishing their autobiographical works

The third problem highlighted in Catherine Pozzi's journal results from the discrepancy in widely held patriarchal notions of femininity and the general status conferred on autobiographers. The popular conception of femininity is that a woman should be altruistic not egocentric, a point stressed by the reactionary psychologist von Le Fort. Writing in the 1940s with the precise intention of dissuading women from the autobiographical genre, von Le Fort argues that 'real women love silence and are themselves silent', and moreover that 'in highlighting personal features, women destroy the eternal appearance of womanhood. The quest for personal identity lies at the root of female sin, the root of Eve's sin.'[5] This has clear implications for autobiography. Unpublished journals and personal accounts are suitable feminine activities as they may give a woman space for self-improvement. In total contrast, the act of producing a published autobiography is deeply transgressive. As Gallop notes, even today there is a general belief that 'women write letters – personal, intimate, in relation; men write books – universal, public, in general circulation'.[6] In assuming the status of autobiographer, the woman writer catapults herself from the relatively lowly position of a woman writing for her own pleasure to that of a woman in whose hands lies considerable power. She controls her own destiny and its representation; it is her perspective, opinions and values which dominate the narrative, and the presentation of those around her is her unique responsibility, for the genre is closed and allows no external contradiction. The author's word is definitive and its printed form adds further weight to the views it conveys. Heilbrun argues that in most western cultures women have traditionally had limited access to this kind of power: 'above all other prohibitions, what has been forbidden to women is anger together with the open admission of the desire for power and control over one's own life'.[7] As a consequence, Heilbrun holds, women autobiographers may feel ill at ease with this degree of authority. In Pozzi's diary there is some evidence for this, in her disclaimer that the only motivation behind her search for and articulation of self-knowledge was pure self-defense (p. 245). She fears that any evidence of an acceptance of power and control would leave her open to attacks of pride, vanity, selfish narcissism and a lack of proper femininity, and, of course, to censure over her infraction of a traditionally male-dominated literary preserve.

For Pozzi, published autobiography has strong links with personal testimony, *témoignage*, and so the problem of authorial status may be further aggravated if the life presented in the autobiography breaches conventional social norms. Given that in the Inter-war era women were faced, as never before, with a wide series of life options which had not as yet been presented in literary or factual works, it is not surprising that this new generation of women writers were wary of inscribing in print lifestyles which varied so dramatically from those of their predecessors. Catherine Pozzi's own life was by no means orthodox, as her brief summary indicates: 'The horrid marriage, the horrid divorce, the war, the martyred fiancé. Years of illness. My father's murder. Last but not least, the love of a madman' ('L'horrible mariage, l'horrible divorce, la guerre, le fiancé, qui fut martyr. La maladie, pendant les années. Mon père assassiné. Enfin, la passion d'un fou') (p. 258). Here it is evident that her life was quite at odds with the traditional notion of the passive domestic bourgeois housewife, the *femme au foyer* or its English equivalent the *angel in the house*. What is of interest is that in leading the life of a non-conformist divorced mistress Pozzi has no qualms; in depicting it in her autobiography she hesitates, as her choice of verb here indicates: 'It would certainly be better not to publish these pages. They might *infect* other people' (my italics), 'Il vaut mieux certainement pas publier ces papiers. Cela *contagionnerait* d'autres gens' (p. 175). While Pozzi clearly acknowledges that her life challenges accepted, traditional behavioural patterns, she sees its representation in a factual authoritative mode as a double violation – an infraction or desecration of a combination of literary, gender and social norms. Pozzi's evaluation of her first-hand experience of autobiographical writing and more especially her study of the tacit pressures of public expectations and opinions faced by the female autobiographer, goes some way towards providing an explanation for the limited numbers of women involved in writing traditional autobiographies, memoirs or journals expressly for a general readership.

Yet some women did pursue this hazardous course. The works of those female writers who ventured into the domain of the traditional autobiography share a common feature, a feature which supports Pozzi's analysis of women's relationship to autobiography: they all exhibit an arsenal of defensive strategies for self-protection, strategies which almost without exception converge on a policy of self-concealment. This general characteristic has been observed by several feminist critics, most notably Spacks who records that women refuse 'to emphasize their *own* importance, though writing in a genre which implies self-assertion and self-display'.[8] Catherine Pozzi's journal certainly supports Spacks's argument that women autobiographers do not reveal or flaunt themselves in the ways that literary critics and historians have frequently assumed, and instead employ extreme diversionary tactics to camouflage themselves.[9] The most common strategies may be classified under two headings: temporal dislocations and displaced or distorted focuses. A survey of select Inter-war works, presented in literary histories as autobiographies, demonstrates these deliberate policies of misdirection at work.

There are two dominant types of temporal dislocations. Most obviously, a writer may deliberately choose to publish her auto-biographical works belatedly at a considerable remove from the period in which they were composed. Such is the case of Catherine Pozzi's journal. Following the explicit instructions laid down in Pozzi's last will and testament and in the journal itself, it became the property and responsibility of her son Claude, who had to arrange that it would be preserved in the Parisian Bibliothèque nationale for a period of fifty years, after which it would be published posthumously. In this way Pozzi hoped that her indictment of Valéry's alleged plagiarism and her exposure of their romantic liaison would be made public and yet would also have a more limited impact on his innocent family. A second tactic adopted by certain writers is the concentration on a relatively unincriminating phase of their lives. This is best exemplified by Anna de Noailles's *Le Livre de ma vie* (1932). As the title suggests, the spotlight falls square on Noailles herself and in accordance with the literalist generic definition of autobiography there is an attempt to depict the growth of an individual – Noailles's birth, childhood and adolescence, her literary and personal interests and influences are all described in considerable detail. However, as in Gyp's *La Joyeuse enfance de la IIIème République* (1931), Louise Weiss's *Souvenirs d'une enfance républicaine* (1938), Rachilde's *Quand j'étais jeune* (1947) and more recently Sarraute's *Enfance* (1983), the autobiography stops short of the period of the author's life which would interest most readers. Although written in the penultimate year of Noailles's life when she was aged fifty-six, *Le Livre de ma vie* comes to an abrupt halt five years before her career as a professional writer took off, that is to say, it chronicles events up to 1896. Some thirty-six years go unrecorded. Noailles gives no insight whatsoever into her adult life, her ambiguous sexuality, her trials and tribulations as a writer, her triumphs in the Parisian salons, the years in which her works were recognized and applauded, or into her declining health and growing obsession with death – subjects of considerable interest to her contemporaries, as the emphasis in biographical studies suggests. In her silence, rather than providing a corrective to the popular mythologized versions of her life, Noailles perpetuates the mysterious aura surrounding her poetic genius. She refuses to present herself as a professional woman writer and, in so doing, she circumvents the entire problem of authorial status found so taxing by most female autobiographers.

The second type of self-concealment, the displaced or distorted focus, also has two quite different guises. A number of writers deflect attention by severely narrowing their focus to cover a single close member of their entourage, such that their autobiographies read more like biographies. The two most obvious cases of this from the Interwar era must be Georgette Leblanc's *Souvenirs* (1931) and Isabelle Rimbaud's *Reliques* (1922). The former dwells largely on the dramatist Maurice Maeterlinck, Leblanc's lover; the latter on the poet Arthur Rimbaud, Isabelle's celebrated brother. The second work is of especial interest not least because of the conflicting guidance provided by the paratext concerning the correct focal point for the reader's attention. Four of the five subsections given by Isabelle on the contents page refer to Arthur and the text itself seems to confirm this emphasis. Yet the portrait which features on the opening page reminds us that the work, in its depiction of the siblings' shared family life and experiences, is equally autobiographical.[10] Isabelle is the sole subject of the introduction, preface and appendix, where three critics try to unearth the key events in her life and cast light on her personality. The main reason for this corrective focus is the fact that Isabelle is quite eclipsed in her own narrative. As Hennique notes in the introduction: 'By the last page, we still do not know the colour of her hair, or strictly speaking anything about her at all.'[11] Even her portrait reveals little – she is dressed in a sombre shapeless cloak, unadorned by cosmetics or jewellery, her hair is neatly tied back, her hands clasped, her body turned to the side such that her eyes are averted from the onlooker's gaze. This stilted picture provides no sign of emotion, feeling or life. From this dearth of information on the author, the critics, like the reader, try to reconstruct an understanding of Isabelle Rimbaud. Méléra, who prefaces the volume with a potted biography, attributes Isabelle's self-effacement in the text to her renouncement of the ego in favour of adoration and glorification of her brother. Hennique, in registering the same fact that Isabelle has effectively written herself out of her own autobiography, claims that her minor ancillary role is evidence of a saintly modest disposition. Her introduction is peppered with adjectives and similes all stressing this supposed character trait, such as 'divinely sculpted', 'like a saint', 'like some kind of miracle', 'like an angelic apparition', 'an evangelical nurse'. Méléra too, employing this religious frame of reference, speaks of Isabelle as her brother's 'first disciple'.[12] The critics singularly fail to see that the sketchiness of Isabelle Rimbaud's self-portrait is related as much, if not more, to the ubiquitous uneasy relationship between women and the autobiographical genre, as to the character traits they attribute to its individual author.

A similar technique, maintaining the displaced narrow focus, lies in creating a traditional self-portrait, while simultaneously shifting the responsibility for the text's conception away from the self. Marie Noël in *Notes intimes 1922–1940. . .* (1959) does just this, acknowledging her obvious part in writing the work but dislocating the twinned concept of author and authority. She justifies recording her thoughts and impressions during moments of spiritual crisis by explaining in the foreword, or disclaimer, that they were conceived as a sort of remedial private confession and only undertaken at the relentless insistence of Abbé Mugnier. He is made solely accountable for the work's inception. Catherine Pozzi goes one step further in her abnegation of responsibility by omitting the middleman. She claims a direct divine calling and throughout her *Journal* there are repeated references to her predestined mission! Likewise, the dramatist Marie Lenéru, whose journal appeared posthumously in 1922, commented 'As you are my witness, Lord, it was not I who chose this path', 'Vous m'êtes témoin, Seigneur, que je n'ai pas choisi cette carrière', again drawing attention away from her own part in deciding to write.[13] Heilbrun offers an explanation for this phenomenon: it is impossible for women 'to admit into their autobiographical narratives the claim of achievements, the admission of ambition, the recognition that accomplishment was neither luck nor the result of the efforts of generosity of others'.[14] Spacks confirms this theory of wilful self-effacement in female-authored autobiography, suggesting that the presentation of a work in terms of a frame of reference external to the author allows her to retreat into an unthreatening ancillary role offering service to a greater man.[15] It creates the impression that she conforms to conservative nineteenth-century concepts of ideal womanhood and consequently it frees her from the charges of personal satisfaction or pride in achievement often levelled at women autobiographers.

The second equally popular technique for self-effacement involving distorted focuses lies in the employment of an abnormally wide perspective. Rather than narrowing and displacing the focus the author extends the centre of attraction to such a degree that the individual becomes camouflaged, little more than one of myriad points of interest. Here Louise Weiss's *Souvenirs d'une enfance républicaine* is of interest. While providing personal, verifiable information on the first twenty-five years of the author's life – on her family background, her childhood in Arras and Paris, her early awareness of political issues such as the Dreyfus affair, her reading, her travels,[16] her introduction to adult sexuality and her interest in journalism, which was to become her profession – it principally examines the nature of female education in France during the Third Republic. Unlike many autobiographical works which paint childhood through a nostalgic filter, Weiss's feminist testimony critically examines her own schooling. Weiss castigates her teachers, the well-meaning, if misguided, women who interpreted Camille Sée's reformatory educational policies to the letter, who sought to instill in her a general culture deemed indispensable for her future role as a wife and mother. She contends that, given the fact that so many women of her generation would not marry (in the majority of cases as a result of the Great War and the reduction in numbers of eligible male partners[17]), women should be educated for more vocational roles. In this, Weiss is in keeping with the spirit of the times. As in Great Britain and the United States, since the late nineteenth century, bourgeois families could no longer automatically expect their daughters to remain at home.[18] Growing numbers of self-sufficient, middle-class girls had chosen to enter the liberal professions – a process accelerated by the military and economic exigences of the Great War.[19] Working-class girls also had vastly altered expectations of their working lives, and many moved away from traditional jobs in domestic service and in the textile and clothing industry to work in the tertiary sector. Educational reforms were needed to facilitate this transformation in the female workforce, and by the date of publication of Weiss's autobiography (1938), although not within the period described in the work, some changes had already taken place: many schools began offering girls career advice in the Inter-war era, in 1924 the Minister of Public Education, Léon Bérard, instituted equal educational syllabuses in French lycées, and in 1935 legislation was passed to give mothers an equal say in all educational matters concerning their children. But Weiss goes beyond asking for legislative change. She progresses to suggest that it is attitudes to female eduction which are most in need of a fundamental overhaul. Again she illustrates this with personal examples. Although much brighter than her brothers, she was offered significantly limited opportunities in comparison: her father insisted on her spending four months in a German finishing school learning housewifery and cooking skills and showed no interest in her school awards for academic excellence. Her final judgement is that so long as men continue to be educated in institutions which have seen no change since Napoleonic times women's position will not improve. In its final pages the autobiography turns from polemic to a more personal note with the death of close childhood male friends. Yet this too is transformed by Weiss into a more universal image of renascent hope in the future of female education rising from the ashes of the Great War. Although throughout the work Weiss grounds this feminist argument firmly in her own unique experience, her final vision transcends the individual. The overall effect is that her social critique and her political argument both mask and justify her autobiography.

The most extreme examples of the wide-angled lens are to be found in the autobiographies of Elisabeth de Gramont, Marthe de Bibesco, Marie Scheikévitch, Marguerite Moreno and Gyp. Despite the presence of a unifying, single, highly personal viewpoint in these works, the authors themselves remain fully concealed. Little, often no, sense of their personal development is conveyed, because the reader's attention is firmly deflected away from the writer herself to the world in which she lives, thanks to an overwhelming wealth of details, be it of contemporary salon life, political machinations, social reforms, or of both worldly and worldwide intrigues. Gyp, for example, having moved as a young woman in cosmopolitan, literary and aristocratic circles in both Paris and the provinces (chiefly Lorraine and Normandy) during the 1870s, is in a privileged position to document the backdrops of high society life. Her highly entertaining two volume *La Joyeuse enfance de la IIIème République* vividly recounts the social effects of the withdrawal of the German occupying forces, the political scheming of their successors and the infighting of the rival monarchists. It provides a wealth of insider information on the foibles and caprices of important statesmen, army officials and their entourage, not to mention particulars on their taste in furnishings, victuals and fashions. As a lighthearted chronicle of the period it is unsurpassed.

Pozzi too explores the possibilities of the wide-angled lens technique in her journals. While she does not provide social documentary information in the same way as do Gyp and Weiss, she does succeed in minimizing her individual importance by presenting her own existential quest as a small part of a much greater autobiographical project. This project, which is concomitantly part of her highly complex philosophical theory, draws together diverse aspects of the lives and ambitions of her forefathers.[20] Pozzi's macrocosmic focus is a perfect foil. A similar technique is employed in Yourcenar's multi-volume autobiographical work *Le Labyrinthe du monde,* which also concentrates on her ancestral past at the expense of her personal present life.

Although these strategies of self-concealment may resolve many of the difficulties women face when writing autobiography, they have their own inherent problems. Sometimes the diversionary techniques employed may be too overpowering, as Pozzi acknowledges in her diary. The final volume of the journal is heavy with a sense of bewilderment, dismay and despair as its author comes to realize that, despite the divine source of her inspiration, her mission has proved abortive. The reader is left unsure whether Pozzi still is in control of her sense of calling, using it as a ruse or rhetorical device, or whether ultimately she is controlled by it. This particular technique for self-concealment is evidently somewhat counter-productive. At other times the stratagems may be so extreme that they in fact contravene the most elementary definitions of autobiography to such a degree that although classified as autobiography several of these works may more fully resemble social documentaries or biographies. In the main, however, the principal effect of authorial self-effacement and misdirection is that female-authored autobiographies assume a counterfeit appearance. They cease to appear as vehicles for accurate self-representation.[21] So it is that Woolf in the Inter-war years categorically states that very few women as yet have written truthful autobiographies.[22] In a sense, the very implementation of the strategies for self-concealment which women find so necessary in the traditional autobiography works against the impetus for honest self-exploration which lies at the heart of the autobiographical impulse.

For a sizeable number of women writers who evidently found the traditional autobiographical genre inimical, given audience expectations of it, there was a possible solution: one means to meet their literary and/or psychological objectives in writing lay in the deliberate blurring of truth and fantasy, in the couching of factual material in a fictional framework. This solution proved highly popular and the period 1920 to 1940 saw the practice of interrogating personal experience in the novel flourish as never before. Naturally enough, critics and literary historians have not been slow to notice the auto-biographical content of much Inter-war female fiction and countless examples of author-centred readings abound. Bethléem categorically portrays Myriam Harry's Siona series, comprising *La Petite Fille de Jérusalem* (1914), *Siona chez les barbares* (1918), *Siona à Paris* (1919), *Le Tendre Cantique de Siona* (1922) and *Siona à Berlin* (1927), as 'her autobiographies', 'her irreligious, improper confessions'.[23] Clouard describes Jeanne Perdriel-Vaissière's work as a barely fictionalized representation of her life; he refers to Antonine Coulet-Tessier's late poems as being autobiographical;[24] and from his deduction that the princess Marthe de Bibesco tells her life-story in *Catherine Paris* (1927) asks if the heroine in *Le Perroquet vert* (1924) is equally a self-portrait.[25] Lucie Delarue-Mardrus's *Le Roman des six petites filles* (1924) is con-sidered by La Rochefoucauld as a personal account of her childhood,[26] while it is widely held that Delarue-Mardrus's *L'Ange et les Pervers* (1930) is based on a love affair between the author and Nathalie Barney.[27] Fleury classifies Gérard d'Houville's fiction in the same way. He writes that 'in all her novels Marie rewrites scenes from her past', and he draws particular attention to *L'Inconstante* (1903), 'her first autobiographical novel'; *Le Brélan*, which depicts a man's love for two sisters, reflecting her relationship with her sibling, Louise, and Pierre Louÿs;[28] *Esclave* (1905), which 'maintains an autobiographical char-acter' in its evocation of her visit to America and her lesbian alliance with Georgie Raoul Duval to whom the work is dedicated; and *Le Temps d'aimer* (1908).[29]

From such typical examples, it is clear that critics have felt justified in their common tendency to read women's fictional works as *romans à clef*, as this approach, with its lengthy historical precedent, has been accorded a certain credibility. As Didier notes, the presuppositions of nineteenth-century criticism grant their modern counterparts the right to 'establish systematically a link between the life and the work, with much less reticence in the case of women writers than with their male counterparts'.[30] In the Inter-war era, editorial marketing strategies, which promoted works through the specific provision of information on the author's life, also played a part in further sanctioning this critical method. While this conception of certain female-authored Inter-war novels is partly warranted – a number of the novels singled out by literary historians are indeed circumstantially autobiographical – in a great many cases, the critical understanding and representation of women's fictionalized autobiographies fail to do proper justice to the works in question. The autobiographical fallacy, which dominates canonical compilations covering the period, is flawed on two counts.

First, women writers' motives are frequently misinterpreted. Larnac, for instance, writing in 1929 comments: 'Most of our women novelists only know how to retell their slightly fictionalized memoirs or confessions through the depiction of a heroine who appears to be slightly different from themselves, but this only in her general appearance, not her deep inner self.' To this he adds 'women who are able to transcend the self to write something different are few and far between', holding that his female peers were quite 'unable to see the world without putting a great deal of themselves into the picture'.[31] He goes on to outline what he sees as the single dominant reason for the absence of any great female literary innovation in the early years of the twentieth century: women's egocentricity, their self-indulgent inward gaze, and its repercussions in their generic choice. In a similar vein, Flat depicts the female author looking at herself, indulging in 'this avowal or confession through which she knows how to reveal herself completely'.[32] Female-authored works classified as autobiographical novels are reduced to a kind of personal avowal, indulgent narcissistic display, or egocentric self-exhibitionism, and as a direct consequence of this these works tend to be dismissed in canonical compilations. How ironic when there is a notable absence of any sense of self-display in women's fiction and when so many women shunned the more direct form of autobiography! Secondly, and perhaps most importantly, all too often criticism prioritizes a purely biographical reading at the expense of a proper valorization of a work's fictional format. Such interpretations, with their disproportionate displaced emphasis, frequently culminate in a highly reductive presentation of women's works.

This type of criticism, which repeatedly comes into play in the denigration of the importance of women's literary contribution, with its neglect or negation of fictional qualities, with its general imputation of narcissistic self-indulgence, was considered offensive by many female authors. Indeed, a number of Inter-war writers, including Colette, Pozzi, Jeanne Galzy, Monique Saint-Hélier and Marguerite Audoux, in reflections on the reception accorded to their literary corpuses, all made a considerable effort to challenge, counter, correct and dilate the critical focus on circumstantial autobiographical detail, to stress the hybrid aspect of their works, and to shift attention from the base material of the work to the final product and the fictional process itself. As an example of this one might consider Pozzi's novella *Agnès* (1927), for which the author claims a dual status. *Agnès*'s earliest audience primarily read the work for its autobiographical elements, and five years later Pozzi reinforced this interpretation by asking that it be read as a literary testimony and introduction to her *Journal 1913–*

1934. Indeed, since the publication of Pozzi's diaries there can be little doubt that *Agnès* is largely a self-portrait; for in terms of setting it faithfully reproduces Pozzi's home and family life. In terms of plot *Agnès* is based on an actual series of incidents from Pozzi's own adolescent years: her refusal at the age of fifteen to go to church with her grandmother to take Holy Communion, and her resultant process of self-education involving studies in theology, science, history and philosophy. The final scene with its theatrical reference echoes Catherine's own honeymoon with the dramatist Bourdet, who produced his first successful work during this break in Cannes. In terms of subject, Catherine and Agnès at times seem to be synonymous. The fictional heroine is unquestionably based on the author for not only does she bear her communion name and share the same interests, she has comparable attitudes to love, marriage and death – the traditional staples of the female life. Both Pozzi and Agnès employ the same recurrent pattern of linguistic and metaphoric motifs. For example, perhaps as a reflection of Pozzi's belief that the self is multiple, individuals are referred to under a wide gamut of names. In the diary the lover is called Ange, Stellio, Desum, Absum, Lionardo, sans toi, tête de Paris, Azéro, no name, Hell, l'Arrivé and le Fou.[33] In the novella the lover is referred to as mon cher, cher amour, cher grand frère, mon fiancé, mon bien-aimé and finally Félix. Likewise, both Pozzi and Agnès use the same nexus of images, of which the most notable are the depiction of life as a sea-voyage which evolves into a shipwreck, death as a means of escape and clothing as a symbol of purity

However, as Pozzi explains in her journal, *Agnès* is much more than a simple self-recording. The novella was originally conceived as 'a fantasy' (p. 331) and in *Agnès* itself Pozzi makes a considerable effort to underline the narrative's fictional quality. While Agnès does closely resemble her creator, Pozzi takes great care to stress that the two, while similar, are not identical or fully interchangeable, that their relationship is considerably more complex. Pozzi sets up a certain ironic distance between herself and her protagonist. In the dedication to the first edition she likens Agnès to a heroine of the Comtesse de Ségur. The latter wrote of idealized children and Agnès obviously fails to conform to such a definition. Irony is equally evident in her choice of register. While Pozzi herself is well versed in Bohr's theory of quantum mechanics, Agnès discusses most contemporary scientific issues in layman's not technical terms. Similarly, her understanding of philosophy is shown to be fairly rudimentary and quite naive.[34] A further means of highlighting the irony in *Agnès* lies in the emphasis Pozzi places on the novella's mock-romantic form. On one level, the romantic plot is debunked because Pozzi focuses on the heroine's life prior to the first meeting with the hero and on their honeymoon. She omits the romance's conventional subject: the lovers' courtship. On another level, the romantic plot is treated ironically in the hyperbolic presentation of ideal love. The relationship between the lovers is suffused with the tropes of the romance for the lovers are pulled together by magnetic forces of destiny beyond their control. Moreover, the hero, to whom Agnès writes in the opening few pages of the novella, conforms to all the standard characteristics of the romantic hero *par excellence*. He is dark and aged between twenty-five and thirty, while the heroine is a tender seventeen. However, Pozzi soon deflates this exemplary picture when it is revealed that the lovers and their relationship are, as yet, only a figment of Agnès's imagination. Pozzi's use of irony, literary parody and this emphasis on the realm of the imaginary further reinforce the impression that the novella belongs to the realm of fantasy as much as fact. Pozzi deliberately calls attention to the work's hybrid nature, and encourages readings which assess both aspects.[35]

A comparable situation occurs with Colette, who, even in her fairly early works, provides several warnings against her fiction being read exclusively as primary biographical source material. In 'Le Miroir' in *Les Vrilles de la vigne* (1908) she ironically depicts an encounter between herself as author and her mirrored image as Claudine her fictional counterpart. In *La Naissance du jour* (1928) she more explicitly cautions the reader against the trap of facile referentiality. *La Naissance du jour* is a first-person narrative set in the author's home in Saint-Tropez. The action is interspersed with largely authentic letters from her mother Sido, and the protagonists are recognizable, named, real-life people including Colette's direct family and friends. What makes the novel arresting is the way in which onto a series of reminiscences of real-life experiences Colette grafts a fabricated plot. Fictional characters – the hero Vial and Hélène Clément, the young girl whose love goes unrequited – interact with flesh and blood protagonists and the work oscillates between fact and fiction, demonstrating the intrapenetrability of generic boundaries. To highlight the deliberately ambiguous shifting status of the novel, and to alert the reader to the danger of reducing the work to a simple *roman à clef*, Colette begins with a striking epitaph: 'Do you imagine when reading my work that I am drawing my portrait here? Patience, it is only my pattern' ('Imaginez-vous, à me lire, que je fais mon portrait? Patience, c'est seulement mon modèle'). Despite the ostensible frankness of the narration and despite the author's limpid style, the differentials separating Colette the writer, Colette the narrator, Colette the protagonist and

Colette as a mirror image of Sido seem intentionally ambiguous, and the reader is left uncertain as to how much of the various self-portraits is genuine, how much is mask.[36]

Jeanne Galzy's response to the autobiographical fallacy is fairly similar. In literary histories, her novels are repeatedly presented as *romans à clef* and explained solely in terms of their factual documentation of the author's life. Lemaître, Bethléem, Lalou, Talvart and Place all concur in their opinion that Jeanne Galzy transcribes her memories, impressions and professional observations in *La Femme chez les garçons* (1919) and *L'Initiatrice aux mains vides* (1929), which both reflect her time as a teacher at the lycée Lamartine in Paris. Her two-year tuberculosis treatment at the Maison des Sables sanatorium in Berck-sur-Mer is seen by these same critics to constitute the unique subject of the prize-winning novel *Les Allongés* (1923). Now Galzy, while freely admitting that her personal experiences provided the basis for her fiction, greatly objected to a purely autobiographical explanation, as her entry in the Prix Fémina compilation indicates: 'I hate thinking of the life I've lived. It wouldn't interest anyone other than myself.' She says of her deliberate choice of a fictional format: 'It was a genre which enabled me to create a world and to avoid being directly myself. That suited a certain need for detachment which I have always had.'[37] Within the novels, to provide an element of self-concealment and to counter prevalent over-simplistic autobiographical readings Galzy rigorously balances her personal circumstances with themes and events of more macrocosmic significance. Thus the violent criminal love scenario of *La Grand'rue* (1925) is given a new dimension through its presentation as a modern enactment of the classical myth of Telemachus and Calypso. The sapphic awakening and initiation of *Jeunes Filles en serre chaude* (1934) is set against a more general judgemental enquiry into female development and in particular the suitability of contemporary educational opportunities for young women, ironically highlighted by the novel's framework which depicts the celebrations of the fiftieth anniversary of female secondary education. The individual affliction depicted in Galzy's *Les Allongés* is twinned with a more general metaphysical investigation and validation of human suffering. Throughout this work, Galzy repeatedly stresses the protagonists' distance from the corporeal, material world, as they are physically immobile, strapped to stretchers or encased in plaster. The reader becomes a party to their inner voyages, their search for self-definition, their evaluation of memory, dream and aspirations, their understanding of physical and mental torment, in short their collective spiritual apprenticeship. It is no surprise then that Galzy, in a retrospective overview of her literary contribution, discusses her work in terms of its thematic investigation of vital philosophical, social and religious issues and in terms of its formal experimentation, implicitly rejecting the narrow egocentric interest attributed to her by literary historians

The same discrepancy in authorial intentions and critical readings may be seen in Monique Saint-Hélier's *La Cage aux rêves* (1932). Here, the narrator Béate is cloistered in her Parisian apartment, where she awaits death from a severe tubercular condition. Physically immobile, like Galzy's narrator, she suffers the imprisonment of the work's title; only imagination, poetic fantasy, memory and dreams may transport her from her narrow, stifling confines. The most interesting aspect of the novel is less its specific content (the heroine's experiences of childhood and adolescence) than its rejection of chronology, its poetic ordering, its structure as what Jean-Luc Seylaz terms an archipelago of scenes,[38] and most importantly its constant fluctuation backwards and forwards, in a style later adopted by Marguerite Duras in *L'Amant* (1985), between a direct first-person interior monologue and a third-person narration. The soliloquizing first-person perspective frees the author from her metaphorical cage and allows her to return and relive her past with greater immediacy. The use of the third-person enables her to explore, pin down, imprison and preserve images from this period. The increasing use of the impersonal 'on' opens up individual experience to provide a more macrocosmic vision of the human condition. This oscillating narrative voice allows the dichotomy of the title to come to represent not just Saint-Hélier's own exhausting illness, but the more general tension between inner strength from memory, love and faith, and the external uncontrollable forces of suffering, disease, and the omnipresent threat of death. The novel, like *Les Allongés*, given its philosophical force and narrative format, is again much more than the autobiographical foundations on which numerous critics focus.

As a final example of the frequent contradiction in the reception of women writers' autobiographical works and how the authors themselves view them we should consider Marguerite Audoux's *Marie-Claire* series. In the Inter-war era the reading public's attention was focused more on Audoux herself than on her literary creations. Both *Marie-Claire* and its sequel *L'Atelier de Marie-Claire* were widely accepted as cryptic *romans à clef* and read for details of the author's personal life. Little has changed in more recent criticism. In his biography *Marguerite Audoux: un coeur pur* (1942), Reyer sets out to redress this situation by providing a detached evaluation of Audoux's work, yet he too intertwines biographical facts with direct textual quotations, thus inadvertently perpetuating the metonymic tendency to read the author's life in place of her works, to confuse the author and her protagonist. Cardellichio, in an article of 1977, despite his claimed esoteric interests, also emphasizes the autobiographical aspects of the texts at the expense of the poetic process through which they are transformed into fiction. Similarly Dumont's thesis of 1985, which compares the representation of the working classes in works by Audoux, Emile Guillaumin and Charles-Louis Philippe, is restricted by a too literal reading of Audoux's fiction. Although Dumont does acknowledge that Audoux's corpus is in fact a fictional representation of her life, she still prioritizes the autobiographical elements, reductively interpreting the novels as schematized plots paralleling the author's life.

While no one would dispute that Audoux's retrospective novels are based on the events of her own life, that they are presented from a single subjective viewpoint, that they focus on the development of the individual and that they are peopled by recognizable self-images, they do clearly transcend purely factual transcriptions. Within the works themselves, Audoux signals their literary quality to the reader in several ways: through intense metaphoric codification and symbolic patterning evident in her recurrent use of prison motifs and images of flight, through her deliberate amalgamation of different levels of reality, and through her rejection of mimetic realism in favour of a systematic employment of a combination of sensory and psychological filters. Furthermore, in *Marie-Claire*, a comparison of the exposition and denouement immediately reveals the extent to which the work is highly crafted and well structured. *Marie-Claire* begins with the death of the heroine's mother, the child's resultant insecurity, her frightening dreams of nakedness and her solitary journey to the orphanage. The key features of this scene are ultimately inverted in a paralleled moment in the conclusion when the heroine witnesses a nun's death and the removal of her vestments. In total contrast to the opening scene, the dead, naked nun, liberated from earthly bondage, is the novel's clearest image of freedom. This scene inspires the heroine and transforms her earlier fears, paving the way for the next stage in her own journey through life, represented by her decision to leave for Paris. The heroine's spiritual and emotional growth is metaphorically articulated through the careful balancing in these two scenes. From this it should be transparent that Audoux's novels merit an evaluation for their literary qualities as much as for their autobiographical source material. That Audoux herself supported this view there can be little doubt. Her biographer Reyer records her total antipathy to purely autobiographical readings of her works. He explains that Audoux was averse to the way in which her life as a disadvantaged, working-class, provincial writer had been accorded legendary status by the critics,[39] and that she resented the way in which this biased emphasis invariably eclipsed all accurate evaluations of her very real literary achievements.[40]

From these five examples, it is evidently the case that while personal material undoubtedly plays an important role in the fictional works of Pozzi, Colette, Galzy, Saint-Hélier and Audoux, the exclusively autobiographical readings provided by literary histories are not only partial and reductive, they also contravene the authors' explicit and implicit intentions. As French Inter-war women writers are at such pains in their works and when writing about them to stress the importance of the fictional format, it is surely time that critics focus on this area and ask what benefits arise from this generic amalgamation.

As we have seen in Pozzi's analysis of autobiographical practices, the major motivation behind many Inter-war women writers' recourse to a fictional format is the aim to sidestep the distinctive problems at the heart of the relationship between women and the traditional autobiography, in particular readerly expectations concerning conventional norms and authorial status. After all, this is the principal area differentiating the two genres. Most obviously, its fictional status serves as a buffer, as a major strategy of self-concealment to protect women writers from the direct public gaze, enabling them in advance to circumvent possible readerly accusations of vanity, egoism, pride, narcissism or unruly self-esteem. Didier, in her study of female writers, confirms this hypothesis. She records the fact that many women writers throughout the history of French literature, particularly autobiographers, have suffered a complex psychological guilt syndrome, resulting in part from an internal conflict between a woman's natural fascination with her own reflected image, be it in a mirror or in writing, and her socially conditioned acceptance of her gender as an altruistic (not an egocentric) relational position.[41] It seems that the move to fiction may play a part in liberating women from this culpability. It could be argued that in representing the self in the third person (or in oscillating between the first and the third person, as occurs in Monique Saint-Hélier's *La Cage aux rêves*) and in distancing the heroine by a degree of irony (as occurs in the works of Galzy, Audoux and Pozzi) the author may overcome the guilt associated with the more direct egocentric gaze of traditional autobiography. This, though, is only part of the answer.

The incorporation of autobiographical material into a fictional framework has several further advantages. As King argues, it may be seen as 'a refusal to conform to traditional genres as defined by the dominant literary culture, or as a subversion of these genres to "deconstruct" their normal significance'.[42] Recent re-readings of both Mme de Sévigné and George Sand which reinterpret and illuminate their decanonization see in their generic choice a similar refusal of mainstream factual forms in preference for minor, less realist genres.[43] Schor's re-evaluation of Sand shows that she is not forced into a minor genre for social or cultural reasons, but that she deliberately selects the idealist novel and this 'signifies her refusal to produce mimetically and hence legitimate a social order inimical to the disenfranchised, among them women'.[44] For these women writers, selecting a non-realist genre allows them to challenge insidiously the enshrined status quo of the patriarchal order. Women's deliberate refusal of the traditional mimetic autobiography may be read in the same way, as a radical critique of dominant ideologies, because the conscious move from memoirs and journals to fictionalized self-portraits results in a freedom to analyse the patriarchal order from a deliberately marginal position

In particular, the shift to fiction enables women to re-examine in a more critical and distanced way patriarchal constructions of womanhood. As King again notes: 'the image of woman created by the male artist is also often the image to which men expect or want women to conform. This image, because it is imposed from the out-side, cannot coincide with a woman's image of herself.' As we have seen, traditional female-authored autobiographies, despite their tacit claim to provide factual documentation, often offer little more than anodyne surface representations, harbouring deeper duplicity, camou-flage and falsification. As a result of readerly expectations, female authors are at pains to quell or negate their emotions, to tone down their life-experiences, in an attempt to conform to paradigms of the passive, domestic, bourgeois woman. Here we should recall the images of saintliness evident in autobiographical works by Isabelle Rimbaud, Marie Noël and Marie Lenéru. As the novel, in contrast, is less subject to prescriptive readerly expectations concerning what constitutes both its 'proper' subject and the 'proper' status of its author, women writers are freed from externally imposed restrictions and demands, and need no longer assume counterfeit self-images. This allows women the possibility to depict their own unorthodox lifestyles, and this is commensurate with a liberation. As Wilson puts it: 'Theirs were to be narratives of truth, and women were to bear witness to the auth-enticity of their lives, a sudden and neglected truth, but all the more subversive for that reason – the testimony now finding expression would cast a new light on the accepted truths of the male world.'[45] Strange as it might at first seem, this move to fiction enables female writers to produce more truthful, sincere and frank personal accounts. In its provision of greater critical distance, the novel also furnishes women with the necessary space to be sufficiently removed from their lives to see them in perspective, to explore them, to judge them and indeed rewrite them.

Following from this, the shift to fiction, most importantly, allows women to employ a dual focus in their works: they may expound on their discontent with the status quo and also explore their own personal, social and political ambitions. We see this in Mme de Sévigné's choice of the epistolary genre in which she rejects mimetic verisimilitude, providing instead a subjective type of self-representation. According to Mann: 'the letter form becomes for the woman who uses it a magnifying mirror which no longer reflects the real picture of her emotions, but an enlarged, deformed image'; 'writing allows her not just to express, but to create through expression an image of herself (. . .) as she would like to be'.[46] Mme de Sévigné's intentionally inward gaze, then, not only signifies a rejection of an inimical external patriarchal realm, it offers in its place an inner world of desires. It allows her to present a new ideal self-image and a more general vision of womanhood as a whole. This projection beyond an accurate self-portrait to the creation of an idealized alter ego is also evident in numerous Inter-war autobiographical novels, where it also enables the author to come to terms with her relational, existential and even psychological problems in a way denied her in more explicitly factual representational modes. Heilbrun, who admits to 'searching for identity other than her own' in her own autobiographical novels, also argues that this is a common tendency in female-authored works: 'the woman writer is, consciously or not, creating an alter ego as she writes, another possibility of female destiny'.[47] Chadwick too, examining the female Surrealists' use of the self-portrait also records this phenomenon where women artists 'in an attempt to overcome the polarity of observer and observed (. . .) often turned to the self-portrait as a device for initiating the same dialogue between inner and outer reality'[48] by projecting inner reality, in the form of desire, onto an externalized version of the self. The dual focus inherent in fictionalized autobiography clearly facilitates this process. It concomitantly promotes the frank testimony of women's discontent with current social orders and encourages their truthful acknowledgement of inner hopes and aspirations.

It is undoubtedly the case that in response to the inimical legacy of readerly expectations left by the autobiography in its traditional nineteenth-century guise few French Inter-war women writers produced and published works which conform to the standard purist definition of the genre. Rather, women chose to present personal material in the more open context of the novel. It is in this area that critics and literary historians do women poor justice. Misdirected by a preoccupation with female authors' lives and by an outdated concept of women's psychological motivations for self-analysis, critics all too often fail to see more in these works than narcissistic, aesthetically conservative *romans à clef.* Such a reading is at once reductive and inappropriate because the prioritizing of autobiographical aspects of female fiction is generally conducted at the expense of any detailed study of either the author's artistry or her possible interest in the major philosophical concerns attributed to male-authored modernist works. The result is a fairly bland and uninspiring homogenized represent-ation of women's writing and this in turn has played a considerable part in the denigration of female autobiographical works. Yet women writers themselves see this hybrid form of creative self-portraiture as enabling and liberating. Its status as fiction is of considerable importance, because it allows a shift away from anodyne, retro-spective, mimetic recordings of the development of the authors' own personal identities. Writers are freed from the constraint of working to a fixed point of closure, for as the concept of selfhood is ever open to fresh interpretations, the emphasis of their self-consciously prospective, open-ended works falls on the difficulties inherent in the active process of gendered identity construction. More importantly, the couching of factual material in a fictional framework means that authors need no longer seek to define themselves in terms of patriarchally approved definitions of femininity; they need not simply reinscribe the values of the status quo. The dual focus of their works allows them to express quite candidly their personal discontent with the limited orthodox life options proposed for women in patriarchal society and, as we shall see in the following chapter, to communicate, in often highly innovative ways, their own personal visions of female needs and desires.

Notes

1. P. Lejeune (1975), *Le Pacte autobiographique,* Paris, p. 14.
2. Simon, for example, in his dismissal of Colette's contribution to the autobiography, stresses that the genre is suited only to import-ant social or political figures. P.-H. Simon (1963), *Histoire de la littérature française au XXème siècle, 1900–1950,* 7th edn, Paris, vol. 2, p. 159.

3. The incident to which Pozzi refers, the murder of Stavisky, made the headlines in the French national press during the early months of 1934. Stavisky, a dealer in forged notes, bonds and fake jewels, before coming to trial, was found dead in Chamonix. To this day it is unclear whether he committed suicide or was murdered to prevent the incrimination of top civil servants, deputies and ministers. He was adopted as a symbol of scandal and government corruption, and following his death, Paris witnessed major street disturbances which culminated on 6 February 1934 when rioters joined forces to storm the French Chamber of Deputies. The right-wing forces called in the *ligues* and after the outbreak of fighting, 15 men died and over 300 were wounded. The event was later described as a 'Fascist riot' by the socialists. They succeeded in coalescing in the Rassemblement populaire, which ensured the return of the left in the 1936 elections in the form of the united Front populaire under Blum. For further details see O. Bernier (1993), *Fireworks at Dusk: Paris in the Thirties*, Boston and London, pp. 126–55.

4. It should be noted that to some extent the concept of autobiography as a simple act of research, recollection and self-recording is chimeric, as writing about the self necessarily involves a degree of self-creation and the generation of a new subject. Just as much fiction subconsciously will have an autobiographical element, given its basis in the author's psyche, all autobiography, even the most referential, is in some sense literary, as there is a constant need to sift, select and order primary source material.

5. G. von Le Fort (1948), *La Femme éternelle: la femme dans le temps, la femme hors du temps*, trans. A. Boccon-Gibod, Paris, pp. 104 and 15.

6. J. Gallop (1986), 'Annie Leclerc Writing a Letter with Vermeer' in N.K. Miller (ed.), *The Poetics of Gender*, New York, pp. 137–57 (p. 139).

7. C.G. Heilbrun (1989), *Writing a Woman's Life*, London, p. 13.

8. P. Spacks (1980), 'Selves in Writing' in E.C. Jelinek (ed.), *Women's Autobiography*, Bloomington and Indianapolis, pp. 112–32 (p. 113).

9. This need for camouflage, although more prevalent in female-authored works, is not necessarily gender specific; we have the celebrated case of Thomas Hardy, who tried to pass of his autobiography as a biography by his wife.

10. The painting was the work of her husband Paterne Berrichon and is dated 1908.

11. N. Hennique (1922), introduction to I. Rimbaud, *Reliques*, Paris, pp. 7–13 (p. 11).

12. M.-Y. Méléra (1922), preface to I. Rimbaud, *Reliques*, Paris, pp. 15–38 (p. 17).
13. See E. de La Rochefoucauld (1969), *Femmes d'hier et d'aujourd'hui*, Paris, p. 147.
14. Heilbrun, *Writing a Woman's Life*, p. 24.
15. Spacks, 'Selves in Writing', p. 113.
16. Louise Weiss studied for a short time in Oxford (at Lady Margaret Hall during the summer of 1911). In this she is similar to both Catherine Pozzi (who spent a year at St Hugh's College, Oxford in 1907) and Nathalie Sarraute (who read history at the Society for Home Students, later known as St Anne's College, Oxford, between 1920 and 1921).
17. Numerical estimates for the number of single French women in the Inter-war era vary from 1.5 to 3.5 million. Hubar calculates that in 1921 marriageable women under the age of thirty outnumbered their male counterparts by a ratio of 6:4. See M.L. Roberts (1994), *Civilization Without Sexes: Reconstructing Gender in Postwar France, 1919–1927*, Chicago and London, p. 154; Cronin suggests that the overall average ratio for the period is 7:5. See V. Cronin (1994), *Paris: City of Light, 1919–1939*, London, p. 42.
18. At the turn of the century France was still some considerable way behind the United States in terms of both the quantity and quality of work available for women. For instance, 1 in every 200 physicians in France was female in comparison to 1 in every 20 in the United States. See A. Klaus (1993), 'Depopulation and Race Suicide: Maternalism and Pronatalist Ideologies in France and the United States, in S. Koven and S. Michel (eds), *Mothers of a New World: Maternalist Politics and the Origins of Welfare States*, London and New York, pp. 188–212 (p. 193).
19. McMillan compares figures for 1906 and 1921. In France, in the commercial sector the number of female workers rose from 779,000 to 1,008,000; in the professional and public services from 293,000 to 491,000; and in the civil service from 100,000 to 200,000. J.E. McMillan (1981), *Housewife or Harlot: the Place of Women in French Society, 1870–1940*, London and New York, pp. 117 and 120.
20. The theory itself (originally conceived as *De Libertate* in 1915, then *Le Corps de l'âme* in 1929) is most fully outlined in *Peau d'âme*, which was published, albeit still incomplete, shortly after her death under the instruction of her son Claude Bourdet
21. French female writers in the era note the existence of only two testimonies which quite openly and sincerely record a full range

of adult human experiences and emotions. Both are in diary form and are not retrospective accounts: the Ukrainian-born Marie Bashkirtseff's *Journal* (Charpentier, 1888) and the Breton dramatist Marie Lenéru's *Journal 1901–1918* (Grasset, 1922 posth.). It is not without significance that even here these intense, tormented, often violent, introspective works were published only after the authors' untimely deaths.

22. V. Woolf (1979), 'Women and Fiction' in M. Barrett (ed.), *Virginia Woolf: Women and Writing*, London, pp. 43–53. This article was first published in *The Forum* (March 1929).

23. Abbé L. Bethléem (1932), *Romans à lire et romans à proscrire*, 11th edn, Paris, p. 132.

24. H. Clouard (1947), *Histoire de la littérature française du symbolisme à nos jours*, Paris, vol. 1, pp. 504 and 164.

25. H. Clouard (1962), *Histoire de la littérature française du symbolisme à nos jours*, 2nd edn, Paris, p. 227.

26. La Rochefoucauld, *Femmes d'hier*, pp. 25–7.

27. Barney writes in turn about Delarue-Mardrus in N. Barney (1960), *Souvenirs indiscrets*, Paris, pp. 147–85.

28. Her family found *Le Brélan* pornographic and the work was never published. Marie destroyed the manuscript at the end of her life.

29. R. Fleury (1990), *Marie de Régnier: l'inconstante*, Paris, pp. 175, 74, 123 and 156.

30. B. Didier (1982), *L'Ecriture femme*, Paris, p. 136.

31. J. Larnac (1929), *Histoire de la littérature féminine en France*, 2nd edn, Paris, pp. 242, 231–2, 241 and 224.

32. P. Flat (1909), *Nos Femmes de lettres*, Paris, p. 72.

33. C. Paulhan who annotates Pozzi's *Journal* (1987), notes (footnote p. 179) that Valéry in turn referred to Pozzi under an equally wide range of names in his *Cahiers*: Karin, K., C.K., ma Psyché, Laure, Le Cygne, Eurydike, X, Béatrice, Bice, Bce and B.

34. This same technique occurs in *Peau d'âme* where the erudite language associated with philosophy is abandoned for the everyday language of two assumed personae, an unsophisticated female student and a crusty university tutor trying to target her ideas at an undergraduate audience. Again neither corresponds fully to Pozzi herself; again Pozzi successfully blurs philosophy, fact and fiction.

35. Pozzi's entire corpus is generically unstable. On the one hand, all of her works (with the exception of a series of scientific articles she produced for *Le Figaro* – 'Les Images parlantes' (9 September, 1929), 'Puits aériens' (6 October, 1929), 'Vénins, poisons régulateurs de la vie' (3 December, 1929) and 'Le Bactériologie

d'Herelle' (26 and 27 February, 1930)), despite their apparent eclecticism in terms of primary subject matter, are governed and unified by an omnipresent autobiographical interest. As her biographer, Joseph, states, her corpus is 'a vast self-portrait' where even her philosophical writing is 'largely an autobiographical undertaking'. See L. Joseph (1988), *Catherine Pozzi: une robe couleur du temps*, Paris, pp. 16 and 297. On the other hand, it is equally clear that Pozzi's *œuvre* has a vital fictional quality. Her philosophical treatise *Peau d'âme* borders on the realms of fantasy, as is suggested by its title, which is so reminiscent of Perrault's fairy tale *Peau d'âne*. Within the *Journal* too there is a move away from the factual mimetic recording of daily occurrences and thoughts, to a more overtly literary form in its enigmatic title: *De l'Ovaire à l'absolu*, and in the inclusion of poems, letters, prayers, theoretical arguments for her treatise and three fictional excerpts – two possible introductions to an imagined novel and a creative retelling of her honeymoon in Cannes with Bourdet.

36. For a fuller discussion of Colette's blurring of the boundaries between autobiography and fiction see N.K. Miller (1988), *Subject to Change: Reading Feminist Writing*, New York, ch. 9, pp. 229–64; E. Marks (1960), *Colette*, New Brunswick; A.A. Ketchum (1968), *Colette ou la naissance du jour: étude d'un malentendu*, Paris.

37. Jeanne Galzy (1954), *Le Prix Fémina: ancien Prix Vie heureuse, Album du cinquentenaire, 1904–1954*, Paris, p. 78.

38. J.-L. Seylaz (1985), introduction to *La Cage aux rêves*, 2nd edn, Paris, p. 16. The novel was first published by Corréa in 1932.

39. This type of reading continues today. Wilson's encyclopedia entry on Audoux opens with the words: 'the story of Marguerite Audoux's success could well be the subject of a novel.' See K. M. Wilson (1991), *An Encyclopedia of Continental Women Writers*, Chicago and London, vol. 1, p. 60.

40. G. Reyer (1942), *Marguerite Audoux: un cœur pur*, Paris, p.11.

41. Didier, *L'Ecriture femme*, pp. 58 and 228.

42. A. King (1989), *French Women Novelists: Defining a Female Style*, London, p. 47.

43. Thiesse and Mathieu describe this phenomenon in which established women writers are being written out of the aggrégation syllabus. A.-M. Thiesse and H. Mathieu (1988), 'The Decline of the Classical and Birth of the Classics' in J. Dejean and N. K. Miller (eds), *The Politics of Tradition: Placing Women in French Literature*, New Haven, CT, pp. 208–29.

44. N. Schor (1988), 'Idealism in the Novel: Recanonizing Sand' in J. Dejean and N.K. Miller (eds), *The Politics of Tradition: Placing*

Women in French Literature, New Haven, CT, pp. 56–76 (p. 73).
45. E. Wilson (1988), 'Tell It Like It Is: Women and Confessional Writing' in S. Radstone (ed.), *Sweet Dreams: Sexuality, Gender and Popular Fiction*, London, pp. 21–46 (p. 28).
46. M.A. Mann (1989), *La Mère dans la littérature française, 1678–1831*, New York, p. 55.
47. Heilbrun, *Writing a Woman's Life*, pp. 111 and 110.
48. W. Chadwick (1985), *Women Artists and the Surrealist Movement*, London and New York, p. 92.

– 4 –

Fictionalized Autobiographies

French female-authored fictionalized autobiographies from the period between the wars demonstrate great surface diversity in subject matter, no doubt because the period saw major transformations in the opportunities available to women, and because more and more women of varied walks of life, and diverse social strata, had now taken up writing as a profession. More significant, though, is the fact that so many of these works share the same principal characteristics.[1] Almost without exception they highlight a range of thematic and philosophical preoccupations converging around the very real problems of personal identity and the more general question of gender construction. While specific details vary, many of these works begin by recording the protagonist's disturbed recognition of her absence or loss of a valid sense of selfhood. Frequently the heroine is emotionally or physically dislocated from her immediate family, and this results in her suffering an acute, all-pervasive sense of separation, loneliness, difference or spiritual alienation, which provides the occasion for the action's inception. For example, in Irène Némirovsky's *Le Vin de solitude* the Jewish heroine is foreign, homeless, and symbolically isolated through language, nationality, creed and gender. In Catherine Pozzi's *Agnès* the heroine, as she undergoes the full throes of an identity crisis, is portrayed in a state of deep psychological disarray, obsessed with her amorphous condition, and quite unable to conceive a single, unified notion of the self (a lack of wholeness reflected in the novella's discontinuous and highly fragmented texture).

The most powerful rendering of this experience is given by Jeanne Galzy in *Les Allongés*. Here the first-person narrator's serious tubercular condition itself constitutes a type of depersonalization, as all the patients in the hospital ward around her appear uniform, anonymous and undifferentiated in their white plaster casts. Their static bodies are repeatedly likened to corpses, and with Death the Leveller as a recurrent motif, the heroine's sense of personal uniqueness is invalidated. The narrator sees herself as a cloistered nun with no material riches, no name and no independent control over the structure of her life. Her condition is aggravated by her overwhelming feeling of fragmentation, highlighted by references to shattered, reflected images. The omnipresent mirrors in the text, rather than reaffirming a fixed identity, present the subject with multiple confused versions of the self:

> Above our elongated bodies, the mirrors slip before our eyes their inverted trembling image. The world which we have lost is dissected into little pieces and limited in the mirrors' nickel frames, and we patiently sew these fragile, shiny fragments in which everything is falsified and diminished back together to create a universe for ourselves.

> Au-dessus de notre allongement, ils font glisser jusqu'à nos yeux leur image inverse et tremblante. Ils découpent en petits morceaux, limités par leur cadre de nickel, le monde que nous avons perdu et nous recousons patiemment ces lambeaux brillants et fragiles, où tout est réduit et faussé, pour nous refaire un univers. (p. 18)

Here there is a disturbing sense of fragmentation, falsification, reduction and loss. The heroine's once clear sense of selfhood is destroyed and even her return to childhood through memory proves futile.[2] Although initially these recollections transport her away from the horror of her invalid state to an earlier period of her life characterized by images of rebirth in a garden world of movement, light and flowers, the narrator realizes that this direction is problematic. She comes to acknowledge that the filter of memory poeticizes past experience to such a degree that the horror of her present reality and the idealized nature of the imagined past become so discrepant as to be irreconcilable. Far from rediscovering her true identity, she experiences a total dislocation from the exalted image of the child, and additionally she constructs a worthless artificial sense of selfhood. Her aim in the remainder of the novel, then, is to rebuild a meaningful, unified, cohesive personal identity.

This notion of self-construction, as opposed to self-recording, which appears in much twentieth-century literature, is especially striking in Pozzi's *Agnès*. Here the heroine, having presented herself as incomplete and unformed, embarks on an active process of self-creation. Her plans follow the schema laid down in Pozzi's philosophical study *Peau d'âme*. The concept of Cartesian duality is rejected, and in its place Pozzi suggests that the individual comprises three interrelated key elements which have to be fully developed and in harmony for the self to feel complete. In *Agnès* the heroine puts the theory in practice and sets up two charts each divided into the three sections marked 'BODY', 'SOUL' and 'SPIRIT', detailing specific areas for improvement. The first table reveals the ideal state, the second Agnès's actual incongruous condition as she sees it. From these charts Agnès develops a programme for self-amelioration which she relentlessly pursues. Of particular interest in this process is Agnès's choice of vocabulary, as her use of terms such as 'an architect's estimate' ('un devis d'architecte'), 'to build' ('bâtir') and 'the construction of Agnès' ('la construction d'Agnès') (p. 26) draws a clear analogy between her controlled, orderly, well-planned self-creation and the careful assembly of a physical edifice.

In many fictionalized autobiographies of the period, this interconnected process of self-creation or self-discovery is articulated metaphorically through images of travel. Marguerite Audoux's *Marie-Claire* series, like the traditional novel of education, shows the protagonist's progression from the country to the town. Marthe de Bibesco's *Catherine Paris* culminates in the eponymous heroine's return to Paris, the city after which she was named. Pozzi's *Agnès* climaxes with two journeys to Lourdes and Cannes. Galzy's *Les Allongés* concludes with the heroine's release from her physically immobile condition in the Sanatorium at Berck, and its sequel *Le Retour dans la vie* (1926) charts her movement between different teaching posts. Némirovsky's *Le Vin de solitude* follows the heroine as she leaves Russia, travels through Scandinavia and finally settles in Paris. Notwithstanding the fact that in each case these journeys have clear biographical correlates, they equally function as more metaphorical odysseys of self-discovery. It is this journeying itself (rather than the final destination) which constitutes the works' focal point, as the emphasis lies less on the fixed point of closure of the author in the here and now, and more on the active, often precarious *process* of self-creation. Indeed, the reader does not know what will happen to Marie-Claire when the atelier is shut down, to Agnès in her married life, to Catherine Paris as she experiences the reality of childcare, to Hélène as she leaves her family and embarks on a new life in Paris. Just as these works lack closure, their fictional format stresses that the possibility of establishing a valid sense of identity is always open to question, and as in all great quest narratives, the ideal path which leads from isolation to genuine connection, from an initially amorphous condition to a heightened sense of autonomy, is often obscured, and the intrepid explorer follows many erroneous directions, undergoes many rites of passage before finding her way.

Although we see a similar pattern in a number of male-authored novels of the Inter-war period, women writers of the era seem to concur in the suggestion that the problems of the loss and search for identity, while not necessarily gender-specific, are especially complicated in the case of a female protagonist. Women not only suffer the same difficulties as men with the general collapse of shared value-systems and external frames of reference resulting partly from the profound social and political upheavals in the aftermath of the Great War, partly from the impact of philosophical theories of phenomenology, they additionally experience two further problems. First, numerous female authors posit the argument that women still had limited access to the realms through which men have traditionally succeeded in finding self-definition, and their works investigate the result of forays into these prohibited domains. As an illustration of this first point we should consider Marthe de Bibesco's *Catherine Paris*. The heroine originally tries to come to terms with her sense of alienation and attempts to create an identity through erudition: 'she receives the sacred teachings reserved for men', 'elle reçoit l'enseignement sacré, réservé aux hommes' (p. 45). It is acknowledged that this is a male preserve and Catherine, comparing herself to Héloïse and Marguerite de Valois, revels in the fact that she can take her place in an illustrious elite of female scholars, as one of a limited number of privileged women allowed to penetrate the special male-dominated world. However, full realization that her chosen path of self-discovery through education is in fact a type of self-betrayal occurs as Catherine gradually perceives that language itself, which lies at the heart of all learning, is male-centred. This first becomes apparent when she realizes that she does not possess a suitable form of speech to express her own sexuality. When, for instance, she attempts to articulate her confused emotions accompanying the onset of menstruation, the patriarchally inscribed words and structures she knows prove wanting. She discovers that the menarche can only be described in religious expressions, medical terms or metaphoric euphemisms. Her disillusionment increases when she begins to perceive that literature, in its perpetuation of the credo of romantic love, is really a deceptive trap for women. On her wedding night, contrary to all her hopes, the sexual act is reduced to a sort of brutal physical domination as is suggested by her emotive choice of vocabulary to describe it: 'wound' ('blessure'), 'victim' ('victime'), 'lethal' ('meurtrier'), 'pain' ('douleur'), 'attack' ('l'attentat') and 'that night he possessed her as a punishment' ('cette nuit-là, il la posséda pour la punir') (p. 117). Yet shortly after this when Catherine discovers a private library in her marital home, a library which significantly comprises only male canonical texts (these are carefully detailed), she momentarily believes again that she too can enjoy the power of this masculine realm, as is suggested in the comment 'at last she owned something', 'elle possédait enfin quelque chose' (p. 124). The reader sees her folly as the reference to possessions recalls the masculine desire for ownership and brutal domination depicted in the first two sections of the novel – on a political level, in the male European aristocrats' greed for the possession of new territories which gave rise to the mass carnage of the Great War, and on a personal level, in her marriage where her sole purpose, in her husband's eyes, is the continuance of the family line through the production of a male heir. Catherine is enlightened to the error of her ways most fully when she takes a lover. He is deliberately chosen to correspond to her ideal and is a composite of aspects of her adolescent reading material: 'an imaginary lover, composed of all the heroes, saints, poets and world leaders she most admired', 'un amant imaginaire, composé de tous les héros, de tous les saints, de tous les poètes, de tous les vainqueurs du monde et qu'elle préferait' (p. 163). But despite all this, he fails to meet her expectations. Ultimately, Catherine understands that the male-dominated preserve of erudition constitutes a false direction in her personal search for a female identity. Patriarchal discourse and the literature it sustains are unable to accommodate her uniquely female experiences, aspirations and needs. Towards the end of the novel, as we shall see later, Catherine realizes that she must reject the male-centred world, that she must redirect her quest for self-definition.

The second reason provided by female writers to explain the more extreme nature of the difficulties faced by women in the creation of a personal identity is that, unlike men, women's condition is rendered more complex by the plethora of often incompatible, externally imposed male-centred roles and distorted images of womanhood through which they must sift to find their true identity. As a consequence of this, for many female characters the attempt to reformulate an identity involves a complex process of recognizing then rejecting inimical social and literary confinement. Such is the case of Marguerite Audoux's fictional heroine Marie-Claire, whose chosen path leads her to confront and investigate several quite different traditional sources of female definition.

As she struggles to create an identity, Marie-Claire first looks for direction from the established values of the Church. Despite the fact that the orphaned heroine does find refuge and companionship in a convent, it is soon patently clear that both the general and religious education she receives here are a poor preparation for a fulfilling adult life. On a spiritual level, Roman Catholicism professes to offer succour and support, yet Audoux ironically suggests that its fundamental tenets are quite fraudulent: the realm of saints encourages unrealistic hopes yet singularly fails to answer prayers; the celibacy of the priesthood is a sham as M. le Curé is involved in a clandestine relationship with Sœur Marie-Aimée; parthenogenesis is mocked through the nun's 'miraculous' pregnancy; and transubstantiation is thrown into question when the scene in which the heroine first takes the host in part one is grotesquely parodied in a brutal pig-killing scene in part two. This first communion ceremony, the event which marks the attainment of the age of accountability and acceptance of the Roman Catholic faith, in practical terms results only in the end of formal schooling. Immediately following this service the convent girls spend all their time learning to sew. Far from heralding a step towards new personal responsibility, it signifies only passive submission as the girls prepare to take up their designated social role as cheap, relatively unskilled labour for the sewing industry. Audoux's treatment of religion is noticeably ambivalent. Marie-Claire, while initially attracted to the Church, ultimately comes to rebuff it and looks elsewhere in her search for identity.

The same pattern of appeal and rejection is seen in Audoux's treatment of nature.[3] Following the exemplar of Audoux's own life, Marie-Claire, discharged from the convent, is sent to work as a shepherdess in a small rural community and here she directly experiences the role of the romantic heroine of the pastoral idyll. For the first meeting between Marie-Claire and the hero, the young bourgeois landowner Henri, Audoux presents the reader with a pantheistic scene *par excellence* in which the heroine becomes one with her natural environment. The suggestively erotic tableau, with its connotations of liquidity, penetration, defloration and the promise of possession, recalls Eden in its topos of the apple tree, river and utopic garden. However, all is not as it first appears. Certain features in the climactic scene forewarn the reader of the possibility of an unhappy outcome. Repeated references to unlocked doors and uncloistered gardens presage danger and discovery, and the particular configuration of objects – a woman, liquid and arborescent forms – recalls an earlier scene in the convent in which these selfsame objects were strongly linked to death. Most importantly, the confusion of limits and boundaries may suggest as much a loss as a discovery of personal identity. These negative undercurrents take a more concrete shape in the second part of the novel. Just as the paradise of Eden was transitory, the real world soon invades this romantic sphere and Henri, under familial pressure, realizes that there is no future in their love. As Marie-Claire attempts to come to terms with her unrequited love and to cauterize her fully developed emotions, the apple tree is shown heavy-laden with fruit and frozen under thick snow. Audoux, in this striking symbol, suggests that the role of the leisured feminine lover, so favoured in romantic idylls, is inappropriate for this working-class heroine. She demonstrates that the tropes of the perfect romantic idyll are in fact traps, and that the static, essentialist roles nature confers on women are ultimately unfulfilling.

Working in parallel with this investigation and rejection of religion and nature as traditional external frames of reference in the process of self-definition, Audoux examines the confrontation with death. In all four of her novels death's presence is ubiquitous, often initiating the quest narrative. In *Le Suicide*,[4] *De la ville au moulin* (1926) and *Douce Lumière* (1931) Audoux examines the cult of suicide (popularized in the early nineteenth century in the works of Romantic writers such as Chateaubriand, whose *Atala* she greatly admired, and in the idolization of Chatterton), and in each case, it is ultimately rejected as a solution to the heroine's existential quest. The reason for this is not what one might expect. Suicide, for Audoux, is invalid not because it represents the logical extension of the heroine's loss of value and identity, nor because it represents the supreme negation of the self. Rather, suicide demands an *a priori* sense of selfhood and an inflated self-worth. It is an egocentric act, presented as a type of escape from earthly hardship, as a total renunciation of responsibility to oneself and to others. It is a luxury in which the working-class woman cannot indulge. Furthermore, unlike her male peers who explore the metaphysical implications of defining oneself through confronting and controlling one's own death, Audoux transposes death from a philosophical to a purely concrete plane. This is especially striking in *L'Atelier de Marie-Claire*. The novel concludes with the repetition of a popular refrain: 'Paris, Paris, Paradise for women', 'Paris, Paris, Paradis de la femme' (p. 269). This is no longer the optimistic jingoistic lyric quoted earlier in the novel. Rather it has become bitingly ironic. The physical inclusion of 'Paris' in 'Par-ad-is' suggests a natural bond. The term is mentioned on only one other occasion in the novel, in the statement 'Today, the cemetery is as beautiful as paradise' ('Aujourd'hui, le cimetière est beau comme un paradis') (p. 74). By implication, Paris is like a cemetery for womankind. For the average proletarian female, Paris offers only unemployment, thankless drudgery, poverty, prostitution, degradation, and perpetual worthless struggle ending inexorably in death and the common grave. The universality of this fate is suggested in a series of increasingly gloomy graveyard scenes. In the last of these, time is shown to move relentlessly on, sparing no one. The crows find no place to perch, and the cypress tree, traditionally used for both coffins and Cupid's arrows, enticingly beckons the mourners. Here, not only does Audoux stress life's transience, but in her disturbingly expressionistic depiction of darkness, mud, rain and rotting vegetation, she underscores the misery of the human condition. A working-class woman's identity, Audoux seems to stress, is conditioned largely by the effects of a very concrete day to day hardship, offset by personal fortitude and a spirit of fraternity, solidarity and camaraderie of the workplace. Self-definition through the Romantic aesthetic cult of suicide or through a more contemporary reinterpretation of extreme situations leading to a heroic philosophical confrontation with death is an intellectual luxury beyond her scope.

In Audoux's novels traditional sources of self-definition, despite being initially attractive, are all finally shown to be invalid. The careful reader will note that in *Marie-Claire* the principal areas investigated by the heroine in her quest for identity share a common feature: they are predominantly associated with the twinned colours black and white. Marie-Claire's entry into the convent is marked by her awareness of the colour of the nuns' attire and this patterning is emphasized when Sœur Néron is described as black and Sœur Madeleine white. At the first communion, when the heroine's disillusionment takes shape, the children are in white and on taking the host the narrator comments that a black curtain falls before her eyes (p. 53). Similarly, in a scene which has received much critical attention from Dumont, when Marie-Claire realizes that the black cow she sees before her is actually a white cow in the shade of a chestnut tree, she discovers not only that empirical knowledge can be deceptive, as Dumont notes, but that the natural world and the images it promotes are not all they might initially appear, this monochromatic pattern again signalling the start of her process of disenchantment with nature. The same occurs with death. The novel opens with the mother's funeral and Marie-Claire and her sister wearing dresses patterned with large black and white squares (p. 15). It ends with the nun's death and the impressionistic scene of the play of white light on a black habit. This black and white patterning, subtly present in each of the key scenes in *Marie-Claire*, takes on a symbolic value, for these antithetical colours indicate the ambivalent quality of the heroine's response. They suggest an opposing desire for the security of established values and roles (be it the chaste bride of Christ, the subjugated ill-educated working-class seamstress, the passive pastoral lover, the woman controlling her own destiny in confronting death) and a concomitant rejection of the same. This conflict between Marie-Claire's psychological attraction to the traditional female images and her more distanced, rational criticism of the ways in which these life options are used to limit women in a patriarchal society is well suited to Audoux's generic choice of the fictionalized autobiography, whose dual status facilitates the binary focus on social criticism and the free articulation of women's deeper needs and aspirations. Moreover, the emphasis on monochromatic patterning also signifies the exclusion of primary colours from the major scenes, and this conveys to the reader the overall impression that the external frames of reference investigated can only ever provide circumscribed images of womanhood. Just as they limit colour, they do not allow a full picture of female potential, and are consequently shown to be of limited value in the construction of a personal female identity. The external agencies of religion, nature, death and suicide in *Marie-Claire*, *L'Atelier de Marie-Claire* and indeed Audoux's corpus as a whole are all signalled as wrong directions on the heroine's quest.

From these examples, it is patent that this search for personal identity and the whole process of gender construction which it underlines and interrogates is particularly complicated for women in France in the period between the wars. On the one hand, as *Catherine Paris* illustrates, women are shown to have only limited access to power, and on the occasions when the traditional sources used to define masculine roles in society do fall within reach, these actually fail to meet women's psychological needs. On the other hand, as is clear from Audoux's work, the social and literary roles engagingly proposed specifically for women in patriarchal society are often in reality far from enabling, highly reductive and quite inimical, again at odds with women's real desires. Given this situation, there is one area which more than any other becomes a major site of conflict in female-authored fictionalized autobiographies, one area which appears with an inevitable regularity in the protagonist's search for self-definition: motherhood.

Early in *La Naissance du jour* Colette recognizes the importance of motherhood, when she recalls a criticism made by one of her husbands: 'But can't you write a book which isn't about adulterous love, half-incestuous collages, break-ups? Isn't there anything else in life?', 'Mais tu ne peux pas donc écrire un livre qui ne soit d'amour d'adultère, de collage mi-incestueux, de la rupture? Est-ce qu'il n'y a pas autre chose dans la vie?'. As an answer to this series of questions, she reflects that beneath the love intrigues in women's literature there are often other secrets plots, as it is not only romantic but significantly 'maternal feeling', 'l'instinct maternel', which together constitute the great themes of a woman's life. She progresses to add that for many female writers, facing maternity (in the guise of their relationship with their own mothers, their personal experience of motherhood or indeed their more general response to the social role) is a necessary, if at times obscured, constant. In *La Naissance du jour* itself, where fact and fiction enigmatically blur, as the epigraph forewarns, filial love does indeed play a crucial part. The novel opens with an imaginary version of a real letter in which Colette's mother Sido declines her daughter's invitation to visit. As is the case in many fictionalized autobiographies, this maternal erasure, and the resultant withdrawal of physical and emotional nurturance, far from constituting a trivialization of the maternal role, actually has a pivotal function in motivating, launching and structuring the voyage of self-discovery.[5] This necessary fictional absence represents the emotional distance Colette must cross in her journey, and the ensuing quest narrative, in which the narrator confronts the complex issue of her sexual identity, is structured around the narrator's oscillation between romantic love for Vial, maternal feeling for Hélène and filial attachment to her own mother Sido.[6]

Several critics, involved to a greater or lesser degree in the study of the autobiographical genre, have recently advanced various explanations for this phenomenon. Didier, in her psychoanalytically grounded study of *l'écriture féminine*, for example, contends that coming to terms with the mother is a necessary basis of all female subject formation, and argues that for women authors writing itself is 'fundamentally an act of identification with the mother'.[7] For Didier the interest in motherhood is chiefly linked to the autobiographer's gender. Mann, in her examination of the representation of mothers in French literature, notes that the popularization of the auto-biographical genre and the social promotion of motherhood both occurred in the same period in the last third of the eighteenth century and that both were directly attributable to the same cause: a change in cultural mores resulting from the rise of the bourgeois class.[8] It is this historical link which, for Mann, results in autobiographical writers' interest in maternity. Lejeune, in his analysis of autobiography, starting from the premise that the fundamental myth in all works of this genre is the return, suggests that in a narrative depicting a reversion to one's roots, to the lost paradise of childhood, maternity naturally will be involved, irrespective of the author's gender. Lejeune records that the phenomenon is particularly prevalent in the Modern period when writers suffer a sense of identity fragmentation and when the concept of unity in symbiotic bonding with the mother attracts the narrator to return to the first moment of separation and difference and to the original source of unity.

Such interpretations might well partly account for the increased, pervasive presence of motherhood in Inter-war French female-authored works. However, they do not indicate why so many women felt the need to explore motherhood in the more open context of the fictionalized autobiography, nor do they acknowledge or offer any explanation of the fact that motherhood is not necessarily by any means a simple solution in the resolution of the heroine's problematic sense of selfhood. Huffer, in *Another Colette: the Question of Gendered Writing*, suggests a further, more productive possibility. Notwithstanding her recognition of the current preference for reading Colette's autobiographical novels as a reappropriation and rewriting of the classical Demeter/Persephone myth, Huffer raises the possibility that Colette's interest in motherhood may have as much, if not more, to do with the specific social and political context in which she lived and wrote. Given that so many women in the era are involved in exploring motherhood in autobiographical works with an explicitly fictional format, and given that their responses to this condition vary so greatly, this explanation seems most plausible and clearly merits further investigation.

As we saw earlier, pronatalist discourse was omnipresent in France following the Great War, with demographers drawing attention to the falling birthrate, and politicians endeavouring to find an accessible means of enabling French citizens to come to terms with the profound transformations in social, cultural, political and gender relations as the country moved towards becoming a modern advanced capitalist society. The ubiquitous bourgeois rhetoric of idealized motherhood, domesticity and the separate spheres was espoused by many militant Catholic feminists, such as Andrée Butillard of the UFCS, in an attempt to arrest depopulation and to reassure both men and women that stable traditional values still had meaning in these times of change. So it should come as no surprise that this exaltation of motherhood is reflected in a certain body of literature of this period of both male and female authorship. Simon notes Jeanne Ancelet Hustache's *Livre de Jacqueline* which gives a 'touching document of a Christian mother's pain faced with the death of her child'.[9] La Rochefoucauld singles out the maternal love poetry of Gérard d'Houville, Cécile Sauvage, Marie Noël and Henriette Charasson who celebrate the trilogy of 'motherhood, Catholicism, and nationalism'.[10] Clouard also praises Charasson's 'spirit of Christian maternity' which is especially evident in *Les Heures du foyer* (1926) and *Deux Petits Hommes et leur mère* (1928). He equally highlights the Belgian poet and novelist Marie Gevers whose *Madame Orpha* (1934) is suffused with 'the poetry of nature and family life'.[11] Moulin similarly draws attention to Marie Gevers's *Les Femmes* and notes that motherhood was a major source of poetic inspiration for many women until around 1925.[12] Larnac cites Sophie Hüe's *Maternelles*, Anaïs Ségalas's *Enfantines*, Magdeleine Marx's *Femme*, Raymonde Machard's *Tu enfanteras*, Mme de Wailly's *Nos Enfants* and *Rimes roses*, Mme Alphonse Daudet's *Les Enfants et les mères* and Mme Catulle Mendès's *Prière sur l'enfant mort*. To this list we could add a considerable volume of romantic fiction, some of which will be discussed in part three.

Not all French Inter-war writers were so keen to provide such a positive evaluation of motherhood. As Larnac notes, in comparison to the total number of works produced by women, there was actually a marked shortage of prose works exalting motherhood: 'Finally, and this seems most strange, our women writers, despite extolling romantic love, seem quite unaware of maternal love. (. . .) We are still waiting for the great maternal book which women perhaps will never give us.'[13] This lack of paeans to maternity is no doubt related to the fact that of all the issues affecting women in the Inter-war era, it was motherhood which most profoundly divided French feminists, with activists such as Pelletier and Roussel strongly advocating a woman's right to control reproduction, and portraying maternity as a physical and intellectual constraint promoted by the patriarchal system, a reactionary cabal construed to curtail female liberation and ensconce women in debilitating cultural stereotypes. Given this political climate, it is unsurprising that when motherhood does appear in Inter-war works of both male and female authorship it is often presented as the site of considerable conflict and debate.[14] Women's fictionalized autobiographies are of particular interest in their investigation of motherhood, because the autobiographical quality of the works creates a sense of personal testimony which lends authority to their message, while the more ostensibly fictional status of the works allows their authors the freedom to express their discontent with the status quo and enables them to propose their own visionary world of desires. Numerous writers active in this domain explore the value of this traditional life option, through their heroines' confrontation with maternity in its various guises during their odysseys of self-creation, and their responses to this role fall into two distinct camps. The first group of writers see the creative possibilities of maternity, and of these, Marthe de Bibesco and Catherine Pozzi perhaps give amongst the most innovative renditions in their appropriation, reformulation and celebration of motherhood. The second group of authors, which includes Audoux and Némirovsky, are more concerned with its inherent social and psychoanalytic problems.

Marthe de Bibesco wholeheartedly proposes maternity as the solution to the heroine Catherine Paris's existential odyssey, and this work is of especial interest because of the way in which Bibesco adopts and adapts the traditional image of the Virgin Mary. Throughout the Inter-war period, many writers and artists spoke out against the Marian cult, which they felt was used to sustain governmental pronatalist policies.[15] Far from being a feminist role model, or even the embodiment of some innate archetypal female nature, the Virgin Mother – defined as an expressly male-centred Christian symbol of de-sexed womanhood – was considered to be little more than a composite of oppressive patriarchal prescriptions for women.[16] As Warner notes, the Virgin Mary was really 'an instrument of a dynamic argument from the Catholic Church about the structure of society, presented as a God-given code'.[17] The Marian cult was seen to limit severely the human potential of women, demanding sexual purity, unqualified love, total devotion, submission, abnegation, humility, passivity commensurate with complete self-sacrifice and renunciation of any personal aspirations.

However, for Bibesco, one particular aspect of the Marian cult was considered enabling: the implied process of parthenogenesis at the heart of the Virgin birth offers a possible means of rejecting outright the crippling patriarchal realm. Within the novel Catherine's pregnancy is the result of an adulterous relationship and this signals a denial of her role as an aristocratic mother who must produce a male heir to continue her husband's ancestral line. Her dismissal of the child's natural father, who is never informed of her condition, and her decision to raise her child alone symbolize an affirmation of complete female autonomy. But Bibesco does not stop here. In a striking *mise-en-abyme*, she metaphorically links all the female characters in the novel to a state of saintly virginity. In the comment 'Saint Anne was smiling at her descendants', 'Sainte-Anne souriait à son descendance', the grandmother in *Catherine Paris* is likened to Saint Anne, mother of Mary, who was deemed by nineteenth-century theologians to have produced her child by an immaculate conception. Catherine's mother is paralleled with the Madonna as she too had pre-natal visions, heralding her child's birth, and it is said of her 'the virgin had had a girl and not a boy', 'la vièrge avait eu une fille au lieu d'un fils'. Finally, Catherine herself is described by the servant as 'the Holy Virgin', 'la Sainte-Vierge' (p. 107), and her own giving birth is said to be 'the Nativity', 'la Nativité'. Bibesco, in her parodic inversion and attack on what she considers the misogyny of Christian culture, feminizes the Holy Trinity and reconstructs it as the perfect embodiment of an exclusively female lineage, presenting the women in *Catherine Paris* as 'the sacred family', 'la sainte famille' (p. 34), 'the Three in One: the mother, the daughter and the granddaughter', 'Dieu en trois personnes: la mère, la fille et la petite-fille' (p. 35).

Bibesco's work proposes the fictional solution of the creation of a would-be separate all-female realm on the borders of patriarchal culture in which maternal inheritances and exclusive female bonding are positively valorized. Her artistic sublimation and celebration of motherhood together with her rejection of the patriarchal world appears on the surface to have much in common with a body of feminist Anglo-American works of the late nineteenth century by writers such as Lady Florence Dixie and Charlotte Perkins Gilman which, as Showalter notes, also depict 'some very peculiar fantasies' including matriarchal states, feminist revolutions and virgin births.[18] However, Bibesco's work in the scope of its poetic vision seems to go beyond these earlier novels because the heroine, in giving birth to a child, effectively gives birth to a new psychological self. *Catherine Paris* ends with a return. Catherine's final destination, Paris, is a city metaphorically described early in the novel as the temple at which Christ first communed with his spiritual father and learned of his true identity. In the final pages of the novel it takes on a special meaning for the heroine. Here in the city chosen as home by all three generations of women in the novel, here in the city after which she was named, Catherine Paris discovers her identity by taking her rightful place in a uniquely female ancestral line. Far from losing her sense of selfhood with the assumption of the Marian image, Bibesco's heroine revises that image, appropriates the aspects she finds most enabling and, in so doing, successfully forges a new personal identity.

Catherine Pozzi's *Agnès*, published in the same year as *Catherine Paris,* also rejects traditional concepts of motherhood and provides an interesting reformulation of the maternal role in the heroine's complex path to self-discovery. As Agnès progresses from dependent child to autonomous adult, the major difficulty she encounters lies in defining personal ego boundaries, a problem aggravated by her fear of the inevitable split away from the family and her dread of adult female sexuality.[19] Gradually the light-hearted irony accompanying the heroine's quest becomes increasingly bleak as Agnès's phobias intensify. This process culminates in the novella's final scene in Lourdes and in the honeymoon epilogue in Cannes. The fortune teller, in the opening pages of the novella, had prophesied that Agnès would travel in order to find her perfect lover and (following the substitution pattern inherent in the text in which the lover exactly resembles the ideal self-portrait) establish her own identity, and so the change in setting alerts the reader to the importance of both events.

In Lourdes, Agnès is distressed when she recalls the lustful admiring glances of passing men. To counter this she prays frantically, and retreats into a spiritual realm remote from the physical world. It is at this precise point that she experiences her first moment of epiphany. The scene is suffused with a subliminal female presence (contrasting strongly with the earlier part of the work where, despite the domestic setting, there is no sense of strong female bonding). Throughout the novella religion as a whole has been systematically twinned with Agnès's maternal lineage (her paternal ancestry has an analogous relationship with science), and in the final pages Agnès is accompanied by her maternal grandmother to a town which is renowned for Bernadette's vision of the Virgin Mary. It is Agnès's prayer itself, though, which most strongly evokes the mother-figure. Prior to this point in the narrative the many letters and prayers which constitute the main body of the work have all been addressed to men. Now this changes, because the heroine's addressee is the chaste and holy Virgin. Agnès prays in the customary way: 'Hail Mary, full of Grace, the Lord is with thee', 'Ave Maria gratia plena Dominus tecum', and the reader should remember that the Ave Maria continues with the words 'Blessed art thou amongst women, blessed is the fruit of thy womb Jesus.' In this prayer Mary is precisely invoked as an embodiment of maternal love. Agnès continues to pray to Mary with the words 'O Fine, ô Pure' (p. 48). These terms do not only apply to the Virgin, they also apply to the heroine herself as the etymological Greek root of Agnès is 'pure'. In one of several substitution scenarios, Agnès realizes that her search for identity, which is now linked to the maternal, actually lies within her. At this point she rejects externally imposed romantic love and instead desires what she describes as the kisses already inside her heart and in the lines of her hands where her ancestral past and future are inscribed. She longs to take her position in a female continuum, both to merge with her own absent mother and to be a mother in turn. Maternity, then, it is suggested, is the true destination in Agnès's quest for identity.

Agnès's positive reappropriation and valorization of motherhood is made much more explicit in the epilogue, where her distrust of the female body is given its most poignant reiteration, when she is at her lowest ebb. Her wedding dress, which traditionally connotes purity, fresh starts and happiness, is described as being dull, drab and black. It is clearly more suited to a funeral than a marriage ceremony and this effectively reflects Agnès's sense of mourning over the loss of her maiden name – the last tangible link with her family – and the death of her ideal self and her illusions. Here, she realizes that the soul and the spirit, which she had taken such pains to improve, are of little use to her now, as only the body is relevant to the act of sexual consummation that marriage entails. Her artificially bolstered self-construction crumbles and she is completely reduced to the body, this body which so repulses her, and her resultant torment is extreme. It is at this moment, in the penultimate section of the epilogue, that

Agnès re-experiences her earlier epiphany. Pozzi emphasizes the importance of this part of the novella by a change from a third-person past historic narrative to a first-person narrative in the present tense. Agnès undergoes an imaginary process of symbiotic bonding in both her imagined return to the womb and her projected embrace of her own potential maternity. The scene is no longer dominated by visual images and Agnès's omnipresent feeling of insecurity. Rather, she assumes a childlike state and the baby's more developed sense of smell is privileged. Agnès is aware only of 'mummy's smell' ('l'odeur de maman') and a sentiment of physical closeness and security as she thinks to herself 'I am so small, I lose myself in you, mummy' ('Je suis toute petite, je me perds en toi, maman'). Then she wilfully, forcefully thrusts herself further back in time from early infancy, back to the foetal position, back to a state of amniotic bliss where her flesh is her mother's flesh, and for the first and only time in the novella there is a lull, a moment of peace: 'I breath, I lose my life, I fall asleep' ('je respire, je perds ma vie, je m'endors') (p. 56). Here in the conjugal bed Agnès comes to terms with her body and what she considered the degrading process of intercourse by replacing the sexual connotations of the scene with maternal ones, by emotionally returning to the mother. Her desire for liquidity (evident in her unquenchable thirst in Lourdes, her unsatisfied desire for a sea view from her hotel window, her prolonged stay in the warm bathtub and her resentment of Félix's dream of saving her from a watery death at sea) is now satiated not so much by her husband's ejaculatory flow, as by imagined uterine fluids. This transposition of mother for lover is suggestively reinforced by Pozzi's choice of name for the husband: Félix, as this term etymologically comes from the Latin word for breast.

In the final section of the honeymoon scene Agnès, in a more rational mode, progresses to reflect on why the real Félix should feel so alien to her and why she needs to substitute the maternal in his place. She realizes that Félix does not share her past. From the start Agnès has believed that her ideal lover is already present in her, visible in the lines of her palm. He must constitute part of her inherited soul, be part of her intimate family, hence the use of the term 'dear big brother' ('cher grand frère') to describe him in several letters. Within the confines of the novella, Agnès's true love can only be her imagined son and it is again in her potential maternity that the solution to her identity crisis lies, in the continuation of her body, spirit and soul, and those of her ancestors, in a future generation. This explains the closing words of the scene in Lourdes: 'Give me love, not the man who is near me to whom I say "no", but the love which is inside me to which I say "yes".' (Donnez-moi l'amour, non pas l'homme qui est près de moi, à qui je dis "non", mais cela qui est au fond de moi, à qui je dis "oui"') (pp. 49-50). . . Although *Agnès* serves as a creative poetic testimony to filial and maternal love, Pozzi does not simply reinscribe patriarchal definitions of motherhood. Rather, she appropriates maternity and shows how it plays a vital role in her protagonist's unique quest.[20] Motherhood works as a resolution to Agnès's journey of self-discovery from a psychological perspective, as it provides a positive valorization of the female body, a transcendence of personal ego boundaries in the creation of multiple versions of the self, and a continuance of family bonds.

It is this notion of inheritance which is especially important in *Agnès*, as it corresponds specifically to Pozzi's own theories on the human condition, based on her reading of the Naturalists and her study of the contemporary science of thermodynamics. Pozzi was firmly convinced that the individual is partly predetermined, foreordained not just through physical biological heredity but just as importantly through a more spiritual inheritance too. Consequently, self-knowledge requires an investigation of one's physical and intellectual ancestry, a questioning of origins and endings, genealogy and generation. Such an interpretation is confirmed by the status Pozzi confers on the epilogue. It makes up part of her own intellectual heritage in that, like her philosophical work, it harmonized her interest in both religion (inherited from her mother, who was staunchly Catholic) and in science (inherited from her father, Samuel Pozzi, a leading gynaecologist of the day).[21] It is also intended as a legacy for her own son Claude to demonstrate her endless love for him. For Agnès, reforging bonds with her own mother and assuming the maternal condition herself represents a continuance of the family line, a positioning of the individual in part of a much greater continuum. Moreover, it is a means to combat the natural force of entropy to which the universe is subject. While Agnès herself cannot personally avoid this process of decay, she can frustrate its wider impact: through reproducing, through playing a crucial integral part in the transmission of body, soul and spirit from one generation to the next, through building on her own inheritance and improving the gifts she passes on to her child. Motherhood clearly is of vital importance in Agnès's self-creation and self-discovery.

Not all heroines in fictionalized autobiographies of the 1920s and 1930s glorify motherhood by transforming it into a trouble-free solution to their existential quest, as do Catherine Paris and Agnès. Often a more qualified response is presented, as is the case of Marguerite Audoux and Irène Némirovsky's fictional counterparts. Audoux's entire corpus, especially her fictionalized autobiographies, demonstrates a fascination with the highly problematic tensions inherent in the state of maternity, and this is an area her protagonists all explore in their search for selfhood. On one level, she recognizes that it is a condition numerous women successfully pursue in order to find psychological and physical fulfilment. She stresses in her work too that many women experience strong inner drives towards motherhood which society as a whole does not fully acknowledge. This is seen in *De la ville au moulin*, when the heroine, Annette, although herself still a child, responds to a natural urge to suckle a crying hungry child. It is also evident in *Marie-Claire* in Audoux's depiction of the nun, Sœur Marie-Aimée, who, despite her status as a chaste Bride of Christ destined to renounce female sexuality, actually follows her instinctive desire for sexual love, and takes a step towards a full realization of womanhood in giving birth to an illegitimate child. Her pregnancy is sanctioned in the text as Marie-Aimée is shown to have all the necessary emotional qualities suited to motherhood; she alone of all the characters befriends and nurtures the heroine. However, achieving the ideal maternal state is complicated. Marie-Aimée, for instance, is separated from her child immediately following the birth and her surrogate relationship with Marie-Claire is also cut short by the Mother Superior. Only on one occasion in Audoux's corpus are we given a picture of exemplary motherhood. In *L'Atelier de Marie-Claire*, we see a photograph of one of the dressmakers, Sandrine, standing behind her husband Jacques and their children, leaning over them to envelop and embrace them in her arms. It is an embodiment of familial bliss in which the mother-figure is presented as a refuge, a harbour. But as the photograph only comes to light after Sandrine's untimely death, the reader is left with the overriding impression that ideal motherhood is either unobtainable or untenable in the real world.

On another level, Audoux acknowledges that motherhood is a state which can all too easily threaten a woman's already fragile sense of selfhood.[22] The problematic conflicting desires for and fear of pregnancy are most clearly illustrated towards the end of *De la ville au moulin* in Annette's prophetic dream sequence, which reflects the period's general interest in the subconscious, irrational associations, interior monologue and nightmare. Within the overall context of the novel, Annette's dream is a disturbed hallucinatory reflection on her inability to breastfeed. It is simultaneously an omen foreshadowing her new-born infant's death. In the course of the dream Annette's body becomes polarized into two opposing versions of the self, one in the first person, the other in the third. The former is an adolescent, depersonalized object, 'a flat transparent body like a pane of glass', 'un corps plat et transparent comme une vitre' (p. 193). The latter is an inadequately constructed wooden replica of a lactating woman, 'naked to the waist, but on her breast made from badly fitting planks of wood, she bears two crystal globes', 'nue jusqu'à la ceinture mais sur sa poitrine faite de planches mal jointes elle porte deux globes de cristal' (p. 193). The sibylline dream consists of the glass girl's impassioned chase after the maternal figure. It can be read as Annette's realization of her loss of selfhood indicated by the split self and the artificial nature of both figures. Or it can be seen as her acceptance of her instinctual needs in her projection of an inner reality — a desire to nurture and be nurtured — onto an external being, in this case, a duplicate self. The outcome of the chase is also ambiguous. The adolescent figure effectively shatters the mother's crystal globes, allowing her milk to flow over a dry, fissured, barren landscape. This act could suggest possible regeneration, but it could equally indicate waste and destruction. Yet Audoux's representation of the experience of maternity is more complex than either of these readings might suggest. What is most significant is that it is an artificial effigy of motherhood (not a real lifelike mother) which is annihilated in Annette's hallucinatory dream, because it is false, idealized images of the mother which most effectively lead to female objectification and irrevocable loss of identity.

Here lies Audoux's main concern, and in her four novels she is at pain to scrutinize this false *image* of ideal motherhood perpetuated in patriarchal society. This explains Audoux's preoccupation with working-class mothers, cracking under the strain of trying to conform to the idealized bourgeois gender stereotypes. It also explains her outright condemnation of the cult of the Virgin birth, and her depiction of the very real dangers of sexual innocence for working-class women. In *L'Atelier de Marie-Claire* one of the minor characters, Gabielle (*sic*), whose knowledge of adult sexuality is minimal, is horrified to discover that she is pregnant following her seduction/violation by a stranger in a night-club. Her poverty is so extreme that she is unable to afford time off work to prepare for the birth, she has insufficient money to nourish herself properly and she is unable to pay for the medical attention she desperately requires following a serious fall. Her child is stillborn and is so badly decomposed that its gender is impossible to determine. Clearly, Gabielle's example is intended to illustrate that women need to have greater access to vital information about reproduction. As a result of the French government's preoccupations with increasing the falling birthrate and with lowering infant mortality figures, *puériculture*, childcare education, had become mandatory for all schoolgirls in the period following the war, but the scope of legislation in this area was fairly limited, especially when compared to the extensive child health and welfare arrangements in place in the United States.[23] Audoux seems to argue that there is need of greater reform, as for her pregnancy should always be the result of an informed choice.[24] Women should be more aware of possible life options (including those which preclude maternity and child-rearing) and of the artificial nature of the idealized bourgeois image of motherhood which should not be accepted at face value.

Audoux's fiction, then, demonstrates an intense, passionate and ambivalent preoccupation with the state of motherhood, and her depiction of this supposed apotheosis of the female condition has certain fundamental reservations. She highlights the dichotomy between the actual experience of motherhood and the unauthentic image promoted in both society and reactionary bourgeois Catholic literature of the period, stressing that motherhood is a state so coloured by images of the self-abnegating Virgin and of the ideal bourgeois *femme au foyer* that for many women, particularly among the working-classes, it is impossible to attain. Even if maternal nurturance may well meet a woman's natural desires and physical needs, and even if it may allow her a means of achieving both self-definition and patriarchal approval, there is a move towards recognizing that this condition may still leave a woman unfulfilled, that it may in reality fail to provide her with a path towards self-definition. The refusal to accept an externally imposed, inimical image, evident in Audoux's corpus and prevalent in many early twentieth-century works, prepares the way for a new direction for female-centred literature. Both male and female writers must be ready to strip away accepted notions of maternity, to look below the exemplary model, to explore the true nature of maternity.

Irène Némirovsky, writing from the late 1920s, extends beyond this to offer not just a more accurate assessment of motherhood as a social phenomenon, but to explore the relationship between the mother and the child from a more psychologically accurate perspective. *Le Vin de solitude*, written in three parts to offer a chronological depiction of the critical stages in the heroine Hélène's quest for identity, explores the role of female sexuality in gender construction, focusing chiefly on motherhood as seen from a daughter's perspective. In part one Hélène becomes aware of her own nascent sensuality when she comes across her mother's torn camisole 'which she inhaled with astonishment, discomfort and a sort of savage modesty', 'qu'elle respirait avec étonnemant, avec malaise, une sorte de sauvage pudeur' (p. 59). From this point, she experiences an enmity towards her mother Bella and this intensifies as she comes to realize more fully the libidinous nature of her relationship with cousin Max. Hélène refuses to acknowledge maternal sexuality in any guise and in part two she systematically denies her mother's erotic appeal and appetites, and this extends to her treatment of her surrogate mother-figure, her governess Mlle Rose. On her deathbed, in part two, Mlle Rose relates her life-story to Hélène, telling her of her love affair, pregnancy, abortion and desire for suicide: 'I too could have had a child. . . He would have been your age. . . I wanted to throw myself in the Seine. . . Love you understand. . .' ('Moi aussi, j'aurais pu avoir un enfant. . . Il aurait ton âge. . . Je voulais me jeter dans la Seine. . . L'amour tu comprends. . .') (p. 145). Despite her knowledge of the truth of this series of events, Hélène poeticizes and purifies Mlle Rose's life and their relationship:

> later she wanted to keep intact in her heart the memory of the only woman she had known who had been pure, peaceful and free from the dirt of desire and whose eyes seemed to have never looked on anything but innocent and happy pictures.

> plus tard, elle voulait garder intact dans son cœur le souvenir de la seule femme qu'elle eût connue, pure et tranquille délivrée de la souillure du désir et dont les yeux semblaient n'avoir jamais contemplé que d'innocentes et souriantes images. (p. 36)

Hélène has suppressed her knowledge of Mlle Rose's sexuality and has blotted out the details of her abortion precisely in order to preserve an image of the ideal nurturing mother, the mother she herself has lacked. Part three of *Le Vin de solitude* goes beyond the conclusion to Némirovsky's earlier work *Le Bal* (1930) in its study of the uneasy coexistence of the sexually active mother and the adult daughter.[25] Bella's continued rejection of the altruistic nurturing maternal role, and the symbolic representation of this in the death of Mlle Rose, forces Hélène to reject her mother, break her filial bond and enter into a heterosexual exogamous plot. When Hélène's first love affair fails to bring satisfaction, she decides to steal her mother's lover Max, thus setting up a highly unstable love triangle governed by sexual and social rivalry. This particular configuration of roles culminates in a striking scene in which Hélène looks at herself in a mirror when kissing Max. She expects to see in her reflection a confirmation of her identity as a lover; instead she sees the image of her mother as a young woman. In attempting to recreate a nurturing relationship outside filial and maternal bonds, and in aiming to replace her mother in Max's affections, Hélène effectively loses her sense of selfhood altogether and becomes subsumed by Bella's dominant image. At this point, in the statement 'I would perhaps one day have a mother like everyone else', 'j'aurais peut-être un jour une mère comme tout le monde' (p. 281), she realizes that she does not want to remove her mother from the love triangle but rather that she wants to supplant the male lover in her mother's affections. Hélène's search for identity, far from following the romance's path of courtship and matrimony, is more a sort of 'maternal seduction'.[26] The heroine's quest for identity is equatable with a search for maternal nurturance, but to achieve this she needs to eradicate maternal sexuality. However, Bella refuses to accept the limiting role her daughter ascribes to her. She asserts her right to choose to prioritize her sexuality over her maternal role, as Max notes: 'she isn't a mother, but she is ferociously womanly', 'elle n'est pas mère, elle, mais uniquement, férocement femme' (p. 249). The novel ends with the death of Hélène's father and Bella taking a new lover. Hélène's quest for identity is incomplete, her situation irreconcilable. The novel offers no solution, coming to an open-ended conclusion with Hélène's solitary departure for Paris. What *Le Vin de solitude* makes eminently clear is the view that mothers and daughters cannot successfully coexist together as adult women. They are forever divided by the fact of maternal sexuality, and in *Jézabel* (1936), published the year after *Le Vin de solitude*, which examines a similar situation from the mother's perspective, the explanation for this situation is clarified.

Here Némirovsky suggests that society's understanding of the maternal role is itself flawed and therefore responsible for the inherent difficulties in the mother/daughter relationship. *Jézabel* opens with a lengthy prelude depicting a court-case in which the heroine Gladys Eysenach (the 'Jézabel' of the title) stands trial and is sentenced for the murder of Bernard Martin, a twenty-year-old man, who is presented by the prosecution as her lover. The main body of the novel investigates Gladys's life and her psychological motive. As the plot untangles it becomes clear that Bernard is actually a blackmailer who is threatening to destroy Gladys's wedding plans by informing her lover of her real age (she has forged her birth certificate and altered the dates on her daughter's tombstone), and of the fact that she is a grandmother (when her daughter refused to abort the baby and when she died in childbirth, Gladys had the child adopted to protect her own assumed image as a young, available woman).[27] Faced with public exposure and a direct threat to her personal identity, Gladys had no option but to shoot Bernard, who, it transpires, is her own grandson. Her motive is finally clear: 'Odious, yes, criminal, yes, but not ridiculous! . . . A monster, an object held in horror, but not that, the grandmother, the old woman, the love-sick witch!' ('Odieuse, oui, criminelle, oui, mais pas ridicule! . . . Un monstre, un objet d'horreur, mais pas cela, la grand-mère, la vieille, la sorcière amoureuse!') (p. 221). Gladys refuses to accept the sacrosanct Proudhonian dichotomy of the mutually exclusive roles 'housewife *or* harlot', 'ménagère *ou* courtisane'. She asserts her right to her own sexuality as a mother and a mature woman. She rejects the literary and social roles assigned to older women.

What makes *Jézabel* particularly interesting is its framework in which the reader is actively coerced into re-evaluating the situation. The courtroom setting is such that the reader is cast as a jury member, and by the conclusion it is clear that it is as much the reader's prejudices and preconceived ideas about womanhood which are on trial. In the prelude, one vital clue to the actual nature of the relationship between Gladys and the victim is given to the court and reader in a citation by the victim's only friend. Constantin Slotis recalls Bernard's reiteration of a neo-classical tragic line: 'My mother Jézabel appeared in front of me', 'Ma mère Jézabel devant moi s'est montrée' (p. 50), a line which informs the novel's very title. The reader, like the jury, though, focuses only on the name's associations of sexuality, and assumes that Bernard is Gladys's gigolo. Athalie's filial relationship to Jézabel, and its parallel in Bernard and Gladys's situation, is overlooked. Némirovsky in this way ingeniously exposes our socially conditioned tendency to see the two roles of motherhood and womanhood as mutually exclusive. It follows that Némirovsky is suggesting that a society which blindly accepts and enforces inappropriate roles is really to blame for women's confusion over their identities. She argues that women cannot establish a valid sense of selfhood so long as the social and literary roles they are offered are so much at odds with the real nature of the female psyche.

In the fictionalized autobiographies of both Marguerite Audoux and Irène Némirovsky the reader sees a fundamental rejection of the way in which motherhood is promulgated in a patriarchal society. Both authors, in their heroines' troubled reactions to maternity, stress the need to represent this condition in a way which is more reflective of women's true social and psychological needs. They suggest that it is only in this way that women can accept all facets of their gendered condition and so achieve their full potential; only in this way can motherhood become a valid female life option.

In many French Inter-war fictionalized autobiographies centred on gendered identity construction, of which the five works examined here are fairly typical examples, it is the traditional maternal role which most frequently constitutes the focus of the protagonists' quest. The representation of motherhood is fully explored in its political, cultural, social, biological and psychoanalytical contexts, and in a significant number of works the overriding message is that patriarchal constructions of the institution of motherhood all require significant modifications to be acceptable to the majority of female writers. Neither the image of the Roman Catholic mother dutifully repopulating the country (sustained by the Marian cult) nor the image of the passive nineteenth-century bourgeois *femme au foyer*, is sanctioned as it stands. Instead, as in Audoux's reformative, socialist presentation and Némirovsky's psychologically realist vision, the maternal role is stripped of the falsely attractive glaze imposed on it by both the Church and Inter-war politicians. Or, alternatively, it is invested with new poetic meaning, as occurs in works by Pozzi and Bibesco, where motherhood is reclaimed and metaphorically reshaped as a means to securing a matriarchal state, or glorified as a uniquely female bodily experience. In either case, it is the fictional status of their autobiographical works which most fully empowers women writers. It allows them the freedom necessary to voice their thoughts openly on patriarchal constructions of gender relations; it liberates them from replicating and reinforcing anodyne, inimical female roles; in particular it facilitates their imaginative reappropriation and reformulation of the concept of motherhood; and most importantly, in a period which did not yet see female suffrage in France, it enables their full entry into the major Inter-war pronatalist debate which preoccupied feminists, demographers, economists and legislators alike.

Given, then, that French female writers' use of autobiography in the period between the wars is so markedly discrepant with its presentation in canonical compilations, is the representation of the relationship between women and romantic fiction equally flawed? Is the romance used in a reactionary fashion to reinforce archetypal female roles, as literary historians suggest, or are the women writers involved in this domain, like those producing fictionalized autobiographies, actually committed to renewing the conventions of the romantic genre and to redefining the traditional gender positions they sustain?

Notes

1. The works discussed in this chapter seem particularly suitable case studies as their biographical foundations are so dissimilar. Jeanne Galzy in *Les Allongés* investigates an adult woman's spiritual and physical experiences during her tubercular treatment. Catherine

Pozzi explores a bourgeois adolescent's dreams of love and court-ship in *Agnès*. The princess Marthe de Bibesco's *Catherine Paris* depicts an unhappy marriage set against a Proustian backdrop of Belle Epoque Parisian salons and the country homes of Europe's privileged, financially secure and leisured aristocracy. Marguerite Audoux, in contrast, presents a world at a complete remove from Bibesco's patrician scenes. *Marie-Claire* describes the early child-hood of a provincial orphaned child and its sequel *L'Atelier de Marie-Claire* details her time spent as a poverty-stricken seam-stress in Paris. Irène Némirovsky, in *Le Vin de solitude*, tells a very different story yet again, of the Russian Pogroms, the flight of middle-class Jews from Russia and the difficulties they faced as immigrants in an increasingly anti-semitic France.

2. The return to childhood is a common feature in many female-authored Inter-war autobiographical works, perhaps because of a new general awareness of the importance of the psychology of infancy, perhaps because the adoption of a child's perspective allows women writers an increased ironic critical distance from which to observe the adult world without the need to interpret or judge overtly, perhaps because child-play may be used as a para-digm for artistic creation (see J.A. Flieger (1992), *Colette and the Fantom Subject of Autobiography*, Ithaca, NY and London).

3. In much early twentieth-century art and literature the traditional bond between femininity and flora is revised and rendered more virile. Radclyffe Hall in *The Well of Loneliness* (1928) presents the heroine Stephen's inversion through her identification with trees, and arborescent bodies feature prominently in the works of the Surrealist artists Rita Kern-Larsen (*Les Deux Demoiselles* of 1940) and Ithel Colquhoun (in particular her parody of the female nude *The Pine Family* of 1941).

4. In 1913 Audoux presented to *Les Cahiers d'aujourd'hui* an early plan of the original sequel to *Marie-Claire* together with a draft of a fragment entitled *Le Suicide*. Her biographer, Georges Reyer, explains that her original intention was to depict her early days in Paris; however, it would appear that she ultimately found writing on this subject too painful and distressing. She abandoned the project and chose instead to concentrate on the happier times she spent working under Mme Marignac and running her own bus-iness. See G. Reyer (1942), *Marguerite Audoux: un cœur pur*, Paris, p. 174. *Le Suicide* has been recently reprinted in D. Roe (1987), 'Marguerite Audoux – un récit retrouvé: *Le Suicide*, 1913', *Les Amis de Charles-Louis Philippe*, no. 45, pp. 55–62.

5. In Galzy's *Les Allongés* this vital maternal absence is drawn to the reader's attention in the paratext, in the work's dedication to a surrogate maternal figure: the mother of a close friend Marianne Segond-Weber. Similarly, the first section of Monique Saint-Hélier's *La Cage aux rêves* (1932) is entitled 'Madre', recalling the woman who came to replace her dead mother throughout her formative years.

6. It is interesting to note the almost total absence of Sido from the literary works produced by Colette during her mother's lifetime.

7. B. Didier (1982), *L'Ecriture femme*, Paris, pp. 259 and 245.

8. In this era aristocratic women were encouraged to relinquish the tradition of sending children to a wet nurse, and as a consequence of this to blur the class distinctions differentiating them from bourgeois women. By the nineteenth century, as the realist novel reflects, family life had evolved. Maternal love and conjugal affection played an increasingly important role in transforming the family unit to resemble its modern counterpart, and by the late nineteenth century the insistence on maternal love became evident in the popular novel. M.A. Mann (1989), *La Mère dans la littérature française, 1678–1831*, Paris, pp. 28, 149, 152 and 205.

9. P.-H. Simon (1963), *Histoire de la littérature française au XXème siècle, 1900–1950*, 7th edn, Paris, vol. 2, p. 94.

10. E. de La Rochefoucauld (1969), *Femmes d'hier et d'aujourd'hui*, Paris, pp. 32, 33, 34 and 50.

11. H. Clouard (1947), *Histoire de la littérature française du symbolisme à nos jours*, Paris, vol. 2, pp. 163 and 391.

12. J. Moulin (1963), *La Poésie féminine de Marie de France à Marie Noël, époque moderne*, Paris, p. 14.

13. J. Larnac (1929), *Histoire de la littérature féminine en France*, 2nd edn, Paris, p. 233.

14. Some recent critics and literary historians note the rejection of the conventional maternal role on social, aesthetic and metaphysical grounds in works such as *Pensées d'une amazone* and *Une Femme m'apparut* by Renée Vivien, and in poems such as 'Femmes' in *Ferveur* and 'Refus' in *Horizons* by Lucie Delarue-Mardrus.

15. One of the most pointed attacks on the glorification of motherhood and the Marian cult is provided by the Surrealist artist Frida Khalo's self-portrait *My Birth* (1932). This oil on sheetmetal work presents an extremely disturbing childbirth scene. The mother is dead and the upper part of her body and face are shrouded in a white sheet rendering her anonymous and suggesting that her experience is universal. At the physical centre of

the work, forming the painting's focal point, is her child's bloody, lifeless head, severed by darkness from the uterus from which it still protrudes. Hanging above the bed, a small framed picture of the Madonna of the Sorrows mirrors the scene below as only the Virgin's face is visible. This triple dislocation of head and body, together with a conspicuously blank thanksgiving scroll placed at the foot of the bed, serves to stress the loss of autonomy inherent in motherhood. Khalo places the responsibility for the self-inflicted suffering portrayed in the work, most evident in the numerous small daggers piercing the Virgin's face, on the Church's deification of the state of motherhood and its endorsement of an image which exalts the degree of self-sacrifice necessitated by maternity. For further details see W. Chadwick (1985), *Women Artists and the Surrealist Movement*, London and New York.

16. The myth of Mary was favoured in France in several historical periods, most notably in the late seventeenth and eighteenth centuries when conjugal not extra-marital concupiscent love was widely championed. In this period of the Enlightenment when death in childbirth was prevalent (Caesareans were almost always fatal) and women were encouraged to think of their future children rather than themselves, the Virgin's self-abnegation helped promote the cult of self-sacrifice. In the nineteenth century too, when the new maternal bourgeois figure came into vogue, Mary's selfless devotion to her child again served as an expedient model.

17. M. Warner (1985), *Alone of all her Sex: the Myth and Cult of the Virgin Mary*, 2nd edn, London, p. 338.

18. E. Showalter (1982), *A Literature of Their Own*, London, pp. 181, 191 and 187.

19. This same experience is evident in Pozzi's diary, in her rejection of physical love in her relationships with Georgie Raoul-Duval, André Fernet and Paul Valéry. The most forceful statement of her disgust for the female body is given in 1914 during a period when she worked for her father in his hospital in Paris. Here she witnesses a laparotomy, a cancerous fibroma and a complete hysterectomy, which leave her reeling with horror. She cannot accept the farcical and tragic fact that the female body can accommodate both passionate love and smouldering putrescence, and she mentally conflates the two states, seeing sexuality as corrupt. C. Pozzi (1987), *Journal 1913–34*, Paris, pp. 71, 80, 97 and 206.

20. In her own life, as recorded in the *Journal*, Pozzi experienced a complicated relationship with her intimate family. Her rapport with Claude, her only child, was fraught with difficulties because

he did not, perhaps could not, live up to her demanding expectations. Her relationship with her mother, Thérèse Loth-Cazalis,
was equally, if not more, strained. She admired her mother's
physical beauty and moral goodness, and actively sought her
approbation. However, she also held her mother in considerable
disdain, scorning her failure to be assertive with her adulterous
husband, and bitterly resenting her demands that she relinquish
her education at Oxford University, which effectively curbed
her first steps to intellectual and emotional freedom. Indeed,
throughout the *Journal* Pozzi is unable to express any tender feelings for her mother until the heart-rending diary entry which
records her death. However, precisely because *Agnès* is a fictionalized autobiography, it can transcend these personal complications
in Pozzi's real relationship with her mother and son, and still posit
motherhood as the principal solution to her heroine's quest for
identity.

21. Pozzi's fusion of religion and her interpretation of the sciences
    of thermodynamics and quantum mechanics was equally seen
    as an extension of the intellectual bequest of her paternal
    grandfather, Benjamin Pozzi, who in several pamphlets and a
    metaphysical treatise, *La Terre et le récit biblique de la création*, argued
    for the compatibility of Christianity and Darwin's theory of the
    origin of species.

22. Surrealist paintings of this era by Dorothea Tanning and Rem-
    edios Varo also focus on the conflicts inherent in maternity as they
    juxtapose the mother's increased interest and pleasure in her own
    body with the dramatic, frightening physical changes initiated by
    pregnancy and lactation which may lead to exhaustion, depletion
    and loss of autonomy. See Chadwick, *Women Artists*, pp. 131–4.

23. In 1912, as part of the Department of Commerce and Labour,
    the United States government set up the Children's Bureau. Its
    priorities were essentially educational, and it operated through
    pre-natal and childcare conferences, the distribution of literature,
    the provision of home visits for confined women, and, in some
    states, the training of midwives and the implementation of
    immunization campaigns. It successfully reduced both infant and
    maternal mortality during the period in which it was in operation.
    Between 1921 and 1928, for example, infant deaths dropped from
    76 to 69 per thousand, and there was a 47 per cent decline in
    deaths resulting from gastrointestinal disease. For further details
    see M. Ladd-Taylor (1993), '"My Work Came Out of Agony
    and Grief": Mothers and the Making of the Sheppard–Towner
    Act' in S. Koven and S. Michel (eds), *Mothers of a New World:*

Maternalist Politics and the Origins of Welfare States, London and New York, pp. 321–42.

24. Some change was afoot in this area. In 1924 Montreuil-Strauss created a committee to institute sex education for girls – the Comité d'éducation féminine. Prior to this date, the Société française de prophylaxie sanitaire et morale had largely concentrated on teaching boys social hygiene and in particular the benefits of prophylactics as a means of preventing the transmission of venereal disease. See M.L. Roberts (1994), *Civilization Without Sexes: Reconstructing Gender in Postwar France, 1917–1927*, Chicago and London, p. 185.

25. *Le Bal* is structured around the interaction of two characters – a mother and her daughter. Each is at a critical phase in her life searching for romantic love at the ball of the novel's title. Antoinette Kampf is a young girl on the brink of adolescence, for whom the family ball is to be her first entry into society. For Mme Kampf this is the last ball she will hold or indeed attend, and it signals her final attempt to find a lover. The action develops when Mme Kampf, acutely aware of her age and convinced that being seen as the mother of a grown child would limit her hopes of taking a lover, refuses to allow her daughter to attend the ball. Antoinette destroys all but one invitation. On the evening of the ball no eligible male guests arrive and Antoinette rejoices in her mother's humiliation. *Le Bal* charts Antoinette's ascendency and Mme Kampf's fall, and this is evident in their final role reversal. Maternal sexuality is destroyed by the daughter's attainment of adult womanhood.

26. This term is borrowed from E. Moers (1978), *Literary Women*, London, p. 232.

27. Jézabel's desire to appear young can be interpreted as a rewriting of the maternal role as proposed in the phenomenally popular bestseller, Victor Marguerite's *La Garçonne* (1922). In this earlier work Monique's mother's sole interest is to look much younger than her actual age, and her egoism is intended to show, as Roberts argues 'that bourgeois society is rotten to its traditional moral core'. In total contrast, Némirovsky's version of the same situation argues a woman's right to enjoy her sexuality and her prerogative to refuse the fashionable cult of glorified motherhood. See Roberts, *Civilization Without Sexes*, p. 52.

Part III

Wedlock is a padlock.

John Ray, *English Proverbs*, 56 (1678)

And in his heart my heart is locked,
And in his life my life.

Christina Rossetti, *Noble Sisters*

– 5 –

Re-reading the Romance

There seems no greater joy to a literary historian than the discovery of a romantic interest in a female writer's work, for it confirms the standard opinion that love is the woman author's natural domain, that women rarely explore unfamiliar literary areas, rarely break new ground. Bertaut, for example, tenders just this conviction when he comments: 'It is unusual for women to venture into new territories, where they feel disorientated; they confine themselves chiefly to the realm of love, passionate drama and all that follows.'[1] To maintain the geographic metaphor, the canon compiler, like the medieval Warden of the Marches, is seen ritually riding out to reclaim and re-mark the fixed posts and boundaries which partition, limit and define the land. Yet regions with their natural and man-made landmarks evolve through time for physical and political reasons; borders change, grounds shift. While it is factually accurate to state that the Fin de Siècle, the Belle Epoque and the Inter-war era did indeed witness an ever-increasing proliferation of romantic works, must one automatically assume, as critics do, that these works remain within pre-set rigid limits? Might these works be read not simply as repeatedly demarcating the same terrain, but rather as altering the genre's outposts, offering new directions, new definitions? The precise nature of Inter-war romantic fiction and women writers' relationship to it can be best understood through approaching the genre from several quite different angles: clarifying the term 'romance' by placing works from the 1920s and 1930s in a historical context, comparing them to both their supposed predecessors and their present-day counterparts; and investigating the underlying reasons for the form's renaissance, growth and ideological stance in the 1920s and 1930s.

Today the most accepted usage of the term 'romance' is to signify a very distinctive and highly specific contemporary Anglo-American novel centred on sentimental love. Applying this term to French Inter-war works may initially seem quite inappropriate as even on a purely linguistic level no direct equivalent exists in the French language for the English word 'romance', and a difference in terminology appears to exist between the present day and the Inter-war period. Nowadays, in France, romantic works are most often referred to by their brand names, generally Harlequin, and this does not seem unreasonable given that the majority of romantic works read in France today are nearly all imported from the United States and translated into French.[2] In contrast, in the 1920s and 1930s a host of French terms were randomly applied – *roman rose, roman à l'eau de rose, roman d'amour, roman sentimental*, to cite but a few. Such a difference in nomenclature should alert the critic to the strong possibility that French romantic fiction of the Inter-war era may indeed differ significantly from the modern romance; however, with this possibility kept firmly in mind, it is nonetheless illuminating to examine the earlier texts from a retrospective position through recent readings of the type of romance which proliferates today. Such an approach has several merits. The slippage in terminology from the adjectival term 'romantic' to the generic term 'romance' all too often goes unacknowledged and unexplained in the literary histories and criticism where it occurs. The many connotations of the modern romance are, as a consequence, perhaps unwittingly applied retrospectively to earlier works to which they may have limited relevance. Differentiating the two periods, comparing and contrasting them, while highlighting crucial similarities and differences, equally allows a more alert and critical appraisal of the general classification and a fuller understanding of the genre as it manifests itself in the eras under consideration.

What, then, is this modern romance; what are its distinguishing features? Although most readers and critics would have no difficulty in identifying a romance, defining it in terms of necessary generic characteristics seems to be increasingly fraught with complexities. Over the past ten to fifteen years, as more and more critics from divergent schools of thought have shown an interest in the genre, there has been an escalation of rival interpretations in which certain detailed structural and thematic aspects are emphasized at the expense of others. Yet, despite the very different approaches to and understandings of this type of literature, there is one area on which most critics would concur: it is almost universally accepted that the contemporary romance is a homogeneous entity. While its uniformity may *manifest* itself, as Coquillat suggests in *Romans d'amour*, within the novels' formulaic plots and distinctive metaphoric patterning, or indeed, as Radway suggests, in her highly influential work, *Reading the Romance: Women, Patriarchy, and Popular Literature*, in the standard nature of reading practices, its homogeneous quality *arises* from largely external factors. Critics unanimously agree that the uniform nature of the modern romance is mainly attributable to the way in which large publishing houses, such as Mills and Boon or Harlequin, systematically target specific readers, tailoring novels to their needs and making these works easily accessible, both physically and financially.[3] This involves a considerable, sustained dialectic interplay of supply and demand.[4] Moreover, it is a process which depends on a solid infrastructure of a highly controlled and developed means of production and distribution, together with the most sophisticated mass-marketing and advertising techniques.

There can be no question that most of the component parts of this complex infrastructure are considerably more advanced today than in the Inter-war era. One might consider, for example, the physical production of paperbacks which, prior to the post-war industrial boom of the 1950s, was relatively time-consuming and costly even with the benefits of the rotary press, as novels were still stitched not glued together; or the nature of sales outlets, which were then restricted to bookshops and direct subscriptions to publishers because supermarkets, the principal outlet today, as yet did not stock popular fiction; or again advertising, which was limited to announcements in journals and magazines, the hard-sell medium of radio playing no substantial part as television now does. However, one crucial aspect of the mass-marketed romance was already firmly established: the need to focus on a specific readership. Despite assertions made by Dudovitz that commercial marketing is 'a relatively recent phenomenon in France, dating only from the post-Second World War industrial boom',[5] the majority of Parisian publishing houses had successfully attempted group targeting over twenty years earlier, as an analysis of Inter-war literary production demonstrates.

Following the First, not the Second, World War, a host of Parisian publishing houses set up *collections* with a select readership in mind, and a particular type of work on offer. By and large, readers were targeted according to gender, as Thiesse notes, citing the examples of 'Collections militaires' (The Military Series) by the Librairie des romans populaires and 'Bibliothèque des grandes aventures' (The Great Adventures Collection) by Tallandier for male readers and, in contrast, 'Bibliothèque Fémina' by Juven and 'Romans célèbres de drame et d'amour' (Famous Novels of Love and Drama) and 'Jolis romans' (Sweet Novels), both by Tallandier, for women.[6] Interestingly, collections specifically destined for a female readership far outnumbered those intended for its male counterpart as the seemingly endless range of romantic series titles indicates: 'Collection l'amour' (The Love series), 'Collection rose des vents' (The Compass Card series), 'Les Romans coeur et vie' (Novels of Love and Life), 'Mon roman complet' (My Complete Novel), 'Fama', 'Graziella', 'Scarlett', 'Le Roman de Madame' (Madam's Novel), 'Bibliothèque azur' (The Azure collection) and 'Bibliothèque d'Eve' (Eve's collection), to name but a few. The gender of the intended readers was not in itself the only factor taken into account by the publishers; social position too played an important part, for the majority of these romantic collections were aimed not at a general female readership, but at the working-class woman. This is attested by the deliberate low pricing of the novels and the fact that many collections belonged to publishing houses which were created purely for the production of works aimed at a working-class readership, such as Fayard, Ferenczi and Tallandier.

For marketing purposes this romantic fiction had to be readily identifiable. As inexpensive works of fiction did not as yet have illustrated covers, both series and individual titles, which often included the additional terms 'roman sentimental' or 'roman de l'amour', were of great importance in themselves.[7] Similarly publicity for these novels almost always had to include certain key words, as Thiesse indicates, namely: *passionnant, passion, émouvant, émotion, poignant, touchant, captivant*.[8] However, whereas today writers of romantic fiction are relatively unknown compared to those producing what might be termed bestsellers, and romantic collections deliberately and completely subsume individual writers, as part of the ethos that romantic novels are not written to be distinguished from other books in the series, in the Inter-war period publishers gave credit to the specific authors who wrote for them. No doubt in this way they hoped to entice both readers of general romantic fiction and devotees of specific writers. So it is that in this era particular authors such as Delly, Colette Yver, Marcelle Tinayre, Lucie Delarue-Mardrus, Michel Davet and Mathilde Alanic have a certain notoriety independent of the principal series for which they write. The combination, then, of astute group targeting and marketing, although less advanced than it is today, was, in effect, highly successful, and these new Inter-war collections proved extremely viable commercially.[9] The publishers Ferenczi, for instance, had some six romantic collections and sold in the region of 700,000 copies a month, 8 million a year, according to figures provided by Olivier-Martin.[10]

Yet this uniformity in the diverse Inter-war series' intended readership does not automatically imply that the content of the works comprised in the collections was homogeneous as it is today. Indeed, a retrospective overview reveals that within each individual series the novels followed a fairly systematic format, but between different collections there was considerable variety. This diversification may be attributable to the specific relationship between individual writers and their fiction. As Miles suggests, variety would result naturally as writers attempted to find a more personal voice within what was by now already becoming a public tradition.[11] There can be little doubt that women writers brought to their writing their own rich experiences. Greater opportunities for women of a certain class to travel resulted in much romantic fiction becoming infused with a sense of the exotic. Here one might recall Myriam Harry's unusual and thrilling settings of Jerusalem, Berlin, Turkey, Madagascar, Syria and Tunisia, or indeed the numerous adventure novels by Ella Maillart, Titanijna, Andrée Viollis, Marcelle Tinayre, Jane Dieulafoy, Jehanne Orliac, Alexandra David-Neel, Magdeleine Cluzel, Fabienne de Croizet, Virginie Hériot and Maryse Bastié.[12]

This said, it should be made clear that the difference between romantic collections, while perhaps related to authorial input, was systematically exploited by the publishers who, in an attempt to improve their sales figures, were at considerable pains to stress the exceptional and momentous nature of their individual series. Most publishing houses, in an effort to differentiate their romantic collections, endowed them with a special distinctive feature, or gimmick in certain cases. For Fayard's 'Le Livre de demain' (Tomorrow's Novel), for example, it was the volume's physical appearance which was its hallmark, as it was coloured a vivid yellow, much brighter than conventional covers, it had a uniquely square contour much larger than standard novels and was illustrated with the latest art deco wood-block prints. The modernity suggested by its series title and its physical guise somewhat belied its contents: reprints of already tested popular works. For new and diverse works the reader had to turn to Ferenczi's popular collection 'Les Œuvres libres' which specialized in promoting largely unknown writers, many of whom went on to become highly successful romantic authors.

For most publishers, professed individuality was signalled not just by the collections' authorship nor by its layout, but most obviously by its stated thematic interest. Gallimard's 'Les Livres du jour' (Up-to-the-Minute Books), for instance, stressed that its romantic works, such as Colette Andris's *La Femme qui boit* (1939), were unparalleled because of their social realist slant; the escapist quality evident in much female romance fiction was highlighted by two series: 'Pour oublier la vie' (Forget Life) and Boursiak's 'Soirs d'oubli' (Nights of Forget-fulness); Albin Michel focused on sin in their collection 'Les Grandes Pécheresses' (The Great Sinners), while Lemerre emphatically exposed its consequences in 'Les Amours tragiques' (Tragic Loves); and Flammarion specialized in romances woven around real historical figures in their series 'Leurs amours' (Their Loves) which included Harry's

La Vie amoureuse de Cléopâtre (1926), Houville's *La Vie amoureuse de la Belle Hélène* (1928) and *La Vie amoureuse de l'Impératrice Joséphine* (1925), Princesse Lucien Murat's *La Vie amoureuse de la Grande Catherine* (1927), Cécile Sorel's *La Vie amoureuse d'Adrienne Lecouvreur* (1927) and the poet Rosemonde Gérard's *La Vie amoureuse de Madame de Genlis* (1927). Clearly, Inter-war popular romantic collections, despite their forward-looking marketing techniques, did not as yet constitute a single, cohesive, fixed category, as does the contemporary romance. The collections, as we have seen, were controlled by too large a number of publishing houses with too many diverse interests to establish any degree of uniformity at this level. So, if Inter-war romantic fiction is in any sense homogeneous, then its uniformity would appear to lie elsewhere than in an *a priori* overall conception of romantic fiction as a genre. It is all too evident that between the 1920s and the 1990s the romance in its fullest sense has greatly evolved, and this in turn highlights the importance of placing the Inter-war romantic fiction in a wider historical perspective.

The English term 'romance' has a second signification which bears a more direct reference to French literature: it is frequently used to denote a grouping of Old French or Provençal works which deal with historical or chivalric deeds and events seen in the perspective of a medieval court, the best example of this being *Le Roman de la Rose* attributed to Guillaume de Lorris and Jean de Meung. This model, however, despite its original characteristic setting, was not in any real sense confined to the Middle Ages, but rather has a lengthy, though not always illustrious, lineage. A brief synopsis of its historical development is enlightening as it provides fresh perspectives on French Inter-war romantic fiction. In medieval times when the romance first flourished it took the shape of a tale of courtly love and chivalric adventure, interrupted by many digressionary anecdotes, climaxing frequently in marriage. The plot often focused on the hero's life and culminated in his assumption of a worthwhile role in a larger social environment, represented by the court. With Chrétien de Troyes's *Erec et Enide* (1160) the emphasis shifted slightly, for the female role which formerly adhered to the model of the passive lady on the pedestal altered with Enide's active demands for love and friendship within marriage. The heroine from this point appeared to move ever closer to centre stage in the romance, such that by the eighteenth and nineteenth centuries the romance appears to constitute a female, not a male, *Bildungsroman* detailing a young girl's personal development and progression from adolescence to adulthood, from isolation to marriage and certain social standing. In parallel with this, the reading

of romances has come to be a largely female preoccupation, as the
heroines of numerous novels of both male and female authorship
attest.

To date, most critics involved in comparative studies of the historical development of French, British and American romantic fiction
have assumed that the type of romance commonly read today has
a single direct cultural lineage and have, as a consequence, largely
avoided the issue of possible portentous divergences in works from
these different countries of origin. Yet, it would appear to be the
case that the rise of the realist novel in the late seventeenth and early
eighteenth centuries marked the beginning of a significant rift in the
Anglo-American and the French romantic traditions which had, until
this point in time, shared a common heritage. While in England, the
romance may be seen to have illustrious precursors (Fowler proposes
Samuel Richardson, Jane Austen, Charles Dickens, Benjamin Disraeli
and Elizabeth Gaskell[13]) and always bordered on the fringes of accept-
ability in the hierarchical literary canon, not so the romance in
France! For the rise of the realist novel marked the romance's unmis-
takable, abrupt decline in status, a relegation which, suggestively, is
also concomitant with its increased feminization (in terms of content,
authorship and readership). From the seventeenth century onwards,
when the novel first emerged, it presented itself in sharp contradistinction to the romance as a more serious type of literature. While
the concerns of love still dominated on the level of plot, gone was the
frivolity of romantic fantasy, gone the happy optimism of the early
romance. The French realist novel, from its inception, borrowed
heavily from neo-classical tragedy which was also in its prime in the
seventeenth century. Not only did it move towards imitating the
Aristotelian unity of action in the honing away of the romance's
digressions, more importantly it shared its conception of desire. Love
was no longer panegyrized and described in and for itself. Rather,
it was depicted as an intrinsic part of the human condition, as a serious aspect of the wider debate on the incompatibility of passion and
reason. Unlike its German and British counterparts, the French novel
from this period shows no taste for *Schwärmerei*, or exuberant emotionally charged language extolling the virtues of ardour and reverie.
Romance is approached with a far greater degree of psychological
lucidity, one might even say cynicism, and throughout the novel's
history the tragic filter persists, emerging most forcefully in Jansenistic,
Romantic, Modernist and Existential works which explore mankind's
estate.

In contrast, the French romance, devoid of these borrowings from
neo-classical works, and still content to champion love in all its guises,

is seen as less weighty, and is consequently considered to be a minor genre. Its decline in reputation is all too evident in the disparaging comments and authorial asides which run through realist novels whose heroines indulge in reading this kind of fiction. Here one should remember the implicit criticism of the deleterious effects of Emma's reading habits in Flaubert's *Madame Bovary*. Indeed, at no time was the romance's name more sullied than in the 1850s. In this era works of a romantic nature, which appeared mainly in *feuilleton* not volume format, were widely considered to be a breeding ground for anarchy, corruption and depravity, a point attested by their having been heavily taxed under the Riancey law from the 1850s, for their encouragement of public immorality. It is the early 1880s, though, which constitute the pivotal moment in the development of popular romantic fiction, and certainly for Inter-war works this period was particularly significant because it witnessed not only a renewed interest in this much maligned genre but as importantly an attempt to rejuvenate it, to break away from the established mould which had become a source of criticism.

This date is of considerable relevance as it coincides exactly with the Third Republic's implementation of secondary education for girls (1880) and with primary education becoming free, secular and compulsory (1881). This is no mere accident or quirk of fate. Rather, it is this single event which is uniquely responsible for the upsurge of a revitalized, modern romantic genre. When schooling was made available to the working classes and to hitherto uneducated women, it was accepted that reading material had to alter to suit a different, wider market. Writers strove to cover subjects deemed to be of particular female interest, as is evident from the proliferation of factual manuals offering women advice on home-management, childcare, fashion and beauty dating from the 1880s onwards. In terms of fiction, for works to be read they had to entice the working-class female reader to give over to them her limited free time, which by the Inter-war era was already being claimed by an array of enticing *divertissements*: sport, driving, attending the jazz-club, the music hall which replaced the café-concert, or the cinema (silent films were very fashionable in the 1920s as were 'the talkies' in the 1930s), not to mention indoor hobbies such as listening to gramophone records and the radio which regularly broadcast popular music from 1926.[14] Fiction targeted at this audience had to be made as palatable as possible and had to be seen to belong to the realm of pleasurable experience.

As a consequence of this, the most obvious characteristic of this romantic fiction, a characteristic which persists today, is its accessibility in terms of language and ideas. The romance is structured in simple sentences, grouped in short paragraphs, punctuated by easy-to-follow dialogues. Within the text there is rarely any ambiguity of meaning or reference, although often the titles are double-edged, their full significance being revealed only in the work's denouement. Moreover, in total contrast to the Inter-war realist novel, with its intellectual vogue of forcing the reader to play a vital role in textual construction, these romantic novels limit the reader's active involvement in the production of meaning. The language of these texts does not serve an aesthetic function, but rather is first and foremost a means to convey the story and so is readily decipherable. Not only does this language help make the works accessible, it may equally play a role in making the reading experience enjoyable. The romance reader's pleasure may stem in part, it would appear, not from literary analysis, but rather from the simpler process of recognizing, deciphering and interpreting linguistic patterns. For example, the hero, according to Coquillat's detailed analysis of works by Delly, may be recognized and distinguished from other male characters by a peculiar metaphoric codification – he is violent, authoritarian, powerful and often described in terms of a predatory animal or even a huntsman; this continues down to the finer details, as the hero's appearance conforms to a pre-set pattern also – he has a blend of Latin and Anglo-Saxon features, wild abundant dark hair and crystal-clear blue eyes.[15] The reader enjoys detecting and assimilating such codes and seeing them repeated from one work to the next.

A further possible explanation for the romance's appeal lies not so much in linguistic identification as in the readers' personal identification with the romantic heroine. From the 1880s revival critics have remarked upon this phenomenon. Bertaut, writing in 1909, for example, talks of 'enthusiastic female readers who find in the depths of their reading matter their own reflection as clear as in their faithful mirrors'.[16] He goes on to suggest that the reader equally assumes that certain aspects of the work reflect the author's life. Consequently, readerly bonding has, he convincingly argues, a dual focus. This interpretation is supported by many articles appearing in Inter-war magazines which discuss the letters sent in to be forwarded to the writers who contribute to it. Here one might consider the highly popular magazine *Le Petit Echo de la mode*. A 1924 article on Zénaïde Fleuriot gives an excerpt from a reader's letter which demonstrates this desired link: 'We love to know about our favourite authors' lives. Their writing has shown us part of their characters yet we are eager to discover even more.'[17] Similarly, an article concerning Mathilde Alanic, appearing in the same year, talks of this empathetic bonding: 'We know for certain that thousands of girls and women feel an ardent, silent attachment to their favourite authors, which brings great comfort to the writers themselves.'[18] In the same article Maroussia describes Alanic's need to write as 'the pleasure of touching, here and there, hearts of unknown friends', stressing the reciprocal quality of the pleasure experienced by readers and writers of romances.

Many critics have attempted to explain how this bonding is engineered. According to the results of Thiesse's survey of Belle Epoque readers it would appear that the presence of a female name in the title helped encourage reader identification. Coquillat argues that the author deliberately leaves the physical details of the heroine vague to enable the intended female reader to see herself in the fictional character, and that the heroines, to encourage empathizing, also tend to be very average, even ordinary. At the same time, almost in contradiction to this, there is often a particularly desirable quality in the heroine, a quality which by and large exists on a metaphoric or symbolic plane. The heroine is repeatedly presented as embodying inner truth, light, beauty or goodness and just as one might desire ownership of an object possessing these qualities so too one imagines the pleasure of owning, or, as the case may be, identifying or fusing with, the romantic heroine. Here the reader's desire for vicarious experience is akin to the kind of consumerism engendered by modern publicity techniques. The period did, after all, witness the shift to a mass-market economy, with elaborate advertising of readily available consumer goods from radios, gramophone records and motor cars to skin and hair-care products, designer and stylish off-the-peg clothes and accessories, and cosmetics, promoted by the burgeoning fashion and beauty industry. Michel Davet's fiction, for instance, sells the fantasy of *embourgeoisement*; her novels, such as *Douce* (1940), are set in upper middle-class or aristocratic society where the decor is sumptuous and the protagonists are leisured, preoccupied only with the personal realm of experience and the pleasurable aspects of domesticity. For the working-class reader this may well have constituted an ideal world at a considerable remove from the actual world of heavy physical work largely centred outside the home.[19]

Whatever the specific means used to achieve readerly identification, its benefits are all too evident, as Thiesse, Radway and Fowler demonstrate in their analyses of reader responses.[20] Their independent studies all note that on the most fundamental level the targeted working-class female reader clearly enjoys, through vicarious identification, the pleasures of escaping for a time her own possibly humdrum life. Throughout her study, Fowler repeatedly stresses that the reader willingly enters into a tacit agreement with the author to suspend disbelief (for she is quite aware that her reading material transcends certain limits of realist fiction) in return for the pleasures of the utopian promise of the escapist fantasy. It is interesting too that in her advice to new writers of the 1990s the novelist Jean Saunders stresses the benefits of this very feature: the romance 'stimulates the reader's imagination and transports her away from her everyday surroundings', it offers 'escapism, wish-fulfilment' and 'vicarious fantasy'.[21] Clearly, then, the pleasure of the reading experience is crucial.

Gratifying entertainment was not the sole aim of the new romance. When it re-emerged in the 1880s, it was not just as a natural consequence of the creation of an enlarged female readership, but rather as a deliberate type of opposition to the specific nature of the new educational opportunities offered to girls. The Third Republic's increase in secular schooling was seen by many as an attack on the Roman Catholic Church's monopoly hitherto on the education of women; Sée, who was responsible for the legislative changes to the education system, made no efforts to disguise his anti-clerical objectives. While lessons encouraged a sense of citizenship, civic duty, patriotism and industriousness, they did so at the expense of the instruction of religious morality *per se*.[22] In an attempt, then, to counterbalance this formal secular education, countless middle-class and aristocratic women put pen to paper with the express intention of defending the faith and offering morally didactic works to the widening working-class female readership. They chose to do so precisely through what one might term popular 'sanitized' romantic novels, works which completely purged their predecessors of their inclination towards licentiousness. Prévost, in the *Revue des bibliothèques* of 1927, in indicating that these romances now met with the approval of the highly influential patrons responsible for financing purchases for the *cabinets de lecture*, who strove to complete the moral and intellectual education of the lower-class female reader, underscores this edifying aim.[23] Certain publishers, in line with this general purpose, targeted their romantic collections specifically at a younger female readership. At the end of the nineteenth century Mégard, based in Rouen, published its didactic series 'Bibliothèque morale de la jeunesse' (The Young Person's Moral collection) which largely featured works by Colette Yver, who by the turn of the century also wrote for the collection 'Pour les jeunes filles' (For Young Girls). By the Inter-war period two further series dominated the market: Fayard's 'Collection jeunes filles et jeunes femmes' (The Young Ladies' and Girls' series), favoured again by Colette Yver, and Gautier Languereau's 'Bibliothèque de ma fille' (My Daughter's collection), which published most of the corpus of the ever-popular Delly.

Yet these works became in the 1880s much more than just manuals of moral instruction focused on ideal models of virtue. They became a vehicle for a particular ideological stance, with three new features distinguishing them from their immediate predecessors: a profoundly bourgeois perspective, extreme Catholicism and excessive patriotic fervour. An explanation for this can be found in the political climate of the 1880s, which they both reflected and reinforced. When Pope Leo XIII (whose pontificate started in 1878) issued a rallying call to reconcile the Church and the Republic many French Catholics were incensed. In response to what they saw as the mediocrity, materialism and moderation of the Church (and as a part of a more general reaction against current tastes for positivism and naturalism) there was an explosion of religious militancy. At the same time xenophobia was rife. France has always had a strong tradition of patriotism, and when the Franco-Prussian War left many French citizens smarting under the ignominy of defeat, significant numbers turned to the revanchist Ligue des Patriotes, founded in 1882 by Paul Déroulède. During the Dreyfus Affair, when anti-semitism reached its apogee, yet more nationalists joined the Ligue de la Patrie Française, founded in 1898. Hatred of Judaism and German Protestantism was framed by the rhetoric of a religious mission akin to the defence of Christendom. This attitude was fuelled by a significant number of influential revivalist writers who exploited current religious fervour to support xenophobic propaganda.[24] Women too played a part in this, as the leagues had a sister movement: the Ligue Patriotique des Françaises founded in 1902. It too championed nationalism, the denigration of Republicanism, the reinstatement of Christian morals, the encouragement of philanthropy, and, in addition to this, it undertook a political campaign for universal suffrage (primarily to enforce retrograde legal measures such as the reversal of the recent laws facilitating divorce and to ensure female subordination). Most importantly it aimed to convert and instruct the lower classes.[25] Its active membership was high: in 1917, between 500,000 and 600,000 members; in 1927 between 730,000 and 900,000 members; and in 1932 around 1.5 million, not including those in the subsidiary section for girls aged sixteen to twenty. It functioned largely through provincial journals, magazines like *La Croix* and *Le Petit Echo de la mode*, and novels by the latter, Bonne Presse and *Les Veillées des chaumières*.[26] Given the League's popularity, its role in the shaping of public opinion in the popular press for women and its link with the literary world, it comes as no surprise that the majority of right-wing religious romances of the period reflected the League's central aims and preoccupations.

This is best illustrated by the work of the most popular Inter-war romantic writer(s): Delly, who produced over a hundred novels from 1907 to 1941.[27] Their readership appears to have been extensive, spanning different generations (as Annie Ernaux's autobiographical work *Une Femme* (1987) attests) and different social groups. Esteem for this writing team was most evident in the Inter-war era and in the period 1950–66, which saw a major renewed interest when Flammarion republished fifteen titles, of which *La Lune d'or* (1966) alone sold 15,000 copies in one day.[28] Delly's appeal, and no doubt success, results from their dependability. The constant in Delly's fiction is not simply evident in terms of the action but is rather to be found in the persistent reinforcement of the same value-system, and their reassurance that in times of change the old values hold firm. However, a closer look at Delly's fiction demonstrates that it does more than simply reinforce the traditional values of the status quo. It didactically expounds the exact blend of bourgeois politics, religion and nationalism seen at the heart of the influential contemporaneous Ligue Patriotique des Françaises.

Perhaps the most explicit example of xenophobic fervour in a Delly romance is to be found in *La Fin d'une Walkyrie,* first published in 1916 and republished during the Inter-war era. The novel is set in the Great War and consequently anti-German feeling runs high. Nationalistic propaganda extends from the opening pages, where German poetry is mocked in the literary salons, to the final climax where the German anti-heroine, Brunhilde Halweg, the Valkyrie of the title, is killed by the hero during his escape from her prisoner-of-war camp. Although this is an extreme instance, patriotism in fact colours much of Delly's work. We see in *Les Ombres* (1925), for instance, Madel's inheritance from her maternal grandmother is a single piece of advice; the old woman's counsel, issued from her deathbed, stresses that above all else patriotism and a genuine love of France should govern Madel's path through life: 'Always love our countryside, Madel, love our old stones, always try to hear what they speak to thoughtful souls, to the real souls of France' ('Aime toujours nos vieilles pierres, Madel, aime nos campagnes, tâche d'entendre toujours ce qu'elles disent aux âmes qui pensent, aux vraies âmes de France') (p. 45). In the final scene of the novel specific details of this excerpt – the architectural metaphor, the link with a special ancestry, and most obviously the importance of country – are echoed when Madel accepts the hero's proposal of marriage:

Now, Bernard, it is you who are my old house. By that I mean that my duty, joy and home are by your side. And all the principles I learned here from my dear ancestors, all the strong traditional French Catholic atmosphere in which I grew up, I find in you, my love, my dear Bernard, who share my beliefs, who are a genuine Frenchman.

Maintenant, Bernard, c'est vous qui êtes ma vielle maison. Je veux dire: c'est près de vous que se trouve mon devoir, ma joie, mon foyer. Et tous les principes que j'ai reçus ici, de mes chères aïeules, toute l'atmosphère de forte tradition française et catholique dans laquelle j'ai vécu, je les retrouverai chez vous, mon ami, mon cher Bernard, qui croyez comme moi et qui êtes un vrai Français. (p. 250)

This statement significantly also stresses the importance of religion in the heroine's vital choice and it is Roman Catholicism which, to an even greater degree than patriotism, dominates Delly's work.

Religion lies first and foremost at the heart of Delly's plots, as the key events which separate the hero and heroine without fail revolve around diverse questions of faith. In *Une Femme supérieure* (1927) the hero, Nathaniel, has to convert from Protestantism to what Delly sees as the true religion before he is acceptable to Liane, the heroine; she, in turn, has to avoid the trappings of the modern worldly society to which her adoptive family adhere before she is rewarded by marriage and the rightful return of her inheritance. In the private and public battle between good and evil, it is the force of good which always triumphs. Olivier-Martin indicates, in his analysis of the historical development of the popular novel, in which a substantial sub-section is devoted to Delly, that popular works traditionally function through this fundamental opposition (the cowboy and Indian, the cop and robber, the detective and the criminal). Where Delly is of particular interest, though, is the unusually minimal coverage given to the depiction of evil which often dominates popular plots. The antithesis of good is always underplayed in Delly's fiction: sin is never presented, only hinted at, and it is never shown as pleasurable or rewarding in any way. Two distinct patterns emerge for the villains: the characters either suffer for their misdeeds, or feel remorse and atone for their sins. If the former, nemesis takes its toll, and the Old Testament belief of 'an eye for an eye' holds true.

Similarly, religion dominates in the presentation of the protagonists. On the simplest level, Delly's heroines share a common feature: their deep belief, and the romances they people are filled with descriptions of this faith in action. One is time and again shown characters as they progress through the different stages of their spiritual growth – devoutly learning the catechism, piously praying, selflessly helping the sick and needy, or teaching and converting others. This religious focus of Delly's fiction interestingly spills over from physical action to the terminology and metaphoric codification used to describe the characters. Madel of *Les Ombres*, for instance, is repeatedly referred to in terms of the purity of her soul (pp. 16, 38, 49, 121, for example), while Aniouta of *La Fin d'une Walkyrie* is actually compared to the Virgin at prayer (p. 165). The hero too always incarnates virtue. Bernard of *Les Ombres* is a typical example in that he manifests limitless faithfulness in the fullest sense of the word, as he is at once loyal and full of spiritual faith. This religious filter also extends to and colours the relationship between the protagonists. Ideal love and ideal lovers, without fail, embody the guiding principles of the Roman Catholic Church. Coquillat's research shows how the female character worships the hero with a devotion akin to religious fervour.[29] This is evident in the conclusion to *Les Ombres*, for Madel admires in her husband-to-be 'loyalty, solid goodness, strong religious convictions and inner moral beauty', 'la loyauté, la ferme bonté, les fortes convictions religieuses (. . .) les beautés morales' (p. 239). She herself is told by her future mother-in-law: 'You must be good and must bear the mark of a strong moral upbringing and serious religious beliefs. Setting up a home without these foundations is like building on sand' ('Il faut être bonne, et avoir réçu de forts principes moraux, une sérieuse empreinte religieuse. Fonder un foyer sans ces bases-là, c'est bâtir sur le sable.') (p. 176). Here Delly, through the use of the biblical parable, most fully conflate romantic love and religious love. This pervades their entire corpus – their character sketches, resolutions of the plot, their language and their depiction of ideal love are suffused with the values and doctrinal teachings of Roman Catholicism.

From the 1880s to the 1930s, then, entertainment and education together became the bipartite aim of this new romantic fiction and their uneasy, awkward relationship helped constitute a highly unusual and at times unstable literary genre, with complex, often conflicting features. At the heart of the romance lay a central paradox fed by these antithetical aims: in being morally didactic it appealed to traditional values; in striving to entertain it appealed to the reader's experience of the quintessentially modern world. The romance authors consequently faced the ubiquitous and seemingly intractable problem of resolving the diametrically opposed need to be modishly progressive yet conservative, and it is interesting to investigate the extent to which they were successful in smoothing out this dichotomy. Fayard's monthly series 'Collection jeunes femmes et jeunes filles' is a suitable point of departure, as in the publisher's explanation of the intended purpose of the series, provided on the cover, it is the modernity of the novels which is stressed. Fayard states its aim as the desire to bring about an evolution in the novel for girls which it believes has remained unchanged since the 1830s! Over and above its declaration of achieving a high literary standard and only the best authorship, it holds that it is moving with the times in its acknowledgement that girls now require more than mere infantile sentimentalism. The novels are targeted at the new modern girl who is 'short-haired, sporty, educated and prepared for life, who sees opening up before her a whole spectrum of career opportunities for which she would be well-suited'. However, this declaration is quite out of keeping with the traditional perspective of individual works forming part of the series of which Colette Yver's *Rose, Madame* (1928) is a typical example.

Unlike the traditional pattern of romance, *Rose, Madame* does not conclude with the marriage of the protagonists, Rose and Martin. Instead, the initial meeting, courtship and wedding all occur in the first fifty pages and the remainder of the romance charts the development of their relationship as each character moves from intellectual and emotional isolation, through a series of misunderstandings all centred on the concept of the female role in marriage, to a denouement of harmonious unity on a spiritual and affective plane. Several aspects of *Rose, Madame* help contribute to its contemporary feel: the events following the marriage take place in an ultra-fashionable home with much-described art-deco furnishings, the hero in the course of the plot, is appointed to a newly created position as personnel manager involved in the implementation of trade unionism in French factories, and Rose is the archetypal highly educated woman of the 1920s who is pursuing further academic research into the advantages of the new higher education system for girls. This particular intellectual investigation, together with the main focus of the plot, allows a philosophical and a practical exposition of the topical debate on the position of women in the era. However, while the subject matter may be modern, its resolution, as we shall see, is not necessarily so.

Within this romance conflicting models of womanhood are juxtaposed. The most extreme vision is that given by Esope Dalizay, Rose's philosophy tutor, who holds that women should be fully emancipated and totally autonomous. His name, Esope, with its connotations of Aesop's fables, together with his professional interest in abstract notions, suggests that his theories are divorced from the real world. In actual fact this proves to be the case as Esope advocates that Rose attend a foreign conference unaccompanied by her husband. While Esope is oblivious to any threat this might pose to Rose's personal security, the Inter-war reader would be all too aware of the possible dangers facing the heroine – the conference setting is Algeria, with its unfamiliar Muslim traditions, its exoticism and its reputation for moral laxity. Although any potential jeopardy goes unrealized, the reader is nonetheless alerted to Esope's lack of care for real people and, as a consequence, the status and worth of his beliefs are thrown into question. At the opposite end of the spectrum, in direct opposition to Rose's mentor Esope, is Martin's mother. She is evoked from the hero's perspective as the perfect woman: she is altruistic to the point of being totally self-sacrificing and is defined completely through her relationship with the husband and eight children she serves. Yet just as Esope's ultra-feminist vision of the female condition is rejected, so too is this ultra-conservative ideal. Martin's mother is only present in the novel in the hero's recollections. As a result of this physical absence, the model woman she represents seems chimeric, illusory, impossible to realize in the society the text reproduces.

Martin and Rose completely base their initial understanding of the female condition on these opposing value-systems. Less ardently feminist than her mentor Esope, Rose is interested in female autonomy and the possibilities of self-development. Although well educated, she first feels happy and fulfilled when she discovers her love for the hero and she has high expectations of marriage to him. However, she comes to understand that her needs and desires for independence cannot be met within this union. Martin too places his hopes in marital bliss. While he acknowledges that Rose is more of an individual than his mother and while he professes to despise men who set out to limit their partners fulfilling their potential, he still longs for his wife to correspond to the traditional female role. But he realizes that his expectations, based on female passivity and dependence, are still clearly incompatible with Rose's. Both characters, it is clear, must re-evaluate their needs and desires, and learn to compromise within their marriage before they can find true conjugal happiness.

Yver brings about this resolution through an intermediary character: Martin's aunt, Sylvie, who ultimately orchestrates the denouement. Throughout the novel, in her advice to the protagonists, she promotes balance and moderation. She is set up to represent the golden mean, a happy blend of modern and traditional values. When she is first introduced these two aspects are highlighted: on the one hand, the reader is informed that in modern vein she has chosen to remain unmarried to pursue a self-reliant lifestyle; on the other hand, she is shown working at a tapestry which suggests a nineteenth-century image of domesticity. By the end of the romance she is seen to occupy the position of right reason and the last comments on the institution of marriage are hers. In a didactic passage in the final few pages she describes the ideal wife:

A woman in love gives up her own ambition, a woman in love takes on the ambitions of her husband, blessing them, caressing them, serving them, for, as the world's greatest moralist has said, 'Man was not made for woman, but woman for man.' All the theories of female pride which promote first and foremost sexual equality do not stand up to this natural basis for marriage.

Une femme qui aime oublie ses ambitions; une femme qui aime adopte les ambitions de son mari; elle les bénit, les caresse, les sert, car, a dit le plus grand moraliste du monde 'l'homme n'a pas été crée pour la femme mais la femme pour l'homme'. Toutes les théories de l'orgueil féminin qui posent l'égalité de la femme au commencement de tout ne tiennent pas contre cette base naturelle du mariage. (p. 217)

This comes as a shock to the present-day reader. Not only does it seem inappropriate to have the only unmarried character in the romance expound on marriage, but her opinion, until now guarded, is not at all what one expects. Sylvie is set up to symbolize the mid-point between the two extreme representations of womanhood, yet her statement, with its heavy reliance on religious phraseology, is still very conservative and is much closer to the image supported by Martin and his mother than that expressed by Rose and Esope, her biological link to Martin's family serving additionally to reinforce this bias.

That Yver advocates this conservative position, there can be little doubt. Unlike the standard romance, it is Martin's perspective, not the heroine's, which dominates the early part of the work encouraging the reader to identify with his opinions. Notably little insight is given to the reasons behind Rose's stance and it is the hero not the heroine who is shown to be misunderstood, maligned and fundamentally in the right. In a work which focuses on women's roles, it is striking too that there is no indication of any female figures in positions of power and that Rose's academic achievement, in its hyperbolic presentation, is ironically undercut. Yver additionally intervenes at a strategic moment at the fulcrumatic mid-point of the action, in a direct apostrophe highlighted by a quite different texture and tonal quality from the surrounding narrative, to warn the heroine of the folly of her independent attitude. In such a way, Rose who fails to heed the authorial advice and curb her egoism, is shown to exhibit a certain arrogant confidence, which the events of the novel ultimately tame and correct. Yver most fully indicates her conservatism when it is Rose, not Martin, who must sacrifice most to achieve marital happiness. In Martin's first statement outlining his vision of ideal womanhood he refers to his wife waiting at home for him at the end of the day like a nurse at a first-aid post. In the events leading up to the denouement, this literally occurs when Rose takes on the actual role of a nurse when Martin recuperates after having been lost in an accident at sea.[30] In total contrast, Rose comes to relinquish her most fundamental belief, that married women should not be forced to conform to the incapable, infantile state they legally hold. In the final page of the romance she states, in response to her husband asking her to evaluate the merits of his political science diploma and his school-leaving certificate, in comparison to her three university degrees, she replies submissively 'Martin, I'm just a little girl compared to you', 'Martin, je suis une petite fille à côté de vous' (p. 250). Rose is forced to capitulate in a somewhat humiliating way and her forward-thinking ideas which she abandons are, it is implied, invalid. The ultimate didactic message of *Rose, Madame* is that it is fine to be educated, but that self-development is inappropriate in marriage where subservience to the man, irrespective of his qualities and abilities, is the order of the day. *Rose, Madame* is highly reactionary and its author, far from being a radical closet-feminist as Waelti-Walters has argued, is very conservative.[31]

So it would appear that even in works which overtly claim to be more modern than traditional, the overriding import continues to be Catholic and bourgeois. The 'Collection jeunes femmes et jeunes filles', in which Yver's work figured, is only forward-thinking in a limited way, not in relation to the changing role of women. The publishers Plon, too, in advertising their collections of romantic novels, which feature writers such as Mathilde Alanic, Henriette Celarié, Alice Decaen, Delly, Eveline Le Maire, Alice Pujo, Yvonne Schultz and Myriam Thélen, offer a similar description of the series and equally lack any genuine audacious modernity and promote only the most circumscribed manner of social change. Clearly the standard Inter-war romance fails to portray with any degree of fairness or accuracy the transformation in gender relations experienced over the course of the Inter-war period and in particular the new needs, values and aspirations held by so many women in modern French society. Belle Epoque Europe had already witnessed the emergence of 'New Women': women who sought economic independence, sexual freedom, cultural radicalism and who frequented avant-garde circles. With the Great War the status of these women, often seen as part of a bohemian fringe, evolved as increasing numbers of women from all social classes aspired to some of the ideals of this pre-war precursor. Throughout Europe and the United States many women no longer felt that they could simply resume their lives as they had been before the outbreak of war, because their range of life-experiences had now changed so radically, as Goldman indicates:

> bereavement; suddenly enforced independence; the paradox of living in a temporary matriarchy yet being powerless to affect matters of life and death; dealing with a new and unsought identity – as bread-winner, perhaps, or symbolic object of patriotic veneration; serving in new professions – policewomen, landgirls, munitions workers, nurses and doctors; having to choose whether to support the war or to oppose it; reconsidering their relationships with men.[32]

During the absence of the men who were serving at the front, many women had experienced new social freedoms, and in the aftermath of war, with the country bereft of a generation of young men, there was a marked increase in single women who had to adapt to changing circumstances and embrace the possibility of greater social, political and economic rights.

When these modern women are presented in the most right-wing Roman Catholic romances, as typified by Delly, they consistently take the role of anti-heroine. Their fate is isolation, rejection, even death. In more modern works, such as those by Maryan, for instance, the heroines, while still following the traditional path towards unity in marriage, assume certain modish qualities: they have wider life expectations and are shown to be autonomous in always directing their own destiny and the outcome of events. When the heroines become fully-fledged modern women, as is the case in Yver's *Rose, Madame*, they are always without exception chastised, corrected and taught to appreciate the traditional bourgeois values of home and family. Despite the fact that these heroines may be more active and militant, the novels in which they feature still do not go so far as to advocate life options other than those which actually enforce more traditional female roles. Like contemporary magazines, romantic fiction fails to reflect the actual feminist conquests of the time. Holmes confirms such a reading, as although the texts 'seem at first to advocate a radical change in the accepted code of sexual behaviour, in fact, the arguments expressed in the novels come full circle, and end by reinstating the monogamous couple as the exclusive ideal'.[33] Here, it would appear, is the root of the problem. Even when the heroines are keen to dispute or disregard traditional roles, the romance's conventional ending fails to offer new or satisfying alternatives.

From the earliest of times romances have concluded with this same narrative convention – the integration of the individual in society, or to be specific, the unity of marriage and the promise of fecundity in childbirth. This, the literary guarantor of the happy ending, the ubiquitous denouement of the comic tradition, is not in itself intentionally political. However, because throughout history the implications of marriage as an institution have varied, it seems highly probable that different generations of female readers' interpretation of marriage as a literary convention may vary accordingly. In France this is particularly marked. With the instigation of the Napoleonic Civil Code in 1804 a married woman held no independent legal status and was considered part of her husband's effects. While in England the Married Woman's Property Act of 1870 gave a woman both the right to control the possessions she had owned before marriage and the right to retain her own earnings, it required a further eleven years before the French government reviewed and gradually began to repeal the most restrictive aspects of the Napoleonic Civil Code – in 1881 it was agreed that women should have the right to hold a personal bank account, and it was not until 1907 that married women were entitled to earn a living without their husbands' consent. As a consequence of the subjugation of married women inherent in French law, marriage itself has taken on certain unpalatable connotations for women. Chiefly it is seen to deny female autonomy. Marriage suggests a renunciation of individuality and progressive feminism. As a literary value it is essentially conservative.

The place given to marriage in Inter-war romantic fiction says much about its conservative nature in this period, for wedlock is elevated to the status of the most fundamental aspect of the plot. As Dudovitz puts it, 'the myth of woman as wife and mother is such an integral part of the narrative structure that without it the fiction would become something quite different, and unpredictable'.[34] Inter-war romantic fiction does not simply present marriage in the final pages as the inevitable conclusion to a non-tragic work, or with an ironic dramatic flourish. Rather, the whole text builds to this climax. The central didactic message is as Holmes, Heilbrun, Dudovitz and Coquillat all confirm, that a woman, in order to be a real woman, must accept the pattern of pre-nuptial virginity, marriage, monogamy and maternity. The romance unquestioningly promotes and perpetuates male primacy, the containment of women to the domestic sphere, and the supreme importance of maternity as both the natural blossoming of womanhood and as part of a woman's patriotic duty to her country, often explicitly presenting these values as a bulwark against and panacea for unemployment, social instability, depopulation and the disintegration of family values. Religion plays an important part in reinforcing this ideological stance. Roman Catholicism places a considerable emphasis on the role played by the individual in a larger collective structure. Marriage, in this scenario, is of vital importance, for it represents entry into the wider community and the general acceptance of its beliefs. In contrast, in Anglo-American works, steeped in a Protestant culture, the emphasis falls on the individual in and for himself; so marriage may be posited as the achievement of personal success and happiness and may be read quite independently of its wider repressive social connotations. French fiction grounded in Roman Catholic mythologies, notably the selflessness of female saints such as Theresa of Lisieux whose cult grew phenomenally in the era,[35] Joan of Arc[36] and of course the Virgin Mary whose role is a patriarchal, prescriptive prototype for womanhood, again lends support to the validity of the role of wife and mother. The romance's portrayal of the *femme au foyer* is undoubtedly reinforced and rendered more innocuous by this religious infrastructure from which it draws strength.

Any attempted modernity in French sanitized romantic fiction of the early 1880s to the end of the 1930s is ultimately crippled by the omnipresence of traditional values in its conception and execution. This is perhaps best illustrated by Raymonde Machard, popular romantic novelist and erstwhile director of the weekly magazine *Journal de la femme*. Machard, in a private correspondence to Louise Weiss outlining how she perceives her role as a novelist, talks of 'the thousands of humble women who read my works, be they workers, servants, country folk, employees, have a great need of guidance. They never stop writing to me to ask my advice.' She notes that in response to this demand she deliberately uses her love stories to offer counsel to her readership.[37] Initially, one might think that the primary didactic purpose of Machard's fiction does not lie in providing moral guidance for her readership. Indeed, in *La Possession, roman de l'amour* (1927), her most widely read work, the romance which is set in a maternity hospital at first seems little more than a foil for Machard to provide technical, practical information on the dangers of caesarean births, eclamptic comas and the problems of lactation, and her detailed exposure of the harsh reality of the female condition seems to run counter to the teaching of most conservative popular romances. However, as the plot develops it becomes evident that all is not as it first appears. The heroine Claude is very much a modern woman. She is educated, pursues a career as a doctor, and is sufficiently liberated to choose her own lover and initiate a pre-marital liaison with him. The drama results when, on being abandoned, Claude returns home to her family where she realizes that she is truly loved by and in turn loves her father's student. The novel ends ambiguously with her decision to follow him to Indo-China. Should the reader see in Claude's departure an exile from the community, a banishment for transgressing certain tacit social laws? Or should her active decision to leave France be read rather as a mark of anti-patriotism and an indictment of the bourgeois society which casts her as a fallen woman and fails to accommodate her need for independence? Or yet again should one understand her final decision to relinquish her profession as a return to the very conformity she has rebelled against throughout the novel? Surprisingly, this seems the most viable reading as Claude's ultimate enlightened re-evaluation of her situation leads not only to her own happiness in a marital partnership described in terms of friendship, companionship and equality, but also to a reunion between her estranged parents. The locus of the traditional happy ending shifts to encompass the maternal figure. Claude's mother rediscovers the joys of her relationship with her daughter and husband. Her long-suffering patience and support is finally rewarded and her chosen role as wife and mother is positively validated. *La Possession* ends with two happy marriages and offers a contrast to the early scenes of physical suffering in maternity in the idyll of the emotional happiness of this traditional female role. Raymonde Machard's novel, despite its striking surface anti-conformism, actually works like most popular romances to reinforce the values of the status quo. There is no genuine attempt to promote the model of the emancipated, forward-looking woman; there is no real sense of progress.

It would appear that romances, whether self-consciously religious like works by Delly, or secular like those by Machard, whether aiming to entertain or aiming to educate, remain deeply traditional, despite any claim to be modern and forward-thinking. This raises a final question: how easy would it have been to read against Inter-war romances' espoused conservative ideology? Determining expectations of and responses to romances read in the 1920s and 1930s is a difficult task, given the prohibitive, inherent problems of a survey-based analysis of reading practices. One solution, though, lies in approaching the Inter-war romance through the experience of present-day readers, as it is possible that the constituent parts which affect their reading may be similar to features inherent in the earlier model. Of particular interest is Radway's controversial theory, expounded in *Reading the Romance: Women, Patriarchy, and Popular Literature,* for although ostensibly specific to American female readers of the 1980s, it is grounded in the belief that individual reading patterns are not idiosyncratic but that women read romances in the same way and for the same purpose.

The most prevalent view on the process of romance reading – a view challenged by Radway – holds that the reader somnolescently ingests alien ideologies, in particular the almost immutable mythic account of how women must find fulfilment in a patriarchal society through marriage and subservience to a single male partner, that is to say, the same reactionary ideology at the heart of the Inter-war romance. Radway's argument, based largely on Chodorovian theories of psychoanalysis, is the very antithesis of this standard interpretation. She begins by maintaining that the dominant ideology behind the romance is not alien to its reader. The lifestyle proposed by the romance's conclusion, that is to say, marriage and motherhood, is the very lifestyle experienced by the average middle-aged married reader, and the events of the courtship detailed in the work mirror the aspirations of the adolescent reader. More importantly, Radway contends that the act of reading, contrary to common belief, is active, and that the intended female reader resists, alters and appropriates the genre's ideology to suit her own ends. The reading process, she argues, is firmly linked to certain aspects of the romance plot. While today story-lines vary from work to work and in the Inter-war era there was an even greater lack of homogeneity at this level, the key elements on which Radway's theory is grounded are archetypal and may be found in many romances from all periods of literary history from late medieval times on, including France in the 1920s and 1930s. The essence of the plot is posited as a quest or voyage of self-discovery. It is articulated chiefly from the heroine's perspective and is composed of three basic phases: a hybrid opening generating multiple possibilities for resolution, a lengthy series of digressionary misunderstandings, and a denouement comprising a moment of self-knowledge and mutual understanding between the hero and heroine. The emphasis lies not on the development of character or event (indeed the characters are 'flat' or fixed and the action of secondary importance), but rather on the protagonists' expansion and clarification of feeling and, most importantly, their growing ability to adopt new perspectives to reinterpret their situation. Two specific elements are crucial to Radway's re-reading of the romance: the specific nature of the heroine's journey and the role played by the hero in the denouement.

The plot, for Radway, charts the heroine's path from isolation to connection. In the introduction she is presented as a solitary figure: sometimes an orphan, almost without exception motherless, often lacking the support of female friends and family. Her life is a physical quest for union and simultaneously, it is implied, a psychological quest to fill this glaringly vacant maternal role. Towards the end of the romance unity is achieved in promises of wedlock. Here the hero's true nature is for the first time fully revealed: he is attentive, observant, intuitive, caring and protective; he both needs and desires the heroine and recognizes her qualities. According to Radway the hero comes to occupy the position of the ideal mother, as yet unfilled within the confines of the narrative – that is to say, in displaying these maternal qualities and adopting a nurturing role in relation to the heroine, he becomes, at once, the subject of both her public and personal inner quest. This pattern is indeed seen in Inter-war romances, a particularly striking illustration occurring in the conclusion to Delly's *Les Ombres*. Madel, the motherless heroine, is asked for in marriage not by the hero, as is expected, but by his mother. The proposal, 'Now, will you be my daughter?', 'Voulez-vous être ma fille, maintenant?' (p. 242), seems to confirm Radway's theory that the heroine's quest for romantic love is as much a search for surrogate maternal love. This has several implications for the romance reader. Most obviously, the effects of reading the romance are transformed from mere escapism to something more akin to therapeutic self-indulgence. If, as Radway's research shows, readers fully identify with the heroine, then by the conclusion they may share the pleasure of the nurturing love the heroine receives from the hero. In the final pages the tables turn and readers, who in real life may be subject to constant external demands to reproduce and care for others, perhaps at odds with their internal limitations or inclinations, for once are themselves nurtured.

Yet, the beneficial quality of reading romantic fiction may be doubled; for readers, according to Radway, not only identify with the heroine, they equally identify with the subject of her quest: the absent mother. Throughout the work readers have been encouraged to visualize themselves as surrogate mother-figures. This effect is systematically achieved by the authorial emphasis on the heroine's unworldiness and solitude, and on the readers' contrasting superior knowledge of the heroine's situation and life in general. The readers, in a relatively omniscient position, unlike the protagonists, are a party to many proleptic clues, which, given their experience of this type of fiction, they are able to read in a way unknown to the characters. Such a superiority, together with the heroine's childlike lack of information and the means of deciphering it, apparently encourages readers to adopt a maternal role and to establish an almost symbiotic bond with the character which in turn gives rise to a further boon. As the general process of nurturance is so fully justified, the reader's real-life role of nurturer is also confirmed as valuable and worthwhile. Just as the heroine attains a legitimate position within pre-established cultural definitions as lover, wife and mother, the reader's own similar position or aspirations are validated. This particular aspect of Radway's theory carries some weight. Harvey, writing on *Backfischbücher*, educative adventure novels for girls in Weimar Germany, comes to a similar result, albeit from a quite different perspective. She also holds that 'the general dominant tendency of such books is to reassure the reader that the traditional feminine role is still an option'.[38] The first phase of Radway's theory, then, that the working-class female reader willingly accepts certain benefits which stem directly from the genre's conservative framework, is quite in line with specific aspects of the genre as it manifests itself in the 1920s and 1930s and with the political climate of the times. The pleasure of romantic literature, the reason for its mass consumption in the Inter-war era, is that in a period of such political uncertainty women read this kind of fiction to expiate their inner feelings of guilt over their assumption of traditional social roles designated for men, to achieve comfort and reassurance on a personal and social level.

In the second, more polemic phase of her bipartite theory, Radway argues that, despite the fringe benefits of conformity, the *way* in which present-day women actually read romances subverts their conservative stance.[39] Here she goes beyond her earlier deduction, in her insistence that readers are not passively endorsing but cognitively exploring and challenging, albeit in a limited way, the dominance of patriarchal forces. She holds that readers, like the heroine, learn the skill of reinterpretation. The heroine re-reads the nature of her romantic attachment, the readers re-read the more general issue of power relations between the sexes. While the heroine accepts a traditional female role in the work's standard conclusion, this role is not seen as subservient nor is this choice shown to be ultra-conservative. Rather, because of the positive re-evaluation of nurturance the heroine's new position of wife and mother is applauded. The denouement consequently marks a shift in the balance of power between the sexes, a point emphasized by the hero's transformation. No longer Coquillat's authoritative, swarthy Latin lover, he is now more akin to the caring maternal figure, converted by the heroine to conform to a more acceptable behavioural code. From this transformation Radway deduces that misogyny and aggressive violence (the excesses of male power), which are often suggested in the demeanour of both the hero and his male foil, are diffused or deflected. Readers may use the romance as a way to cope with deep-rooted fears of masculine domination, which the romance goes some way towards domesticating. Consequently, it displays the benefits of conformity and simultaneously allows women to challenge, albeit in a limited way, the dominance of patriarchal forces. It provides a strategy for women to make their situation acceptable without a substantive reordering of society itself.

This second part of Radway's argument, while perhaps apt in its depiction of current reading practices in America, is out of keeping with the French Inter-war romance and its readership on several grounds. Most obviously, the genre is not necessarily enabling for the reader, who may at best experience a degree of momentary power, as the plot focuses largely on courtship where women see themselves as central. Even this is not without attendant problems, as Heilbrun notes:

> women are allowed this brief moment in the limelight – and it is the part of their lives most constantly and vividly enacted in a myriad of representations – to encourage the acceptance of a lifetime of marginality. And courtship itself is, as often as not, an illusion: that is, the woman must entrap the man to ensure herself a centre for her life.[40]

In many French Inter-war works courtship certainly is a prelude to a much less heartening literary denouement where it is without fail the heroine, not the hero, who is tamed and controlled in the final pages. However, the discrepancies between works of these two periods actually lie much deeper still – in the very nature of their conservatism. The contemporary Anglo-American romance is reactionary chiefly because of its increasingly rigid in its formulaic nature. This in turn results from its gradual steady evolution throughout history, and, more specifically, from the fact that it is mass-produced, rigorously controlled by omnipotent publishers (which results in a restriction of authorial freedom), and subject to market forces and audience expectations – all of which blunt its critical edge. While innovative, politically revolutionary writing is limited, there may still be some opportunity for a greater degree of subversive intent on the part of the readership precisely because of the romance's built-in formulaic rigidity, as Radway argues.

In complete contrast, the French Inter-war romance does not share the same development pattern, the same lengthy, immutable conservative precedent. While in the English-speaking world the current genre's formation was very gradual, its history in France has been particularly disrupted especially in the extremes of the licentious days of the 1850s and religious revival of the 1880s to 1930s.[41] Indeed, it is reactionary chiefly because of the predominant Roman Catholic values deliberately adopted at the time of its renaissance. Its conservatism is at once more insidious and ubiquitous. While the Inter-war romance may appear relatively open and heterogeneous and while in theory it is more able to reflect and discuss current progressive issues (as is evident in the debate conducted in these works concerning the position of women, as we have seen), in practice the parameters of the debate were often fairly circumscribed because of the authors' aim of moral edification. Further to this, the role of the reader is also limited. Precisely because the early twentieth-century French romances were more varied in terms of content, precisely because their conventions were less set and rigid, their plots less formulaic, their linguistic codification less standardized, their tone more flexible, the reader is denied the possibility of re-reading fixed generic features in a subversive manner. Consequently, French Inter-war romances, unlike their present-day counterparts, are not incipiently oppositional. They do not offer any real possibility of seditious readings. They are, instead, politically limiting in the fullest sense. It is the case, then, that the popularity of French Inter-war romances and the great success of the collections to which they belonged undoubtedly lies in the fact that these works filled a basic human need in the era: reassuring women of the validity of traditional life options in what was a socially and politically troubled, unsettled epoch.

The link between gender, genre and period, which resulted in the French romance's religious purification and revival, which guaranteed its wide acclaim over a span of some fifty years, also proves to have brought about its equally marked decline; for this particular type of romance, with its rigid, dominant conservative ideology, proved unable to move fully with the times. It was powerless in freeing itself from its ideological fetters. Any attempts at modernity were hampered or indeed thwarted. By the post-war period, which saw the rise of secular socialist feminism, the Inter-war romance, with its religious, patriotic, bourgeois values, had become, once and for all, too distanced from current concerns, dated. As a consequence, it fell out of favour and from the 1940s onwards was superseded by the secular American romances which continue to flood the French market today. It is indeed the case, as Benisti affirms, that 'the popular novel such as existed at the beginning of the century no longer exists'.[42]

It follows, then, that Bertaut's suggestion, with which this chapter opened, that romance, a woman writer's sole domain, is essentially a static limited area, is evidently flawed. Despite the fact that in the romance's evolutionary chain from medieval to modern times, the now extinct French Inter-war romance may appear somewhat aberrant, it should not be forgotten that the genre in this era, thanks to countless women writers, underwent considerable new definitions and directions, in terms of both its conception and execution. Yet for many pioneering women writers, extending generic boundaries was insufficient in itself; those interested in the literary, political, philosophical and social issues of the day, no doubt finding limited opportunity in this conservative type of work for full investigation and debate, transcended it. In exactly the same way, and, significantly, for the same reasons that women moved from the autobiography to fictional representations of the self – a resistance to reactionary ideologies, and a concomitant desire to explore and re-evaluate the implications of social and cultural change on gender relations – women also moved from the romance to works exhibiting romantic elements. While love and indeed certain fundamental aspects of the romance still feature in their work, as we shall see, these come to play a very different part. Women, contrary to Bertaut's claim, do extend into new lands; there they do not wander aimlessly, but rather deliberately explore, with great daring and certain innovation, the new terrains love opens to them.

Notes

1. J. Bertaut [1909], *La Littérature féminine d'aujourd'hui*, Paris, p. 7.
2. See R.L. Dudovitz (1990), *The Myth of Superwoman: Women's Bestsellers in France and the United States*, London and New York, p. 100.
3. Over the past fifteen years there has been a marked increase in the homogeneity of American romantic fiction as Harlequin Publishers merged with Mills and Boon (established 1910) and took over the production of Silhouette. It now dominates the market, making $11 million profit in 1977, selling 168 million copies globally in 1979. For further details see G. Paizis (1986), 'The Contemporary Romantic Novel in France', unpublished Ph.D. thesis, University of London.
4. Writers at the heart of this process are very aware of the expectations of both the reading public and the editors, thanks to an abundance of advice from varied sources: personal letters, publisher's recommendations, writing classes, bulletins from special romance organizations and, of course, manuals by present or former successful writers.
5. Dudovitz, *The Myth of Superwoman*, p. 51.
6. A.-M. Thiesse (1984), *Le Roman quotidien: lecteurs et lectures populaires à la Belle Epoque*, Paris, p. 127. We should note that while women were the privileged readers of romantic fiction, they were not necessarily its sole readers.
7. A few paperbacks by women writers in the period do have pictorial

covers. These include historical biographies which depict a black-and-white portrait or photograph of the subject. Significantly, these works were more expensive than fictional works belonging to collections.

8. Thiesse, *Le Roman quotidien*, pp. 99 and 97.
9. Average print runs for popular novels in the period averaged out at around 15,000 copies, the same number as for novels by well-known writers published by Flammarion. See M.L. Roberts (1994), *Civilization Without Sexes: Reconstructing Gender in Postwar France, 1917–1927*, Chicago and London, pp. 47 and 244–5.
10. Y. Olivier-Martin (1980), *Histoire du roman populaire en France de 1840–1980*, Paris, p. 237.
11. R. Miles (1987), *The Female Form: Women Writers and the Conquest of the Novel*, London and New York, p. 33.
12. See A. Sauvy (1986), 'La Littérature et les femmes' in H.J. Martin, R. Chartier and J.P. Vivets (eds), *Histoire de l'édition française: le livre concurrencé, 1900–1950*, Paris, vol. 4, pp. 242–55.
13. Fowler sees no distinction in the French and English traditions. She acknowledges the romance's medieval French roots, and from the eighteenth century onwards focuses exclusively on English works. She posits the common characteristic of the cited proto-romantic writers as their depiction of female financial dependence. This focus on class and capital is not in any sense unique to the romantic genre, appearing as it does in so much nineteenth-century realist fiction, nor is it in fact explicitly present in most French romances of the early twentieth century. Fowler's examples also pertain quite specifically to an English tradition. Richardson is generally associated with the Protestant introspective narrative which is at odds with the Roman Catholic basis of the French romance. Dickens, Disraeli and Gaskell are renowned for playing a cardinal role in the realist 1840s' 'Condition of England' novel, depicting social inequalities in Victorian England, and this again seems totally remote from French romantic works of the period between the wars. See B. Fowler (1991), *The Alienated Reader: Women and Popular Romantic Literature in the Twentieth Century*, London and New York, pp. 50–100.
14. See J. Forbes and M. Kelly (eds), (1995), *French Cultural Studies: an Introduction*, Oxford, p. 65.
15. M. Coquillat (1988), *Romans d'amour*, Paris, pp. 27–32.
16. Bertaut, *La Littérature féminine*, p. 8.
17. Francelisse (26 October 1924), 'Figures féminines: Zénaïde Fleuriot', *Le Petit Echo de la mode*, no. 43.

18. Maroussia (21 September 1924), 'Mathilde Alanic', *Le Petit Echo de la mode*, no. 38.
19. Recent research into early twentieth-century working-class women's lifestyles, prior to the invention and spread of household electrical appliances, has revealed the astounding proportion of the day spent outside the home carrying out domestic chores.
20. Thiesse surveys French Belle Epoque reading habits, Radway looks at American women in the early 1980s, while Fowler examines the reading practices of female working-class Scottish readers in the 1990s.
21. J. Saunders (1991), *The Craft of Writing Romance: A Practical Guide to Writing Contemporary and Historical Romantic Fiction*, London, pp. 9–12.
22. See K. Offen (1987), 'Feminism, Anti-feminism and National Family Politics in Early Third Republic France' in M.J. Boxer and J.H. Quataert (eds), *Connecting Spheres: Women in the Western World, 1500 to the Present*, Oxford, pp. 177–86 (p. 180).
23. See Thiesse, *Le Roman quotidien*, p. 58.
24. See R. Griffiths (1966), *The Reactionary Revolution: the Catholic Revival in French Literature, 1870–1914*, London, ch. 11; F. Baldensperger (1943), *La Littérature française entre les deux guerres 1919–1939*, Marseilles; and A.D. Sertillanges (1908), *Féminisme et Christianisme*, Paris.
25. A.-M. Sohn (1984), 'Les Femmes catholiques et la vie publique en France (1900–1930): l'example de la ligue patriotique des Françaises' in M.-C. Pasquier (ed.), *Stratégies des femmes*, Paris, pp. 97–120 (p. 97).
26. *Le Petit Echo de la mode* was especially successful. By 1928, some fifty years after its inception, it claimed to have the highest turn-over of copies, an astounding 1,125,000 a week. See D. Holmes (1977), 'The Image of Women in Selected French Fiction of the Inter-war Period: a Study of Literary Responses to the Changing Role of Women, 1918–1939', unpublished Ph.D. thesis, University of Sussex, p. 15.
27. Delly is in fact a brother and sister writing team. Fréderic Petitjean de la Rosière invented the plots while his younger sister Marie wrote the romances based on them.
28. See Olivier-Martin, *Histoire du roman populaire*, p. 239.
29. See Coquillat, *Romans d'amour*, pp. 112 and 118.
30. This set of references recalls a number of novels produced during the First World War which explore and update the Proudhonian 'bad woman/good woman' schism in terms of the sexually prom-iscuous woman who is indifferent to male suffering and the

self-sacrificing mother/nurse. Rose moves between these two antithetical positions: there are clear sexual undercurrents in her early trip to North Africa, while her final role as nurse signals her return to female virtue, loyalty and devotion. Roberts notes that this polarization of female roles gains extra validity in male-authored wartime literature because of the soldiers' tendency to conceptualize the world in stark opposites: peacetime/wartime, the French soldier/the German enemy, the home front/ the battle front, and she bases her very interesting argument on the reading of a range of texts by Gaston Rageot, Roland Dorgelès, Raymond Radiguet, Pierre Chaine, Henri Barbusse, André Beaunier, Paul Tuffrau and Francis Forest. See Roberts, *Civilization Without Sexes*, ch. 1.

31. J. Waelti-Walters (1990), *Feminist Novelists of the Belle Epoque: Love as a Lifestyle*, Bloomington and Indianapolis, p. 15. Waelti-Walters bases this opinion on her reading of *Dans le jardin du féminisme* (Paris, 1922) as a 'tour de force of accommodation'.

32. D. Goldman (1993), *Women and World War 1: the Written Response*, London, p. 6.

33. Holmes, 'The Image of Women', p. 133.

34. Dudovitz, *The Myth of Superwoman*, p. 110.

35. Saint Theresa was canonized in 1925. Lucie Delarue-Mardrus's fiction bears witness to her popular appeal, as Theresa appears as a leitmotif in her corpus, featuring as the subject of two biographies and being present in many of the works set in the author's home of Honfleur, lower Normandy – here one thinks particularly of the celebrated *L'Ex-voto* (1922). Most surprisingly, she even has a place in Delarue-Mardrus's beauty manual. While the author states that the saint would no doubt be surprised at her inclusion in such a work, she does have a place, as Theresa has the secret of true beauty – an inner radiance, calmness and serenity.

36. Joan of Arc, who was canonized in 1920 some 500 years after her martyrdom, was adopted as a mascot by various women's movements in the period. The Action sociale de la femme, a reactionary association which aimed to promote women's social responsibility in areas of family and child welfare, formed the Congrès Jeanne d'Arc, a coalition of women's charitable institutions. See A. Klaus (1993), 'Depopulation and Race Suicide: Maternalist and Pronatalist Ideologies in France and the United States' in S. Koven and S. Michel (eds), *Mothers of a New World: Maternalist Politics and the Origins of Welfare States*, London and New York, pp. 188–212 (p. 192). Joan of Arc also appealed to

more radical feminists, who admired her cropped hair and sexual ambiguity. See Roberts, *Civilization Without Sexes*, p. 63.

37. Machard's comments from a private interview are quoted in L. Weiss (1938), *Ce que femme veut: souvenirs de la IIIème République*, Paris, p. 43.

38. E. Harvey (1991), 'Private Fantasy and Public Intervention: Girls' Reading in Weimar Germany' in J. Birkett and E. Harvey (eds), *Determined Women: Studies in the Construction of the Female Subject, 1900–1990*, London, pp. 38–67 (p. 61).

39. Neither Thiesse nor Fowler draw these conclusions from their similar studies of reading practices. Indeed, Fowler, following Frank Kermode's analysis of formulaic endings, insists that the readership of modern popular romances, with its demand for the traditional ubiquitous happy ending, is in fact demonstrating a naive trust in the governing social order. Romance reading, she holds, is 'firmly linked to higher levels of political and gender conservatism'. Fowler, *The Alienated Reader*, p. 173.

40. C.G. Heilbrun (1989), *Writing a Woman's Life*, London, p. 21.

41. It is noteworthy that America in the 1930s, in complete contrast to France, saw a marked decline in organized religion.

42. E. Benisti's comments from a private interview of 18 February 1985 are presented in Dudovitz, *The Myth of Superwoman*, p. 100.

– 6 –

Revising the Romance

Simone de Beauvoir, promoting ideal reciprocity and equality between the sexes, an acceptance of otherness and difference, but a refusal of hierarchies based upon this, argued that 'In order to free women, one must stop imprisoning them in the relationships they make with men', 'Affranchir la femme, c'est refuser de l'enfermer dans les rapports qu'elle soutient avec l'homme.'[1] For many French women writers in the first half of the century, the creed of male centrality was largely attributable to the widespread impact of romantic fiction. It was this genre, above all others, they believed, which actively promoted and perpetuated the myth that a woman's entire significance and true destiny must be centred upon a man, that her self-discovery must invariably culminate in monogamous heterosexual marriage. In much realist, feminist fiction of the period, then, the romance's values were openly challenged. A number of authors contended that true love is chimeric and only possible in forbidden situations not sanctioned by society. Anna de Noailles, for example, depicts the ill-fated, clandestine relationship between a nun Sœur Sainte-Sophie and a bohemian artist in Le Visage émerveillé (1904), while Rachilde portrays a young girl's passionate liaison with her disguised religious confessor in La Femme-Dieu (1934). It is incestuous love which dominates in Marthe de Bibesco's Le Perroquet vert (1924), where the heroine perpetuates a line of incestuous couples in her direct family as she experiences intense spiritual love for her dead brother Sacha and a more troubled physical bond with her estranged half-brother Félix. This theme of sibling attraction is also explored in the relationship between Bertille and Malique in Michel Davet's Le Prince qui m'aimait (1930) and in Marguerite Yourcenar's Anna, Soror . . . (1925).[2]

More pointed criticism was directed at the popular romance's promotion of conflated marital and maternal love. Claire Sainte-Soline's Les Sentiers détournés (1937), which details the heroine's four unhappy marriages, shows how a woman's dream of nurturing a man and child can so easily lead to her physical, financial and emotional depletion, a point underlined when the novel's artist figure relinquishes his dream of painting blooming, fecund maternity and opts instead for disturbing images of skeletal, de-sexed bodies. Marcelle Auclair's *Toya* (1927) depicts the tragic life of a modern-day Cousine Bette who waits in vain for ideal romantic and maternal love. Likewise, Josette Clotis's *Le Temps vert* (1932), which significantly opens with a largely female environment under the auspices of an aunt who read sentimental novels which fuelled impossible expectations of life, charts the heroine's growing disenchantment with this world of make-believe. As more male figures are introduced, Clotis juxtaposes the romantic ideal with a bleak picture of heterosexual relationships which are characterized by lovelessness, adultery, deceit, exploitation, sexual harassment and prostitution. Her earlier work *Le Vannier* (1946 posth.) similarly details the impact of a male outsider on a small, close-knit, rural community. Valbruge's arrival, which initially inspires no less than six amorous liaisons, succeeds ultimately in releasing a spirit of wanton cruelty, supreme hedonism, licentiousness and rivalry which finally climax in patricide. This same examination and exposure of the fraudulent promise of happiness in romantic relationships equally dominates Irène Némirovsky's eclectic corpus. Her earliest novel, *Le Malentendu* (1926), attacks the genre's salient conventions, and *Deux* (1939), an extrapolated rewriting of this earlier work, criticizes the romance's optimism, replacing the exalted state of unity, harmony and fecundity with alienation, suffering and death. Wedlock in *La Comédie bourgeoise* (1932), *Le Pion sur l'échiquier* (1934), *Films parlés* (1934), *Les Biens de ce monde* (1947 posth.) and most obviously *David Golder* (1929) is shown to be a social institution constructed entirely on inauthentic values. Romantic love, particularly in *Film parlé* (1931) (which focuses on prostitution) and *La Proie* (1938), is shown to be a type of suppression, possession, dominance and cruelty.

However, it is not only in realist fiction that a dissatisfaction with the romantic credo is espoused. What is perhaps more absorbing is that certain writers of the romance themselves acknowledge and protest against the limits of male-centred roles, and show an interest in female emancipation. As has been demonstrated in the preceding chapter, although many Inter-war romantic writers strove to embody some of the more liberating aspects of feminist ideology in their work, their success was somewhat limited, as the genre proved too resilient to lend itself readily to subversion. Be that as it may, a number of the more daring authors discovered that the same did not hold true for appropriation and adaption; so rather than reject the romance outright, they chose instead to work within it. In the early part of the century, a range of what might be termed 'revised romances' emerged. These works share with their more conservative prototypes a dominant sentimental interest and an array of the more salient formulaic characteristics, yet, in their specific configuration of the problematic relationship between the sexes, they provide innovative alterations and amendments. Their principal focus lies in reformulating and restructuring the standard romantic relationship and the corresponding balance of power, questioning the fundamental premise of inevitable female dependence and subservience. In so doing, they aim to offer new perspectives of the female condition, new liberating definitions of womanhood. Two revisionary reversals are of particular note: sexual inversion and gendered role swapping.

From 1897 and the discovery of important papyrus fragments of Sappho's poetry in Egypt,[3] to the late 1930s' exodus from Paris of the American Lost Generation, a significant number of women writers saw in this revived Hellenic figure a model for their own life and literature. They not only embraced Sappho's vivid passionate poetic language, but also her intensely ardent love of nature and her equally fervent, if more conspicuous, love of womankind. With the emergence of Benstock's in-depth, exhaustive study of women writers of the Left Bank, certain misconceptions concerning this sapphic movement have been redressed, the chief of which was the tacit assumption that there existed a homogeneous 'bond of sisterhood among lesbians of the Paris community that transcended all other differences'.[4] From Benstock's analysis it is evident that there was a profound schism in sapphism in the early part of the century, and that there in fact coexisted two quite distinct and conflicting movements. The first of these, which saw its apotheosis in the Belle Epoque period, encompassed Liane de Pougy, Colette and Anna de Noailles, as well as many expatriate writers and socialites such as Nathalie Barney, Renée Vivien, Eva Palmer, Sylvia Beach, Adrienne Saint-Agen and Alice B. Toklas, who elected to see their self-imposed exile as a declaration of emancipation and a celebration of alterity. The second faction comprised the circle of writers who joined Barney's 'Académie des Femmes' (founded in 1927), including Lucie Delarue-Mardrus, Elisabeth de Gramont, Jeanne Galzy, Romaine Brooks, Janet Flanner, Dolly Wilde, Radclyffe Hall, Una Troubridge, Janine Lahovary, Hilda Doolittle and Margaret Anderson.[5]

The principal literary manifestation of this division lay in their divergent treatment of romantic love. The Belle Epoque sapphists sought an alternative literary tradition for their sexual orientation outside the patriarchal order, and certain writers such as Renée Vivien, in her use of first-person plural female pronouns, ostensibly addressed and privileged an elite female readership. They disregarded hetero-sexual paradigms, exalted and glorified female sexuality, and celebrated the unique pleasures of reciprocated love between ultra-feminine women, stressing similarity and synthesis. The relationship between the female protagonists generally revolved around a young girl's desire for and need of an older, more experienced woman, and often emu-lated the model of mother–daughter love, with lesbian rapports being enacted in a distinctively female environment: Colette's *Claudine à l'école*, Myriam Harry's *Siona chez les barbares* and Audoux's *Marie Claire*, for example, are given the popular setting of a single-sex school; Audoux's sequel *L'Atelier de Marie Claire* takes place in a dressmaker's workshop; while Lucie Clairin's somewhat prurient depiction of the lifestyle of Parisian mannequins is staged, like many of Jean Rhys's short stories, in the female dressing rooms of *haute couture* fashion houses. In each case there is a sense of a special maternal world, at once comforting and reassuring, enabling and liberating. Belle Epoque sapphic novels, despite their preoccupation with sentimental love, bear little resemblance to the popular romance. Unlike this genre, they do not focus on courtship leading to union, but give a wider depiction of a woman's voyage of self-discovery, from childhood, through adolescence, to adulthood and maturity. Again, Siona, Claudine and Marie-Claire, whose fictional life-stories cover several volumes, are fairly typical examples. Most importantly, in such novels, male figures play a very minor role, and are, by and large, displaced, de-centred or confined to the wings. This became a trademark of much early twentieth-century sapphic romantic fiction.

In complete contrast, the second group of writers, active mainly in the Inter-war era, wholeheartedly rejected this utopic segregated vision of sapphism, and chose to examine lesbian relationships within a wider context.[6] To do so, they adopted the popular romance and employed it, in a striking fashion, as a vehicle to depict homosexual love. Jeanne Galzy, whose eclectic corpus spans the period 1917–76, provides a classic illustration of this new development. Her con-struction of lesbian relationships deliberately seeks to undercut the Belle Epoque notion of an ideal perfect love characterized by freedom, joy, support and fulfilment. In *Jeune Filles en serre chaude* (1934) Galzy denounces the inappropriate nature of symbiotic maternal love as a model for lesbianism, and refuses to validate the ideal Belle Epoque image of the nurturing, protective, separatist all-female environment, beyond the jurisdiction of the patriarchal world. The typical Belle Epoque Dionysian setting of the protective enclave of an all-girls' boarding school, here the famous Ecole de Sèvres, the hothouse of the title, serves as a backdrop to the relationship between Isabelle

Rives and her English teacher Miss Gladys Benz.[7] The latter is introduced as a mentor, a watchful mother-figure, who will guide the innocent girl through the complications of adolescent life to the joys of sapphism. However, their relationship is fraught with tensions, jealousies, inequalities and duplicitous lies. These climax in Gladys's ultimate betrayal, which in turn results in Isabelle's nervous breakdown and permanent emotional scarring. Jeanne Galzy rejects the Belle Epoque model of ideal sapphic love, and depicts, instead, inversion as a sort of mimicry of a masculine–feminine axis. While Galzy does not depict physically virilized heroines, while she does not explore the sexual ambiguity of a woman in male attire seducing another woman, her novels do clearly replicate heterosexual patterns of dominance and submission within the homosexual couple.

First, the sapphic passion between Gladys and Isabelle, unlike the gift economy of Belle Epoque love, or its more recent equivalent in Violette Leduc's *Thérèse et Isabelle* (1966), is based on the paradigm of heterosexual love as violent and penetrative. This is signalled to the reader through metonymic codification when, early in the work, Gladys squeezes Isabelle's shoulder, bruising her. Isabelle's stifled cry of pain and pleasure is suggestive of lost virginity, and the blood-red mark acts as a symbol of possession. The young girl, initiated into new adult pleasures, is at first overcome with the effect of this physical contact, then delighted with her nascent sexuality, until gradually she becomes a more responsive, willing accomplice. Soon it is she who plays the dominant part and her imagination allows a symbolic penetration of her mentor Miss Benz. She visualizes herself moving along the corridor to find the teacher's private bedroom:

> She was down there, in the east part of the house, following the corridor to the bedrooms, looking for the unknown door. Probably at the far end of the corridor. In her thoughts she entered the obscure, unknown room.

> Elle était, là-bas, en train de suivre le couloir des chambres, dans la partie de l'est, de chercher la porte inconnue. Tout au bout du couloir sans doute. Elle entrait en pensée, dans la chambre ignorée. (p. 96)

This imaginary encroachment on Gladys's personal realm, with the metaphorical crossing of the unknown threshold, recalls an earlier scene when Isabelle is overcome by the invasive effects of Gladys's heady perfume, only now the balance of power is overturned. Isabelle casts off the role of protégé and usurps her schoolmistress's position of dominance. From this point forward, it is now Isabelle who attempts to control the other characters. This culminates in Isabelle breaking into Gladys's room uninvited. In a scene which mimics brutal sexual penetration, even rape, Isabelle leaves her mark, reminiscent of the earlier bruise, as she tears Gladys's dress to shreds. The use of pronouns in 'she wanted to tear it/her to pieces, to destroy it/her', 'elle voulait la déchirer, la détruire', the repetition of these verbs, and the personification of the dress: 'and the lacerated dress hung in her hand as if it had been murdered with violent blows', 'et la robe lacérée pendit dans sa main, comme assassinée de coups furieux' (pp. 267–72), stress the brutal, invasive, injurious nature of Isabelle's action.

Secondly, Jeanne Galzy superimposes heterosexual patterns on the homosexual couple through a series of substitutions. *Jeunes Filles en serre chaude* is structured around a love triangle. The third protagonist, the hero Marien, is repeatedly described as being womanly, and it is his femininity, much in evidence in his relationship with the sapphic lovers, which permits Isabelle to achieve full penetrative sexual union with Miss Benz. Isabelle imagines Marien having intercourse with Gladys; she fuses his image with her own, supplanting him in her fictitious phantasmal world; and in this way consummates her own relationship with Gladys:

Had she created a sort of chain between them the day when she had imagined him leaning over Miss Benz? Had he felt from afar that she had substituted her self, her real self, for this image of him leaning over Gladys which she had created? Was he instinctively attracted by it or made jealous? Had he felt this substitution of which he knew nothing?

Le jour où elle l'avait imaginé penché sur Miss Benz avait-elle crée entre eux une sorte de chaîne? Avait-il senti de loin qu'elle s'était substituée, elle réelle, à cette image de lui qu'elle avait créée et penché sur Gladys? Etait-il instinctivement attiré ou jaloux? Avait-il senti cette substitution ignorée? (pp. 117–18).[8]

For Jeanne Galzy's heroine, full possession of Miss Benz requires the penetration of heterosexual love and Marien's physical presence is essential.[9]

The question arising from this is what are the achievements and limitations of such sapphic romances? On the most general level, the revival of Sappho meant that a female literary and historical tradition could be founded outside patriarchal canonical constructs, because, as Benstock claims, an appreciation of pre-Christian Greek culture provided an alternative to the heterosexual imperatives of modern Western civilization. Renée Vivien, for example, made painstaking efforts in her literary corpus to place Sappho in ancestral line with prominent fictional and factual figures as diverse as Lilith, Eve, Cassiopeia, Aphrodite, Bathsheba, Cleopatra and Lady Jane Grey. Sapphism also allowed a reappraisal of patriarchal representations of womanhood. Inter-war lesbian literature successfully placed a question mark over the traditional depiction of the relationship between the sexes inherent in the romance. Writers such as Galzy helped revise the romance in their tacit refusal of the dominant cultural pattern of always defining a woman in relation to a man. In rejecting the male-centred relational role imposed by patriarchal society on women, these authors liberated their fictional heroines, unfettering them from externally imposed prescriptive definitions as subservient lover, ancillary wife or self-effacing mother. Moreover, sapphic romantic fiction in the displacement of the hero, or his replacement with a 'female hero', provided a positive valorization of female bonding and solidarity, held out the promise of symbiotic female nurturance, promoted female autonomy, and championed the firm opinion that women were as competent as men to play a dominant, vital role in both the personal and the public spheres.

Contemporary male critics interpreted such sapphic romances as threatening, as jeopardizing patriarchal power structures. Most popular romantic fiction, it had been universally assumed, posed no threat to the prevailing political climate. With its reactionary utopic promise of marriage and fecundity, it was seen to uphold the values of hetero-sexual love, and correspondingly to support the societal status quo based on these values. Sapphic fiction, however, which eulogizes romantic love but which contravenes the standard male–female relationship at the heart of most romantic works, was seen to attack not just the institution of wedlock, but the more general socio-cultural framework to which it belongs. Ever-increasing demands for female-authored romantic fiction evidently gave certain critics cause for additional concern. Assuming that the romance had an exclusively female readership, and convinced of its didactic purpose, critics such as Flat and Bertaut express fears of a general indoctrination of young women to immoral, anti-social and politically radical codes of behav-iour. They explicitly attribute the rise of both sapphism and feminism to the catalytic effects of improved educational opportunities for women. Such interpretations are by no means new and have a lengthy historical precedent. Beizer talks of a 'time-honored theological pre-cept that equates ignorance and innocence, book knowledge and carnal knowledge', which has become 'meshed with the fabric of societal mores', citing as examples of this phenomenon the eighteenth-century *querelle du roman*, Rousseau's prefatory pronouncement in *Julie ou la Nouvelle Héloïse* (1761) that 'no chaste girl has ever read a novel' and Sylvain Maréchal's *Projet d'une loi portant défense à lire aux femmes* (1801), re-edited as *Il ne faut pas que les femmes sachent lire* (1853). In the early twentieth century the fear of literate women continues and is compounded by the growth of sapphic writing.

A fairly typical attack on the literary embodiment of female homo-sexuality came from Maurras in 'Le Romantisme féminin', one of a series of right-wing, anti-democratic, traditionalist essays in *L'Avenir de l'intelligence* (1905), which examined the troubled relationship between culture and politics in the modern world.[10] In this treatise Maurras initially focuses on the poetic works of four prominent contemporary authors – Renée Vivien, Gérard d'Houville, Lucie Delarue-Mardrus and Anna de Noailles. In the fifth and final chapter, by extrapolating his interpretation of their sapphic tendencies, and current trends in female literary production in general, Maurras fore-casts the nature and dimensions of the imminent 'lesbian risk':

> It is nonetheless true that a city of women is in the process of organizing itself, a secret little world where man only appears as an intruder, a monster, a lecherous and comical toy, where it is a disaster, a scandal that a young girl should think of becoming engaged, where the announcement of a marriage resembles a funeral, where a bond between a woman and a man is considered the most degrading misalliance. Under the pallid Phoebe which illuminates this land, girls and women are sufficient unto themselves and arrange all romantic matters on their own.[11]

With its outlandish theory of conspiracy, its deformed caricature of the lesbian, its ludicrous characterization of the hero, its hyperbolic examples and its governing ironic tone, the passage is at once mocking and alarmist. For Maurras, the central problem lay in his belief that the sapphic writer loved to 'copy man, play the man, become a little man herself'. In short she aimed to replace the men she imitated. This equalled a deliberate style of male-centred inverse misogyny, and was tantamount to a direct challenge to the hegemony of male power in both the literary and social domains.[12]

Despite the alarmist nature of Maurras's prophetic, vitriolic attack, the threat posed by sapphic romantic fiction to the patriarchy's status quo was, in effect if not in theory, limited in several fundamental ways. The most obvious problem with the conception of the 'sapphic hero' was that this image of women had already been employed by men in the realms of art and literature throughout the previous century, and that male configurations of womanhood pre-emptively defused both Belle Epoque and Inter-war constructions of the lesbian. According to detailed research conducted by Dijkstra, in the early nineteenth century educators 'posited the existence of close friendships among women as one of the principal sources of the development of humane sentiment in society'. By the 1860s and 1870s sexologists were redefining female sexuality in relation to autoerotic desire, of which lesbianism was considered a natural extension. This change was reflected in the visual arts where the popular mid-century image of what Dijkstra terms the 'household nun' was on the wane, replaced initially by a host of images of women kissing their mirrored reflections. This solipsistic, narcissistic interpretation of lesbianism posed little threat to male writers and artists depicting or viewing it. Rather, woman's ability to satisfy her own sexual needs freed man from certain obligations, certain onerous responsibilities 'allowing him once more to enter into voyeuristic, passive erotic titillation within a soothing, undemanding context conducive to a state of restful detumescence'.[13]

Sapphic literature of the Belle Epoque was read through the standard tropes of nineteenth-century depictions of the androgyne and the lesbian. So, in Maurras's work for example, Renée Vivien and Lucie Delarue-Mardrus are envisioned as young girls who prefer childish pleasure to reasoned thought; the universe they inhabit and depict, 'like the cradle', reflects their nurturing maternal instinct, their love of nature; all four writers are shown to embody the female virtues of 'resignation, gentleness, patience' as pronounced by Michelet; while both Renée Vivien and Anna de Noailles's heroine Sabine of *La Nouvelle Espérance* are portrayed as Narcissus gazing in a mirror. Maurras imposes on these intelligent, sophisticated, cosmopolitan women writers a whole gamut of the previous generation's concepts of the ideal woman as childlike, confined to the private realm of home and garden (i.e. interior and inferior), submissive to the men against whom she is defined and, most importantly, obsessed with egocentric love.[14] For Maurras, in devotedly, passively looking inwards, the woman writer is oblivious to the external patriarchal world of oppression. She has no need to rebel. It is this notion of sapphism, as a solipsistic extension of self-love, of narcissism, which renders it altogether inoffensive.

Inter-war images of the male-styled lesbian were similarly deflated.[15] From the 1880s onwards, painters such as Egon Schiele, Pierre-Georges Jeanniot, Louis Schryver, Eliseu Visconti, Picasso and Edmond Aman-Jean became more sexually explicit in their depiction of lesbian scenes and by the Fin de Siècle, when sapphic poetry was revived, this sexual preference came to be seen in quite a different light, as a transgression of the natural order, and a threat to male power. Women who relinquished their self-sacrificial male-centred relational roles were condemned as guilty not just of vanity and self-absorption but of wilfully destroying the masculine ego. At the turn of the century, this self-reflexive love became the evidence of women's enmity towards men and their intent to usurp the male role and threaten patriarchal order. So, in an attempt to minimize women's encroachment into what was considered the jeopardized realm of male supremacy, male writers and artists parodied the image of the viraginous lesbian, describing her part in the perpetual battle of the sexes, through a range of images – the wild animal, the sphinx and the ever-popular Amazonian warrior. Sapphic authors had to compete with the all too memorable, inaccurate, reductive, unfavourable and offensive representations of the lesbian as a stimulus for male voyeuristic titillation, an exaggerated incongruous comic figure, and an object of derision or censure. These rival male-authored interpretations of female homosexuality pre-emptively undercut the sapphists' attempted reformulation of the romance and its construction of the relationship between the sexes.

This was not by any means the only difficulty faced by Inter-war sapphist writers. While Miles argues that 'lesbianism is almost invariably feminist in its application if not in its original orientation' because 'the lesbian is gifted with a *uniquely* liberating, *single* vantage point, from which to criticise and analyse the politics, culture, and language of patriarchy' (my italics) her case is flawed.[16] Contrary to Miles's claim, sapphic writers did not assume a 'single' position; their literature, like their homosexual lifestyles, was far from homogeneous. Not only were there major discrepancies in sapphic works of the Belle Epoque and 1920s, as already indicated, but French homosexual women writers, unlike Gertrude Stein and her Lost Generation united under the banner of Modernism, did not adhere to any single literary school. Inter-war French sapphists, unlike their predecessors, did not assume a 'unique' position from which to evaluate both the personal and public self, but rather duplicated heterosexual patterns, with all their implications of duality, inferiority and otherness. Sapphism's links with feminism are also much less clear-cut than Miles suggests. Belle Epoque lesbianism, with its retreat to a uniquely female environment, does not address the specific problematic issues of patriarchal power; while Inter-war sapphism, in its duplication of power relations, seems to compound the problem rather than offer a real revision of the patterns of heterosexual romantic love.[17]

While sapphic writers' modification of the romance proved somewhat ineffective, because of their reinforcement of the genre's heterosexual pattern, many women authors working precisely within this heterosexual frame of reference had a greater degree of success. By self-consciously examining the romance's traditional formulation of the ideal couple, and by altering the male-biased balance of power within that relationship, these writers made a more consequential contribution to the genre's revision. Already in the nineteenth century, with the improved condition of literary markets and the dramatic rise in the number of professional female writers, women's preoccupation with gender reversal was becoming increasingly patent. It was apparent in their escalating use of asexual or male pseudonyms, and in their fictional works, where female protagonists assumed positions of power through the adoption of male names and, more importantly, stereotypical characteristics. By the Belle Epoque and Inter-war era, virilized heroines proliferated in number as never before. Particularly memorable examples of this phenomenon might include Gyp's assertive, self-assured Chiffon; Renée Dunan's sexually demanding, audacious Mademoiselle Louise de B.; Daniel Lesueur's Nietzschean superwoman Joselyne; Marcelle Tinayre's intractable heroines Josanne of *La Rebelle* and Hellé; and a number of assertive female characters from the extensive works of Colette.[18]

The corollary of the virilized heroine, the effeminate hero, also became a customary figure in romantic novels of the 1920s and 1930s. Colette, for example, in this era gives equal weighting to both male and female protagonists, and her heroines' acquisition of masculine attributes is almost always at the expense of the heroes, who are emasculated in inverse proportion. This balanced symmetrical reversal of characteristics is most manifest when her heroines, contrary to romantic conventions, willingly take the sexual initiative. When in *La Chatte* (1933) Camille (whose ungendered Christian name alludes to her transgression of feminine norms) commands Alain on their wedding night, he finds her mastery and insouciance a source of discomfort and embarrassment. The eponymous hero in *Chéri* (1920) feels prudish and insecure with his more mature lover, Léa. Similarly, when Camille Dalleray first seduces Phil in *Le Blé en herbe* (1922), she engineers and controls the situation, while he is 'paralysed by one of his feminine crises', 'paralysé par une de ses crises de féminité' (p. 315). Following his first night of love at Ker-Anna, as he looks at his mirrored reflection expecting some visual evidence of his having crossed the threshold into adult manhood, he is confronted with a face 'less like that of a man than of a young bruised girl', 'moins pareil à ceux d'un homme, qu'à ceux d'une jeune fille meurtrie (p. 337). The author explicitly reduces Phil to an infantile dependent status and quite pointedly offers a contrast in his sweetheart Vinca, who remains relatively unaffected when her virginity is surrendered. Colette's characters are held in a dynamic equilibrium; despite the fact that their personality traits are diametrically opposed and inverted, their relationship still offers a harmonious, balanced picture.[19]

Not so the work of several less conventional Inter-war writers, such as Lucie Delarue-Mardrus. Her depiction of amorous relationships is deliberately one-sided. In what appears to be an attempt to redress the long-standing inequality between the sexes, she tilts the balance of power in favour of women, in her recurrent depiction of gendered role reversals. *L'Ex-voto* (1922), considered Delarue-Mardrus's most popular novel, shows the autonomous, assertive heroine, Ludivine, deriving considerable personal pleasure from inverting traditional power structures and enforcing her will on the hero, Delphin, whom she sees as 'her defenceless prey, her plenary possession', 'sa proie sans défense, sa possession plénière' (p. 168). Unlike Colette's male protagonists, he is not innately weak, feminine or androgynous. Rather, as an orphan living in Ludivine's home, he is both emotionally and financially dependent on her, thus subject to her control. Delarue-Mardrus justifies Ludivine's ascendency over Delphin in several ways. Her dominance directly echoes and inverts her parents' relationship: her mother is subject to habitual male violence from her irresponsible, drunken, penniless husband, and is portrayed as being pitifully bruised, bent and dejected. Ludivine's simulated masculinity results in her assumption of the traditional function of breadwinner for her destitute family, and this is clearly praiseworthy. Additionally, at the beginning of the novel, Delarue-Mardrus explicitly sanctions role reversal on the grounds that in Normandy working-class women are often forced by circumstance to play a more dominant role in the domestic and public spheres: 'women hereabouts very often have the souls of leaders', 'les femmes, chez nous, ont très souvent les âmes de chefs' (p. 7).

In Delarue-Mardrus's later works the hero is diminished and emasculated to an even greater extent. The three male characters of *L'Amour à la mer* (1931), part of Lemerre's 'Les Amours tragiques' (Tragic Loves) series, are all defined purely through their relationship to the heroine Clémence. As she becomes increasingly vengeful, insensitive and brutalized, that is, as she develops what Delarue-Mardrus considers typical male flaws, the men in her life are given a diminished subordinate role. Her husband, whom she repeatedly cuckolds, is powerless. The first subject of Clémence's adulterous passion, the swarthy Marie-Pierre, is increasingly referred to by the single female name Marie. The second lover, of whom Delarue-Mardrus writes 'she was the man, and he was the young girl who totally surrendered herself to him on a whim', 'elle était l'homme, lui la jeune fille qu'un coup de folie lui livre sans défense' (p. 92), is clearly cast as the innocent virgin the heroine will deflower and possess. At the end of the novel only the ascendent Clémence survives: her husband is brutally murdered by her first lover, who himself dies of sorrow, while her young gigolo flees in fright to the realm of oblivion.

Given the biased partial nature of Delarue-Mardrus's construction of gender, one might ask to what extent such depictions of virilized heroines and emasculated heroes succeed in reshaping the romance's construction of the relationship between the sexes? In theory, role reversal may have several positive effects: it may result in the establishment of powerful images of dynamic vigorous women, it may serve the polemic purpose of highlighting the nature of stereotypes, and it may consequently challenge women's inferior literary and social standing. In practice, however, gendered role reversal is in itself insufficient to suggest any radical revision of either the romance or its portrayal of womanhood; as Lefanu notes, 'role reversal stories, despite, in many cases, a progressive if not a feminist aim, tend to corroborate gender differentiation'.[20] The very concept of swapping gendered power positions requires the differentiated oppositional positions to remain intact; thus the existence of a division in the site of power in male-dominated society is not contested or challenged in and for itself. Binary logic remains in place and the phallocentric power base is not threatened. Cranny-Francis also argues that such literary role reversals often amount to little more than an 'effective apology for patriarchy', as 'attempts to construct a female hero based on simple substitution fail badly. A female hero who is as bloodthirsty (i.e. brave) and manipulative (i.e. clever) as her male counterpart does nothing to redefine that characterization and the ideology it naturalizes; she may even reinforce it by lending it a new legitimacy.'[21] The emphasis on sadistic sexuality, on power struggle, as seen in Delarue-Mardrus's fiction, actually perpetuates the restrictive positions of master and servant. Irrespective of the inverted nature of the sexual inscription of these roles, they still do little more than duplicate reductive configurations of inequality and altereity.

Furthermore, as with the image of the sapphic hero, Inter-war attempts at revisionary role reversal also are impeded by the fact that this literary strategy is not new, but has a lengthy precedent. Praz records that it is commonplace in nineteenth-century literature to find women defying societal mores in the adoption of male attire and in their infiltration of the public realm designated as a male domain.[22] It would have been virtually impossible for women writers in the Inter-war era to appropriate role reversal without their readers recalling the misogyny of the Decadents' model. Although the Decadent movement reached its peak in the Fin de Siècle, the sustained production of Decadent works throughout the early twentieth century continued to fire the popular imagination with their perpetuation of an arresting representation of the relationship between the sexes. For the Decadents, the model heroine was the gynander, defined by Dijkstra as the 'woman who strives for male characteristics, the sexual usurper', 'the destroyer of souls', 'a creature with near magical power of seduction', 'the forager into the realm of the male soul'. Their archetypal hero was a degenerate consort who 'chose to wallow in agonized masochistic submission to the "unnatural acts" of the gynander in order to demonstrate [his] self-sacrificial virtue in the cause of masculine evolution'.[23] Undoubtedly, many women writing in the aftermath of this movement, who wished to depict powerful autonomous heroines, through the attribution of stereotypical male attributes, faced a considerable predicament: despite the marked difference with the Decadents in terms of their intentions, the effects they achieved often proved indistinguishable.

The reception of works by Rachilde serves as a good illustration of the plethora of rival interpretations engendered by this situation. Rachilde began her writing career in the heyday of the Decadents and produced on average one work per year from 1881 (*Les Femmes du 199e Périgueux*) to 1947 (*Quand j'étais jeune*). Her interest in the exaggerated polarity and reversal of sexual positions is evident in the very titles of several of her works, titles such as *La Marquise de Sade* (1887), *Madame Adonis* (1888), *Monsieur Vénus* (1884) and *La Femme-Dieu* (1934). Of these it is *Monsieur Vénus* which secured Rachilde's reputation and which, as a result, attracts most interest from critics desirous to classify and reclaim the novel as either Decadent or feminist. *Monsieur Vénus* tells a tale of female dominance. The aristocratic gynandrous heroine, Raoule de Vénérande, takes an unknown, untalented artist, Jacques Silvert, as a lover. She instals him in a studio apartment where he is kept as an inamorato to satisfy her sexual demands. Towards the end of the novel, in accordance with the romance's formula, he becomes her husband. The plot moves further into the realm of the bizarre when, following a series of melodramatic scenes of blackmail, prostitution and mistaken identity, Jacques is killed in a duel at the hand of his rival Raittolbe, and his dead body is preserved by Raoule, who becomes a reclusive necrophile. Role reversal is evident throughout the novel in the lovers' personality traits, their professions, financial conditions and social status, not to mention their enthusiastic experimentation with cross-dressing. Most importantly, it is manifested in the way they employ language. By chapter three the protagonists have swapped inflected nouns, personal pronouns and adjectives, in such a way that gendered elements of linguistic codes are inverted to reflect the characters' inversion of social and sexual roles.

Explanations of these transpositions vary tremendously. Simone de Beauvoir argues that any young girl whose sexual initiation is moulded on the pattern set by Raoule is demonstrating neither an innate superiority nor a dissatisfaction with the balance of power between the sexes. According to Beauvoir, the opposite is in fact the case: her attitude – 'she only becomes attached to men who can be treated as women' – marks a retreat akin to lesbianism, and is the direct result of her fear of the potent adult male.[24] Frappier-Mazur, although considering the novel from a similar theoretical standpoint, offers a quite antithetical interpretation of the *Monsieur Vénus* scenario. She sees Raoule as a feminist paradigm, and judges Rachilde's use of systematic role reversal to be a clever type of subversion, in which the novel 'can be read as an attempt to leave behind ordinary notions of bisexuality and as an experiment in the radical scrambling of definitions. Rachilde seems to adopt gender stereotypes unquestioningly only in order to demonstrate their absurdity.'[25] In complete contrast Dijkstra, placing Rachilde in relation to the Decadents, argues that *Monsieur Vénus* offers no serious revision of the movement's depiction of womanhood: 'Its role reversal theme was not meant as a serious critique of the state of nineteenth-century male–female relationships. Instead, the narrative is an early example of the unthreatening reversal games which, during the past century, and especially among the French intelligentsia, have too often taken the place of serious social criticism.'[26] Indeed, according to Dijkstra's definitions, Raoule and Jacques are full-blooded examples of the Decadents' model protagonists, the dominant independent woman and the impotent masochistic male. Birkett's analysis of Rachilde's fiction, again seeing it in its historical context, confirms this viewpoint, for even when women like Raoule apparently play the more dominant role, they continue to be victims 'by signalling their connivance with their executioners'.[27] Rachilde, according to both Birkett and Dijkstra, like her heroines, far from challenging Decadent models, colludes with them. Whichever reading (lesbian, feminist or Decadent) is more accurate in terms of Rachilde's intentions, it is impossible to decide from the text itself. This ambiguity of interpretation haunts Inter-war female-authored works such as those by Delarue-Mardrus.

However, role reversal, despite such seemingly intractable difficulties, need not necessarily be a completely redundant method for highlighting, undermining and invalidating the stereotypical image of women as inferior other, promulgated in romantic fiction. Indeed, under certain circumstances, when combined with other strategies, it may prove effective. The most recent re-reading of *Monsieur Vénus*, Beizer's *Ventriloquized Bodies: Narratives of Hysteria in Nineteenth-century France*, while acknowledging these inherent interpretational ambiguities, does also suggest a new approach. Beizer draws attention to Rachilde's use of 'extra and intratextual destabilizing contexts'. The first of these involves the novel's dialogic and deconstructive relationship with Barrès's preface of 1889, which foregrounds the norms of contemporary reading practices. The second, more striking technique is Rachilde's use of italics in her novel. Beizer argues that these pervasive textual markers, whose status varies over the course of the novel, not only call into question the linguistic codes or conventions that assign gender, but also highlight the fact that the novel works chiefly through citation. She shows that some of the italicized quotations are attributed, while others represent an 'anonymous pool of social discourse', and she convincingly suggests that the entire novel, through this process, becomes a caricature of Fin de Siècle stereotypes. The ubiquitous parodic nature of much of the novel's topoi, then, serves to denaturalize common concepts of gender. Reversal, when used as one of many ironizing strategies, and when 'subordinate to the regime of repetition', can have a destabilizing effect on the reader.[28]

We see a similar situation in the early fictional works of Louise de Vilmorin.[29] Explicitly working within the confines of romantic fiction, she too foregrounds the issues of generic convention and reading practices, and in so doing offers a radical metamorphosis of the romance and its standard depiction of the relationship between the sexes. Literary histories do Louise de Vilmorin little justice. Canon compilers, noting her interest in love and fantasy, dismiss her corpus and disregard the original contribution she makes to the revision of the romance. According to the influential literary historian Peyre, for example, she is an author who 'lays no claim to importance as a novelist or to a revolution in the traditional picture of the second sex'![30] Louise de Vilmorin's first two works in prose, *Sainte-Unefois* (1934) and *La Fin des Villavide* (1937), appear to contradict such an interpretation. Far from confirming the genre's dominant conservative ideology, they serve as a radical critique of it. Both novels, through a series of highly self-conscious, technically innovative, daring inversions, have more far-reaching consequences than the varied reversals employed by the majority of her peers in their reworking of the romance and its portrayal of womanhood.

The most extraordinary trait of Vilmorin's fiction is the extent to which it inverts the nature of romance reading practices. While the popular romantic genre is chiefly renowned for its transparency, Vilmorin's novels, in complete contrast, prove intellectually demanding.

In *Sainte-Unefois* the reader is alerted to the vital interpretative role to be played when the heroine asks 'what can you do with my thousand reflections, my thousand bodies, my thousand words?', 'que faites-vous de mes mille reflets, de mes mille corps, de mes mille mots?' (p. 130). Similarly, early in *La Fin des Villavide* the reader is forewarned of its unorthodox nature through a discussion of a scholarly work owned by the hero's father entitled: '*How to Unlearn to Read in Thirty Volumes*, which scholars from many far off lands travelled miles to consult', '*Méthode pour désapprendre à lire en trente volumes*, que des savants de tous les pays venaient de loin en loin consulter' (*sic*) (pp. 15–16). This not only prepares the reader for the major comic inversions to come, it suggests that Vilmorin's novel, like this supposedly celebrated tome, will act as a catalyst to a destabilizing 'unlearning' operation. In both *La Fin des Villavide* and *Sainte-Unefois* the reading process is highlighted and made deliberately complicated, at times impossible.

While no single generic classification can be exclusively imposed on *Sainte-Unefois* or *La Fin des Villavide*, a problem with which many literary historians have tussled – both are works of extreme elasticity, capable of stretching to envelop a variety of different literary genres – it is unquestionably romance which dominates.[31] In *Sainte-Unefois*, the heroine Grace is a budding romantic novelist. Her study is consecrated to love: its decor contains all the clichéd trappings of the romantic scene, with its frivolous ribbons, silver candelabra, its exotic dried palms and Scottish shawl (recalling the great Romantic writer Sir Walter Scott). A second central narrative strand revolves around Grace's own troubled courtship, which strongly resembles the type of fiction she is trying to invent. The plot is starred with customary love tokens, misunderstandings, jealousies and manifold amorous events. In places the excessively hyperbolic outpourings echo the traditional German Romantic taste for *Schwärmerei*. The characters are stereotypical, a point stressed when they are likened to Romeo and Juliet through allusions to an ill-fated family feud which separates the lovers, a balcony scene in which the hero Milrid suggests an elopement, and the reference to Juliet's lines on Romeo's name in the Shakespearean tragedy. The comic exaggeration is so omnipresent that it soon becomes clear to the reader that *Sainte-Unefois* is no ordinary romance. However, the full extent to which the novel should be read as a parody of the romance is left deliberately enigmatic until the denouement. This ambiguity of intention is intensified by Vilmorin's elliptic style, for the novel is infused with a variety of salient characteristics of other fictional genres. There are, for example, assorted recounted tales, reflecting Vilmorin's interest in oral traditions and folklore, and most obviously diverse borrowings from the fairy tale. Not only does the title *Sainte-Unefois* bear a reference to the traditional opening lines 'Once upon a time' ('Il y avait une fois' or 'Il était une fois'), but Grace frequently adopts the persona of a fairy-tale princess. She surrounds her true identity in mystery hiding, like the Sleeping Beauty or Rapunzel, in an ivory tower where she dreams of the handsome modern-day prince (he does in fact appear and attempt to rescue her, but Grace announces that she prefers her solitude, which is figured as a means to self-knowledge and contentment). The related realm of escapist fantasy is also much in evidence, as is the world of the supernatural, evoked by references to dreams, apparitions, visions of angels and, of course, the fleeting presence of the 'Transparents' who regularly pass through Grace's home.

The principal function of this generic fusion is to draw the reader's attention to the romance's own literary conventions.[32] Indeed, throughout the novel, Vilmorin places a considerable emphasis on the construction of the narrative, hence the *mise-en-abyme* choice of a novelist for a heroine. This has a singular effect: certain fundamental features of the genre, those most taken for granted, are given a new prominence. They are then most wittily investigated, contorted or reversed. Particular scrutiny is given to the traditional use of a single, causal, linear narrative, meaningful symbols, the espousal of a certain code of values and a reliable narrator.

Sainte-Unefois is composed of multiple narrative strands, some of which are mutually contradictory, like the two versions of the family feud, which are explained in terms of Oedipal tensions, and conversely, as a somewhat bathetic squabble over stamps. No guidance concerning the status of these rival versions of events is given to the reader. At times information concerning the nature of the narratives, needed by the reader to enable the deciphering of fact from fiction, the unravelling of multiple interconnected layers of meaning, is withheld. Instead, most of the various threads – dreams, daydreams, escapist fantasies, narrated events, recounted tales, the thoughts of a madwoman, fantastic inventions such as the tale told to Milrid by a wasp – are equally weighted and frequently blurred. As a result, the novel resembles a frustrating jigsaw puzzle where many of the segments are ill-fitting, the key pieces are missing and where several parts disturbingly fit the same slot. Furthermore, logic is conspicuously flouted in the author's occasional undermining of causality and temporal continuity. Some events, for instance, seem governed by wish fulfilment: in the third chapter the heroine states a desire to be orphaned, in the following chapter her parents are said to have vanished and ultimately they are referred to as being dead. There are gaps in the narrative and chronological jumps. The logical conscious world seems to be supplanted by the impossibly complex realm of the mind with all its tricks and subterfuges. Working in parallel with this, the whole gamut of objects, images, symbols and leitmotifs which appear in *Sainte-Unefois*, from guns to ghosts, pebbles to birds, Russian boots to pink writing paper, prove no more helpful. Their description is tantalizingly enigmatic, particularly when the objects recur and are juxtaposed, and the reader's attempts to look behind them, perhaps to find some proleptic purpose, to establish links between them, to explain their significance, to understand their function, are systematically thwarted. These symbols beg interpretation but no logical explanation is possible. Unlike Surreal objects, whose bizarre, eccentric, miscellaneous quality they recall, they do not lead the reader beyond surface fact into a greater reality. They simply defy the attribution of meaning.

The reader, in an attempt to create order from disorder, to make sense of the novel's irregular pastiche texture looks to the text for guidance. A clue to Vilmorin's artistic strategy appears to be given in the scene in which Grace reorganizes the positions of the ancestral paintings. While to the uninitiated onlooker there is no semblance of order, a certain governing principle is still at work, although it is itself quite arbitrary: Grace uses as her governing criterion degrees of ugliness. Likewise, the messages from the Fiancé Espagnol, who transpires to be a tattered scarecrow, are given by a series of blinks, described by Grace as 'a silent language which only I understood', 'un language muet que j'étais seule à comprendre' (p. 42). This again suggests that behind the surface events of the romance, as in the major novels of Stendhal, there is a concealed but meaningful design, available to Vilmorin's 'Happy Few'. At the ball which ends the novel, the norms of social etiquette are uproariously reversed.[33] Uninvited guests are welcome; it is considered both mannerly and flattering to ask the hostess's age and comment on how worn her clothes are; female refinement is demonstrated by spitting food under the buffet; while gallant, genteel men in the company become breathless when dancing, perspire freely and refuse to remove their outdoor clothes. This direct reversal of values is reflected linguistically when compound words are inverted such that we have 'souris-chauve' (p. 115), and when mutually exclusive answers – 'Yes and no' – are given quite naturally. However, although in this example right reason is replaced by its antithesis wrong reason, this is far from systematic throughout the novel. The reader is deliberately confused as criteria, order and values change constantly, undercutting all possibility of readerly control.

The reading process in *Sainte-Unefois* is rendered more complex by the absence of a reliable single controlling perspective. The reader, schooled in romantic literature and a party to the heroine's thoughts, is encouraged to adopt her outlook, to read her life-story as the selvage, holding and binding together the other narrative threads. However, Grace's perspective, following the major preoccupation of Inter-war realist writers, is partial, subjective and inaccurate (science of the time proved that the act of observing altered the actual state of the object observed). She herself ironically comments that she is in search of a 'point of view', to control her ever-shifting and multiple perspectives, and Sylvio, in his rejection of Grace's version of events, noting her lack of lucidity and cogency, states that she is 'lacking in discernment, confusing love and fantasy','sans discernement, confondant l'amour avec sa fantaisie' (p. 31). Towards the end of the novel, Grace's own story is definitively debunked and the status of the whole novel is thrown into question when it becomes clear, firstly, that Sylvio, her source of inspiration, her motivation, is in fact nothing more than a figment of her own imagination; when, secondly, in chapter nine Grace states that the narration has no foundation in reality, but is simply a winter's dream; and thirdly, and most importantly, when it is revealed that she herself has been dead for some time. External events corroborate this: a Transparent claims she is one of them and her writing room is already covered in dust. The most disturbing aspect of this is that Grace has been recounting her life from this untenable position, which makes all of her comments, especially those referring to death such as 'moving when you are dead isn't fun, but what else can you do to come back to life', 'bouger quand on est mort n'est pas gai, mais que faire pour revivre' (p. 122), and 'I partly open my lips to reveal my pretty skeletal teeth, and that's a smile', 'j'entr'ouvre les lèvres sur mes jolies dents de squelette, on appelle ça sourire' (p. 133), completely paradoxical. These statements, in their very utterance, are invalidated. At the close of the novel the unsettled reader is aware that there is no single narrative, no definitive causal sequence and consequently no single site of knowledge. The posthumous publication of Vilmorin's *Carnet* (1970) – a gamut of disconnected maxims, autobiographical musings, reflections on the writing process and fragmented fictional passages, some of which concern the characters in *Saint-Unefois* – far from explaining or illuminating these difficulties, make them seem even more irresolvable.

To what purpose these inversions? As conventional romance structures are broken down the reader is forced to supply another organizing shape, becoming an active collaborator in writing the book, as is common practice in the twentieth century. Faced with a confused picture of the literal world, we are encouraged to investigate the freer metaphoric patterning in the novel, to perceive connections which the characters do not. When our interrogation of the novel's nexus of imagery proves no more fruitful, we are left with the implication that the world of objects and symbols does not give signification, meaning or permanence either. As all attempts to provide stability in inner and outer worlds, past and present, real and imaginary fail, as all attempts to supply meaning are invalidated, we are left to turn in upon ourselves. Vilmorin's irony, like that most notably employed by Swift and Céline, is far from stable. Initially the reader is encouraged as onlooker to construct a tacit pact of complicity with the ironic overviewer, in this case Grace. While the reader's stance is constantly challenged and unsettled as information is proffered but meaning and significance are constantly denied, our superior, omnipotent, voyeuristic position of stable irony is fully overturned at the end of the novel when Grace is shown to be a highly unreliable narrator. The reader, at this juncture, must relinquish control of the text and must adopt the position of least knowledge, that of the victim of Vilmorin's anarchic irony. When Grace's own situation and status as a female romance writer are undermined, the reader's corresponding position (as both romance reader and active contributor to the production of this particular romance text) becomes the true target of the irony. Consequently, we are coerced into analysing our own culturally imposed ideas. Our readerly expectations and assumptions are highlighted and challenged, and we are forced to re-evaluate and perhaps ultimately surrender some of our own preconceptions, primarily those concerning the twinned issues of the romantic genre's conventions and its representation of gender.

As important as Louise de Vilmorin's attack on genre is her attack on gender stereotypes, which again is executed through a series of destabilizing techniques. In *La Fin des Villavide,* the author, in an attempt to emphasize and repudiate inauthentic female roles and images, focuses on the most offensive, long-standing characteristics attributed to romantic heroines: passivity, or at its most extreme, inanimacy. The reduction of female characters to an object condition dates from the Middle Ages, when in the earliest romantic works the ethics of gallantry placed the heroine on a pedestal, giving her the semblance of pre-eminence while in reality setting her back in the realm of minors. From this period onwards many of the heroines in both realist and romantic novels have been described as static, fixed images (one need only think of the portrait of the Princesse de Clèves, the painting of Adolphe's lover Ellénore, the picture of Lucille

Bucolin). At no time is this objectification more pronounced than in the mid to late nineteenth and early twentieth centuries, when it proliferated in a variety of guises. Depersonalized women were familiar figures in bourgeois realist fiction, and this for reasons related more to the social and political environment of France than to literary precedent *per se*. Again it was the entrepreneurial atmosphere recorded by, if not engendered by, the Napoleonic Civil Code which was responsible, as Dijkstra notes: 'The notion of woman as man's personal property and the sweet dreams of servitude that notion implied were very pleasing to the middle-class male, with his well-developed acquisitive urge and its concomitant aggressive energies.'[34] Similarly in the world of art, at the close of the nineteenth century, the pre-Raphaelites, with their remodelling of chivalric themes, specifically recalled female objectification fashionable in medieval works. However, the most striking insistence on female anatomy and corresponding denial of female autonomy was launched by an Inter-war school: the Surrealists.

Whitney Chadwick, in an excellent study of female Surrealist art, indicates that while the Surrealists exalted *woman*, they did not equally revere *women*, and suggests that this ambivalence reached new heights in the 1930s. Writers and artists transformed woman into a Muse, a source of poetic stimulus for secret male fantasies and aspirations; they glorified the innocent *femme-enfant*, who in her purity could tap into her own unconscious, and thereby provide access to this realm for the male observer:

> Fuelling the male imagination by projecting it onto woman, Breton and Peret turn her into an abstract principle, a universal and an ideal. Passive and compliant, she waits for the world to be revealed to her. What they give us, finally, is not a role for woman independent of man, even as they acknowledge her power and her proximity to the sources of creativity, but a new image of the couple in which woman completes man, is brought to life by him, and, in turn, inspires him.

The Surrealists, in limiting the role of the female artist as a creator in her own right, sought to silence women and to objectify them through a Sadeian corporeal metamorphosis: 'their wombs and breasts tortured and destroyed, their bodies torn apart and re-created (. . .) the ravaged female, denied her normal sexual, emotional, and procreative functions, became the theoretical basis of the Surrealist object'.[35] This is evident in their actual depictions of women, which do not only replicate and perpetuate the Proudhonian myth of 'ménagère ou courtisane', 'housewife or harlot', as Suleiman correctly argues, but which effectively reduce women to a state of mute inanimacy.[36] Particularly commanding examples of this include René Magritte's decapitated women in *La Folie des grandeurs* (1961); the life-size plastic doll suspended from the ceiling of the Surrealists' meeting place in 1924, a doll which significantly had no arms or head, implying that women are incapable of worthwhile action such as writing or painting, or independent thought; Roland Penrose's *Portrait de Valentine* (1937), in which the eyes and mouth of his wife, the Surrealist author, are replaced by butterflies; and André Masson's *Girl in a Black Gag With a Pansy Mouth* (1938), a doll's head (who knows, perhaps that of the decapitated body in the Surrealist central meeting place!) which is caged and gagged with a *cache-sexe* to prevent freedom of movement or speech. As in the painting of Valentine Penrose, Masson's doll has inserted in her mouth a flower, which suggests that women are restricted to the world of nature, and that this silencing of women is natural.

As might be expected, the Surrealists' specific configuration of womanhood, together with the general increase in numbers of inanimate female characters in art and literature in this period, was found particularly distasteful by many feminists in the 1920s and 1930s, precisely because so many women were ardently, actively protesting, through their adoption of the latest fashions and through more overt political action, against the image of woman as a silent male appendage, against the specific configuration of woman as prize, prey or pretty-doll. So a number of female authors in the period played a significant part in wholeheartedly rejecting the credence given to the persistent ubiquitous reduction of woman to her biological, sexual or physical body. Writers such as Yver, Tinayre, Némirovsky, Vioux, Machard and Delarue-Mardrus endeavoured either to provide a mimetic representation of the way in which society and literature construct the image of the passive woman, or to record the specific nature of feminist opposition to this objectification, and in consequence, to reaffirm and re-establish female autonomy. Even Rachilde's work entered the debate, as *Monsieur Vénus*, in its extensive attack on cultural stereotypes, takes issue with this process of female-objectification. Jacques literally becomes an object at the end of the novel, when on his death he is transformed into a wax effigy to satisfy Raoule's sexual desire. Throughout the novel he has been linked to this notion of the silent site of representation. When he first appears in the novel, he is pictured in his sister's flower shop, garlanded with artificial roses, his shapely legs and fine ankles on display. In short, he is introduced with all the imagery associated with nineteenth-century painted ladies. He is even framed, like a real picture, by the doorway through which

Raoule and the reader gaze. A little later his body is described as a poem, then a palimpsest, a work of art and finally a masterpiece or *chef d'œuvre*. In this, Rachilde is clearly reversing aesthetic conventions.

More interesting still is the contribution made by Louise de Vilmorin to the debate, as her appropriation of artistic objectification directly challenges Surrealist practice. Vilmorin's connections with the Surrealist movement have all too often been misrepresented.[37] For certain critics, such as La Rochefoucauld and Lemaître, Vilmorin's use of fantasy, her vivid character sketches, bizarre juxtapositions, verbal acrobatics, light and lively irony, her violent disruption of the traditional relationship between words and meaning, and her manifest concern to reach beyond surface reality, all result in her work being 'very close to Surrealist games'.[38] Yet a closer analysis of Vilmorin's work, in particular her treatment of the object, reveals that despite surface similarities, the author, far from reinforcing Surrealist stereotypes, in fact actively seeks to reverse them, in much the same way as do several female Surrealists (such as Valentine Penrose, Frida Khalo, Leonora Carrington, Ithel Colquhoun and Rita Kernn-Larsen) from the 1930s onwards.

La Fin des Villavide constitutes Vilmorin's most effective attack on the objectification of women. Its foregrounded action is fairly typical of the Inter-war romance. The heroine, Aurore, is first introduced as an object – in this case a miniature painting of her scantily clad body. It is no surprise to learn that Julien Villavide, courting on behalf of his son, is a collector who wants no more than to possess and imprison her, and to this end he places a proviso on the marriage between Aurore and his only child, Robin: she may never leave Villavide, their ancestral home. Aurore, though, is a modern girl. After only a few years of marriage, following the death of her father-in-law, she is consciously dissatisfied with life. Tired of the trappings of wealth and rank, she longs for freedom and, most importantly, wants to be accepted for herself. When a former lover, aptly named Raphaël Désire, unexpectedly appears at a propitious moment, they elope at Aurore's behest. Finally, in a scene recalling and revising the conclusion to Edgar Allan Poe's 'The Fall of the House of Usher', she forgets her marital promises and contentedly smiles as she watches her home, Villavide, burn to the ground with her master, Robin, still inside.

La Fin des Villavide, though, is by no means as conventional as this plot synopsis may have suggested. As in *Sainte-Unefois*, the governing atmosphere is disturbing as reality and fantasy merge. The romance is framed by a fairy tale in which the old Duke Julien Villavide and his wife, having no heir to their name and fortunes, decide to create a successor. Many female suitors come to seek his hand, but, following literary traditions, none meet with the duke's approval. This precipitates a dangerous search over hill and dale for the ideal maiden. The quest ends at the medieval castle of the Chevalier Arthur, and his innocent ward Aurore is selected to be the future duchess. She accepts, longing to live in a world of dream and fantasy and to achieve legendary status. This at least is guaranteed because the future duke, much to the reader's surprise and amusement, is not a man, but an armchair. Robin, the 'armchair-son', the 'fils-fauteuil', is made up of various parts, but each piece is specifically linked to the Villavide family, so that Robin is never the alien, the outcast, the repulsive other of, say, Dr Frankenstein's creation. If anything, the exaggerated nature of the components used to construct Robin is a source of considerable fun. He is made from César, the tree under which the duke was born, a tree which 'had played a crucial role in each generation of family life', 'avait a chaque génération joué un rôle dans la famille' (p. 21). He is fashioned by the duke, who expressly learns the skills of marquetry, and the duchess too contributes to his creation: for years she has shorn her pet sheep, died their wool and made tapestries. These become the covers for the chair and they are stuffed with boxes of the duchess's hair, which she has again preserved over the years. When on Easter Day the duke announces 'Here is our work, (. . .) our inheritor, our son', 'Voici notre œuvre, (. . .) notre héritier, notre fils', 'a perfectly distinguished armchair', 'un fauteuil d'une distinction parfaite' (p. 31), the duchess expires, almost as if she had died in childbirth.

Although initially Robin is conceived principally as a means of making the Villavide name live on, and although he is perceived solely in terms of his inanimate object state, gradually he evolves from his artifact state. When on the duke's death he is put in mourning, wrapped in dust sheets, the heat under his cover is so great that he begins to crack and his inlaid jewels fall out. Aurore repents for her unthinking cruelty and begins to show affection for the chair, at which point, as the firelight plays upon his encrusted jewels, he begins to appear more lifelike, to assume human attributes, to display human emotions. On Midsummer Day when Raphaël Désire returns from his quests, this humanizing process reaches its cataclysmic climax when Robin is roused to such heights of jealousy that, as literal and metaphoric meaning blur, he catches fire and is simultaneously inflamed with love. Aurore has a part to play in this metamorphosis, as Lefanu's analysis of formulaic features of fantasy monster stories suggests: 'Within monster stories women have a specific role: they provide the excuse for vanquishing the monster, for they inflame it with lust, and, as in *King Kong* for example, at the same time humanise it. In such stories women are at once available and forbidden; the lust they arouse is fearful in its power and must be contained.'[39] Not only does Aurore inspire love, she provokes envious rivalry and the hero-armchair is ultimately victim of his own emotion; his passion can ultimately only be contained by the fire which destroys him.

In *La Fin des Villavide*'s exaggerated comic reversals, Louise de Vilmorin extends beyond generic parody and, more importantly, provides an ironic commentary on Inter-war France. The Villavides, whose very name suggests sterility, are excessive in their attempt to procreate, and this reflects comically on contemporary pronatalism. Most of the social satire falls on patriarchal conceptions of ideal gender relations. Womanhood, as a social construction promoted by bourgeois morality, and perpetuated in both realist and romantic fiction, is openly satirized. For example, the sexual double standard of infidelity is exposed. No comment is made by the duchess when Julien Villavide, like his ancestor in the picture gallery, has numerous affairs, but when it is Aurore who elopes, her misadventure has serious repercussions. Similarly, the institution of marriage is caricatured. The most telling remark is that made by Aurore's guardian: 'and don't forget that it is the wife who belongs to her husband and not the contrary', 'et puis n'oublie pas que c'est l'épouse qui appartient à son mari et non le contraire' (p. 130). It is highly paradoxical that Aurore will, on marrying, become her inanimate husband's property. This is given a further ironic twist after the ceremony when, following the hyper-metropic duke's comment 'aristocrats see far: only the union of great houses counts', 'les gens de haute naissance voient loin: seule l'alliance comptait' (p. 36), scandalized aristocrats accuse her of 'marrying into money', of making 'un mariage d'intérêt' (p. 123), of marrying the armchair for its name and fortune. Not only is this comic as Robin has nothing else to offer, it is equally satiric for it raises the question: why should a woman marry for wealth when in this very act she becomes part of her husband's belongings, when rather than having joint power and control of this capital she becomes equated with it? The reader, although amused by Vilmorin's hyperbolic incongruous portrait of the couple, cannot but see in it a sardonic reflection of the actual legal objectification of married women in contemporary French law, which despite the constitution of the Fourth Republic continued well into the 1970s.

Vilmorin most effectively highlights this combined emotional, psychological, spiritual, civic and political repression suffered by women in society through her employment of physical transformations. In an oral tale recorded by Chalon, her biographer, this same female objectification is parodied when a wife and mother is shown to be a commodity defined exclusively through her male-centred relationship: 'He was a man who had married a large cupboard and in each of its drawers was a child', 'C'était un monsieur qui avait épousé une grosse armoire et dans chaque tiroir de l'armoire, il y avait un enfant.'[40] Here, as in her early novels, the mosaic of fantastic and realist literary genres enables the reader to suspend disbelief sufficiently to enter into the utopic world where the borders of fact and fiction blur, only to be forced to see in this magical fairy-tale world a contorted, exaggerated and consequently striking reflection of actual life. In *La Fin des Villavide* Vilmorin's satiric depiction of the relationship between the sexes is made particularly pointed by her decision to represent the hero as an armchair. This choice is not as fanciful or arbitrary as it might first appear, because in the art world women have all too frequently been equated with this particular object. The two much-acclaimed drawings by François-Rupert Carabin (1862–1932), exhibited at the Paris Salon des Beaux-Arts 1893 exhibition, are fairly typical:

> The first of these drawings shows a naked woman, who serves as support for the backing of a chair. The other is even more straightforward: The molding of an armchair has been placed on the back of a young woman who grimaces in pain as she leans forward, pressed in upon herself by the weight of the chair molding she must carry and whose sole, agonized support she is. This drawing represents in the most literal way imaginable the twisted turn-of-the-century dream of masculine mastery which insisted on seeing woman as merely a piece of household furniture.[41]

This reductive Fin de Siècle image was purloined by several artists, most notably the Surrealists.[42] Magritte's *Threatening Weather* (1928), for example, juxtaposes a trombone, a female bust and a hard-backed chair, while in the January following the publication of *La Fin des Villavide* Kurt Seligmann's *Ultra-furniture*, a stool composed of four stockinged female legs, was displayed at the International Exhibition of Surrealist Art in the Galerie des Beaux-Arts in Paris. In equating woman and chair, the artist suggests that woman's function is to suffer silently, that she has a purely minor utilitarian value, unless she is re-created as art by the male genius. Vilmorin's equation of the male protagonist with this particular object, the most memorable aspect of the novel, recalls and reverses the Surrealist image. It exposes the covert sexism inherent in the objectification process, the double standard at play in the denial of female autonomy. The novel's most telling comment – 'he disliked people discussing his body', 'qu'on parlât de son corps lui déplait' – highlights the paradox, as the duke readily reduces the heroine to her bodily state, but cannot accept that a man suffers the same treatment. The humiliation inherent in the dehumanizing process is also emphasized in the events leading to Robin's death when Raphaël states: 'what a magnificent piece of furniture you have there, Aurore. It is a real museum piece', 'quel magnifique meuble tu as là, Aurore. C'est une pièce de musée.' In denying Robin's human qualities, Raphaël undermines his mental capacities and precipitates his bodily destruction. This cautionary tale warns against objectification and female acceptance of it.

Vilmorin's use of gender reversal in this process is more than just a criticism of bourgeois morality or Surrealism, it is as importantly an attack on the Inter-war period's cult of heroism. For writers such as Malraux and Saint-Exupéry, who coincidentally were both for a time Vilmorin's lovers, heroism implied masculinity and was gender-specific. For them, 'as for many generations the man of action *par excellence* [was] the soldier', as Winifred Holtby, writing in 1935, explains:

> For the most part society takes care to see that the leader is masculine. The peculiar nature of this cult demands it. Virility, combativeness, physical endurance, power to impress all types of person, are the qualities demanded, and since quite sixty per cent of humanity is at present irremediably predisposed against submission to a woman, the odds are enormous.[43]

The female role in this general scenario is limited and subordinate. For the most part women merely assist in permitting what Virginia Woolf, again writing in the Inter-war era itself, terms male 'looking-glass vision'. The female function, expounded and decried by Woolf, is to reflect and enlarge the male ego and for this women must necessarily be inferior in the eyes of men, as this subservience is 'essential to all violent and heroic action'.[44] In the burning of the hero, *La Fin des Villavide* is not unique but joins a growing tradition of celebrated canonized works of female authorship, from Marguerite de Navarre's *Les Prisons*, to the nineteenth-century classics Charlotte Brontë's *Jane Eyre*, Charlotte Yonge's *The Clever Woman in the Family* and Elizabeth Barrett Browning's *Aurora Leigh*. Unlike these precursors, in Vilmorin's work the degree of violence against the male oppressor is significantly more intense, and the castigated, wounded male protagonist does not find redemption in the heroine's love. The balance of power is not so much redressed as reconstructed to reveal a dominant, omnipotent heroine and impotent hero. In the outlandish, immoderate nature of its attack, Vilmorin's treatment of the cult of heroism is far from conventional.

It would appear, then, that in the period between the wars, a number of French women writers endeavoured to revise the relationship between the sexes as promulgated in the romance. This was not always easily accomplished. While authors such as Jeanne Galzy and Lucie Delarue-Mardrus did produce works which effectively disputed phallocentricity and endorsed powerful autonomous women, they also encountered several difficulties in their venture. The revolutionary potential of their portrayal of sapphic and virilized heroines is somewhat undermined by the fact that these selfsame images had been common currency among anti-feminists in the nineteenth-century art world. The gender reversals they propose in their depiction of effeminate heroes and 'lesbian heroes' can also be read against authorial intentions, and understood, not as contesting, but as reinforcing binary logic and replicating traditional power positions. These problems were more successfully circumvented by Louise de Vilmorin in her early works. As is the case with Rachilde's *Monsieur Vénus*, her variant on gendered role reversal is convincing because the radical revision and remodelling of the hero as a castrated, silenced site of representation had no misogynistic precedents with which to contend. The transformation of the male hero into an inanimate *objet* also draws strength from the critical parodic dialogue it establishes with contemporary male-dominated literary movements. In addition to this, Vilmorin's early novels, unlike those by Rachilde, are much less open to reactionary interpretations. This is chiefly due to the multiplicity of interconnected destabilizing narrative techniques she employs. Not least of these is humour. Her employment of the traditional comic techniques of repetition, incongruity and exaggeration, together with her special configuration of vivacious ironic reversals, witty satire and literary parody, has a fundamentally destabilizing power. The particular type of laughter she generates can be seen to anticipate Hélène Cixous's anarchic *écriture féminine* as outlined in 'Le Rire de la Méduse':

> A female text cannot but be subversive: as it is written it is necessarily volcanic, resulting in an upheaval of the old property crust, the carrier of masculine investments; there can be no place for it (. . .), if it is not to smash everything, to shatter the framework of institutions, to blow up the law, to contort the truth with laughter.[45]

Most importantly perhaps, Vilmorin positions the reader in such a way that the standard romantic tropes become limpidly clear. The result is that conventional reading practices are frustrated, and the reader is coerced into re-evaluating and ultimately deconstructing the genre's dominant ideology. Interpreting the text becomes aesthetically and intellectually challenging. The reader is encouraged to question cultural representations of womanhood, to scrutinize the romance's perpetuation of the phallocentric creed of male dominance and female dependence, and to reflect on the replication of this scenario in the wider context of Inter-war French society as a whole. In all of this Vilmorin's success clearly demonstrates that even the most apparently reactionary of literary genres can be used as a vehicle for the promotion of political and social change.

Notes

1. S. de Beauvoir (1976), *Le Deuxième Sexe*, Paris, vol. 2, p. 662.
2. *Anna Soror. . .* was written in 1925, included in *La Mort conduit l'attelage* (1935) and republished with minor alterations in *Comme l'eau qui coule* in 1981.
3. Acclaimed translations from the original Greek were produced by Pierre Louÿs and André Lebey. For an overview of Sappho's reception see J. Dejean (1989), *Fictions of Sappho, 1546–1937*, Chicago and London.
4. S. Benstock (1987), *Women of the Left Bank: Paris, 1900–1940*, 2nd edn, London, p. 175.
5. Ibid., pp. 306–7.
6. While a number of Colette's early novels fit the Belle Epoque sapphic mould, with their emphasis on sensuous female settings and empathetic bonding, there is a definite shift in her position *vis-à-vis* sapphism. In terms of her own biography, she moved away from Barney's lesbian circle, and in her literature, in particular *Ces Plaisirs* (1932) whose title changed to *Le Pur et l'Impur* in 1941, she paints a very unflattering picture of Renée Vivien and of her former lover of 1906–12, Missy (the Marquise de Belbeuf). The focus of Colette's later works widens to explore love and desire in a fuller social and literary context.

7. It is frequently the case in Inter-war novels that the more radical female characters, be they feminists, suffragists, New Women or virulent lesbians, are English or American, as these women were seen as being more socially and sexually liberated.

8. This looks forward to the celebrated voyeuristic substitution scenario in Marguerite Duras's *L'Amant*, where Hélène Lagonelle plays the same part as Galzy's Marien: 'I'd like to give Hélène Lagonelle to the man who does that to me, so he may do it in turn to her. I want it to happen in my presence, I want her to do it as I wish, I want her to give herself where I give myself. It's via Hélène Lagonelle's body, through it, that the ultimate pleasure would pass from him to me.' M. Duras (1986), *The Lover*, trans. B. Bray, London, p. 79.

9. We see the same heterosexual substitution pattern in Galzy's *La Grand'rue* (1925) where the heroine Hortense, on witnessing the incestuous relationship between the hero and his mother, experiences a transfer of desire. Her passion for Vivien becomes conflated with an infatuation for his mother. Hortense's latent homosexual lust is fired by images she spies across her courtyard of the woman's hands caressing her son's hair. In the denouement, when the hero and heroine are united, Hortense, rather than kissing the hero as is the norm in romantic fiction, unexpectedly bites into his hand. As the hand metonymically evokes the incestuous mother, the hero is effectively supplanted. Hortense's decisive and peculiar deed, through this heterosexual substitution pattern, may be read as a consummation of the quiescent, obscured homosexual romance between the heroine and the 'female hero'.

10. Maurras's influential treatise was re-edited and reprinted throughout the early twentieth century. It first appeared in 1905 as *L'Avenir de l'Intelligence*, published by Albert Fontemoing as part of the collection Minerva; then as *Romantisme et révolution* in 1922 and 1925; and again under its original title in 1927 and 1942 by Flammarion.

11. C. Maurras (1925), *Romantisme et révolution*, Paris, p. 199.

12. Marks notes Maurras's fusion of anti-feminist and anti-semitic rhetoric when he classifies lesbians as 'inevitable and inferior, 'feminine and superstitious', 'a monster, a thinker, someone who breaks the natural order', 'a powerful disruptive force' and 'a dangerous phenomenon'. E. Marks (1988), '"Sappho 1900": Imaginary Renée Viviens and the Rear of the Belle Epoque' in J. Dejean and N.K. Miller (eds), *The Politics of Tradition: Placing Women in French Literature*, New Haven, CT, pp. 175–89 (pp. 182, 185 and 178).

13. B. Dijkstra (1986), *Idols of Perversity: Fantasies of Feminine Evil in Fin-de-siècle Culture*, Oxford, pp. 67, 152 and 78.
14. Maurras, *Romantisme et révolution*, pp. 146, 131 and 194–5.
15. For full details see Dijkstra, *Idols of Perversity*, pp. 150–7.
16. R. Miles (1987), *The Female Form: Women Writers and the Conquest of the Novel*, London and New York, p. 188.
17. Robinson suggests that the Belle Epoque lesbian writers, whom he classifies as separatists, also depict unequal partnerships which reflect and perpetuate dominant and submissive positions, and even Colette (classified by Robinson as a proponent of the continuum approach to lesbianism) in the 'Ladies of Llangollen' in *Le Pur et l'Impur* criticizes the replication of heterosexual power structures in long-term sapphic relationships. See C. Robinson (1995), *Scandal in the Ink: Male and Female Homosexuality in Twentieth-century French Literature*, London, chs 7 and 8.
18. For further examples of works featuring dominant virile female protagonists see J. Waelti-Walters (1990), *Feminist Novelists of the Belle Epoque: Love as a Lifestyle*, Bloomington and Indianapolis.
19. For discussions of this role reversal see M. Biolley-Godino (1972), *L'Homme objet chez Colette*, Paris; and J. Duffy (1989), *Colette: Le Blé en herbe*, Glasgow.
20. S. Lefanu (1988), 'Robots and Romance: the Science Fiction and Fantasy of Tanith Lee' in S. Radstone (ed.), *Sweet Dreams: Sexuality, Gender and Popular Fiction*, London, pp. 121–36 (pp. 124–5).
21. A. Cranny-Francis (1990), *Feminist Fiction: Feminist Uses of Generic Fiction*, Cambridge, p. 9.
22. M. Praz, (1933 reprint 1970), *The Romantic Agony*, trans. A. Davidson, Oxford.
23. Dijkstra, *Idols of Perversity*, pp. 272–4.
24. Beauvoir, *Le Deuxième Sexe*, vol. 2, p. 154.
25. L. Frappier-Mazur (1988), 'Marginal Canons: Rewriting the Erotic' in J. Dejean and N.K. Miller (eds), *The Politics of Tradition: Placing Women in French Literature*, New Haven, CT, pp. 112–28 (p. 122).
26. Dijkstra, *Idols of Perversity*, p. 337.
27. J. Birkett (1986), *The Sins of the Fathers: Decadence in France 1870–1914*, London, p. 173.
28. J. Beizer (1995), *Ventriloquized Bodies: Narratives of Hysteria in Nineteenth-century France*, Ithaca, NY and London, pp. 228, 235 and 237.
29. Louise de Vilmorin was announced winner of the Grand Prix Littéraire de Monaco in 1955 and commandeur de la légion d'honneur in commemoration of her literary corpus as a whole.

Her most celebrated works date from the 1950s and their popularity, in part at least, seems related to their affinities with the
nouveaux romans in vogue in this era. Of these works *Migraine* was
recast as an *opéra-comique*, while several novels were made into
films, namely *Madame de. . .* by Max Ophuls, *Juliette* by Marc
Allégret and *Le Lit à colonnes* by Roland Tual. Vilmorin's early
works remain relatively unknown.

30. H. Peyre (1955), *The Contemporary French Novel*, New York and
Oxford, p. 334.

31. Critics, confounded by Vilmorin's fine blend of dream, reality,
supernatural, yarn, myth and fairy tale, tend to shy from generic
classifications and choose instead to draw comparisons with other
writers, Vilmorin's name being frequently linked to her peers
Monique Saint-Hélier, Germaine Beaumont, Michel Davet, and
by Chalon to the story-teller Karen Blixen. One might add to this
list the 1980s writer Marie Redonnet, whose fictional works most
closely resemble Vilmorin's in their fusion of literary forms and
the multiplicity of interpretations they encourage.

32. The author's specific choice of non-realist forms may provide a
further ironic commentary on the romance, suggesting that sentimental love can only ever be fictional and confined to the realm
of make-believe.

33. This anticipates 'La Débutante', a short story by the Surrealist
Leonora Carrington, in which a hyena is substituted for a young
girl attending a ball. Carrington, while living in Provence with
Max Ernst in the late 1930s, produced two collections of short
stories, *La Maison de peur* (1938) and *La Dame ovale* (1939), both
in French, and the novella *Little Francis* (1938) in English.

34. Dijkstra, *Idols of Perversity*, p. 111.

35. See W. Chadwick (1985), *Women Artists and the Surrealist Move-
ment*, London and New York, pp. 33, 65, 107 and 110; see also
S. Alexandrian, *Surrealist Art*, trans. G. Clough, London and New
York.

36. Suleiman sees in Man Ray's photograph of *La Centrale surréaliste
en 1924* 'two poles of femininity between which male desire
hovers: the chaste asexual wife/mother and the burning-eyed
whore'. S.R. Suleiman (1988), 'A Double Margin: Reflections
on Women Writers and the Avant-garde in France' in J. Dejean
and N.K. Miller (eds), *The Politics of Tradition: Placing Women in
French Literature*, New Haven, CT, pp. 148–74 (p. 159).

37. Her biographer records Vilmorin's tenuous links with the group:
her friendship with Elsa Triolet and Louis Aragon, and her interest in the works of Max Ernst. See J. Chalon (1987), *Florence et*

Louise les magnifiques: Florence Jay-Gould and Louise de Vilmorin, Monaco.

38. E. de La Rochefoucauld (1969), *Femmes d'hier et d'aujourd'hui*, Paris, pp. 43–4.
39. Lefanu, 'Robots and Romance', p. 131.
40. Chalon, *Florence et Louise*, p. 138.
41. Dijkstra, *Idols of Perversity*, p. 118.
42. It also occurs in the relatively recent pop-art imagery of Mel Ramos and Allen Jones.
43. W. Holtby (1978), *Women and a Changing Civilization*, Chicago and London, pp. 102 and 160.
44. V. Woolf (1977), *A Room of One's Own*, London, p. 36.
45. H. Cixous (1975), 'Le Rire de la Méduse', *L'Arc*, no. 61, pp. 39–54 (p. 49).

Conclusion: Missing Links?

In what way are you different? Are you saying there haven't been artist-women before? There haven't been women who were independent? There haven't been women who insisted on sexual freedom? I tell you there is a great line of women stretching out behind you into the past, and you have to seek them out and find them in yourself and be conscious of them.

Doris Lessing, *The Golden Notebook*

They are not dead, but full of blood again,
I mean the sense, and every line a vein

Henry Vaughan, *On Sir Thomas Bodley's Library*

Contrary to the standard opinion expressed by Suleiman, Cixous and Peyre, with which this study opened, on the supposed dearth of quality French female-authored works prior to the emergence of Simone de Beauvoir, there were indeed many outstanding, innovative, prolific women writers in France in the first half of the century. Through no fault of their own they have been partly eclipsed by the reception accorded to their Anglo-American Modernist counterparts, and more importantly they have been marginalized by the way in which they have been represented by the literary establishment. It is the omnipotent self-perpetuating canon which is largely responsible for the way in which female fiction has been lost with passing time.

An overview of canonical compilations reveals a definite male bias in terms of numbers, and suggests that the supposedly objective selection procedure is deeply flawed. Feminist critics in recent years have proffered assorted, rival hypotheses for this. Some have speculated that female marginalization results from a general intellectual inertia; members of the literary establishment may simply prefer to discuss and teach already established authors, whose works are readily available and on whom critical material abounds. Others, such as Koppelman, attribute canonical omissions of female writers to 'epistemological solipsism', whereby critics with no personal knowledge of a subject assume that the field of enquiry does not exist.[1] Benstock observes that 'literary activity in the years following World War I was characterized by variously competing "isms"' and, as a consequence of this, male writers are habitually catalogued in terms of their relationship to these rival literary schools.[2] This has lead to difficulties for their female peers, because the majority of women writers did not identify themselves with recognized movements. Not only did this result in women missing out on publication opportunities at the time, more importantly it also meant that even commercially successful female writers often failed to make a mark at all in anthologies and literary histories.[3] Spender more polemically contends that there is a systematic, comprehensive, discriminatory exclusion of women writers. She argues that women as a group suffer from invidious suppression and censorship, because 'under the guise of scholarship and the dogma of "objectivity" literary men have been playing politics, protecting their own power base by providing preferential treatment for their own sex'.[4] Spender's conspiracy theory, based solely on the author's sex, is modified by other critics who suggest that it is the gender of the intended readership which determines the hidden agenda behind the canon's selection procedure. Such sweeping theories seem somewhat unrefined and alarmist.

Yet attitudes to gender do play a covert, complex role in canonical selection procedures. Not only is there an extreme degree of under-representation of women writers, but even in the presentation of the chosen elite there is a marked privileging of works considered masculine, be it in terms of writing style, subject matter or generic choice. While certain individual women writers benefit from and consequently collude with this, the majority suffer. These authors are consistently homogenized and viewed as quintessentially dependent feminine creatures, whose thematic interests are limited to the private realm of domesticity, love and nature. The genres they reputedly favour, namely the autobiography and the romance, are both consistently denigrated and dismissed in the canon's hierarchies of classification. Even token works by acclaimed 'feminine' writers are trivialized in this way. However, although the romance and the autobiography are both downgraded in what appears to amount to unjust, institutionally constructed segregation, a more detailed study of these genres suggests that it is not simply a problem of (intentional or subconscious) misogyny or anti-feminism. Nor is it only a question of masculine tastes or values prevailing, as many critics have argued. A more qualified explanation suggests itself.

Women's literary contribution, when included in canonical compilations such as literary histories and anthologies, is frequently distorted in various ways by the classification process itself. Often categorizations are plainly inaccurate and inappropriate. While critics correctly note an autobiographical and romantic interest in much Inter-war female-authored fiction, they singularly fail to recognize that significant numbers of women writers are unhappy with the corresponding, so-called feminine genres. There is no record of the strikingly limited quantity of autobiographies conforming to purist definitions. No mention is made of the numerous women writers rejecting the 1880s-style reactionary romance in favour of more innovative revisionary works. With the canon compilers' appraisal of novels of an autobiographical nature there is an additional failure to note that many works are not confined to any single genre, that they in fact transcend generic boundaries. Inter-war women writers, as a result of their strategies of self-concealment, juxtapose, overlap and combine elements of personal testimony, social chronicle, biography, social satire, romance, fantasy and wish fulfilment. Far from being slaves to rigidly defined literary categories, female authors of both romantic and autobiographical works often deliberately toy with generic features, in an ironical, innovative, intelligent way. As their self-reflexive works explore, fuse, superimpose, flout, exaggerate or parody literary conventions, they force the active reader to re-evaluate the genres, the values they advocate and the reading practices of their devotees. With romantic novels there is a further complication. Tracing the developmental pattern of the romance reveals that popular works of the 1920s and 1930s are far from homogeneous, given the lack of systematized marketing and authors' conflicting aims to educate and entertain, to appear modern while reinforcing traditional values. It also, more significantly, shows that licentious pre-1880 romances, their morally upright Inter-war counterparts and potentially subversive present-day romances are far from identical. Yet despite this, the same narrow, restrictive generic term is applied to all of them. Fixed, insufficiently flexible labels cannot adequately reflect the nature of literary genres which are so mutable through time.

These problems are aggravated and perpetuated as literary histories seem to build on previous canonical compilations without fresh recourse to the actual texts described. Not only does this reinforce already inadequate, poor classification, it gives rise to a situation where critics, unaware of the real content of much female-authored literature, confidently claim that these 'feminine' works are of limited value. Many Inter-war works, rather than reinscribing and endorsing the quintessentially feminine, as canonical compilations assume, actively explore the very nature of cultural gender construction. Eighteen-eighties-style romances, with their xenophobic, patriotic, Catholic bourgeois governing ideology, although ultimately failing to accommodate the unorthodox aspirations of modern women, do present their readers with more dynamic heroines and reflect the variety of new life options available to Inter-war women. The period's more innovative works go further in their reappraisal of literary and social representations of womanhood.

These heterogeneous works unite in challenging Proudhon's sacrosanct dichotomy, which casts women in one of two mutually exclusive roles: as selfless, ancillary mother-figures, or as sexual creatures expressly destined to ensure male pleasure. Their authors reject these outdated, stereotypical, essentialist images of women as either 'housewife or harlot', 'ménagère ou courtisane', on the grounds that this portrayal of the female identity, as altruistically male-centred, constitutes an offensive objectification and denial of personal autonomy.

Fictionalized autobiographies focus on the first half of the equation; they examine and re-evaluate women's function in the domestic sphere, in particular motherhood. Their heroines, who confront multiple alien images of womanhood in their quest for self-discovery in a world of collapsing value-systems, converge almost without exception on maternity. For these protagonists, the role as it stands is inimical; it has to be redefined. It may no longer be accepted as a male-oriented relational position imposed on women by a patriarchal society. Instead, it must be reconstructed as a celebratory female bodily experience, as a positively valorized type of female bonding or as a means to achieving a uniquely female matriarchal realm. The period's revised romances, which focus on woman as a sexual being (the Proudhonian courtesan figure), offer new representations of womanhood through their reconstructions of the relationship between the sexes. Chiefly they alter the dynamics of the balance of power within the couple, with female characters assuming the hero's role in sapphic romances, with dominant gynandrous heroines challenging the sovereignty of effeminate heroes in works by Delarue-Mardrus and Rachilde, and most strikingly with the total reversal of the inanimate objectified hero in de Vilmorin's ironic novels. Némirovsky's works, in their depiction of the sexual mother-figure, deliberately transgress the Proudhonian schism. All in all, these diverse Inter-war novels share an overriding aim of reformulating or rejecting traditional, reactionary notions of female identity. They wholeheartedly repudiate the persistent reduction of woman to her biological, sexual or physical body, and seek to re-establish and reaffirm female independence.

The most important aspect of the classification problem, then, is not just the existence of competitive male-biased hierarchies. Rather, French Inter-war women writers have been read in terms of outdated notions of femininity and categorized in relation to genres which fail to reflect the true nature of their production. It seems particularly ironic and unjust that they themselves should ultimately fall victim to critical 'miss'-representations, given their interest in revising, reformulating and redefining the concept of both genre and of gender in the period.

So what place should the Forgotten Generation hold in canonical compilations? Clearly certain writers, given their strong connection with established movements – Rachilde and Decadence, Audoux and Populism, and de Vilmorin and Surrealism, for example – merit more prominence. However, it is clearly not enough simply to reinsert individual women writers into the canon as it stands. Rather, a more radical change needs to come about in the way in which our literary heritage is understood. Showalter argues that minor, often-neglected writers constitute the missing links in women's great literary lineage, and urges feminist literary historians to construct an exclusively female historical tradition.[5] As a result of this process, women authors would no longer feel that they were writing in a vacuum, but rather would have a greater understanding of their part within a larger movement. They could learn lessons from the errors of the past, and both benefit from and build on their rich cultural heritage. This process is eminently possible.

Robbe-Grillet argues that 'the writer must bear his date with pride, in the knowledge that there are no masterpieces in eternity, only works in particular historical contexts; and that they only survive in so far as they have left the past behind them and have heralded the future'.[6] While Inter-war female-authored works do bear their date, there are in fact many ways in which the Forgotten Generation may be seen to resemble and anticipate its present-day counterparts. This may be partly attributed to the fact that there remain marked similarities between French society and the position it confers on women writers in the Inter-war era and in the present period. Despite some shift in the hegemony of power in the world of publishing, little has really changed. Chantal Chawaf's satirical depiction of the tense relationship between the inexperienced author Elwine and her publisher Pierre Duval in *Elwina, le roman fée* (1986) suggests that many women continue to face the same difficulties outlined by Suzanne Normand some sixty years earlier in *Cinq femmes sur une galère* (1926). For instance certain women writers today still provoke interest more for their lifestyles than for their literature. This is evident not just in their critical reception but in the lengths they will go to in order to promote their works and render them more amenable to the tastes of current markets.[7] While a significant number of women are commercially successful (and widely read by what is still a predominantly female readership), they are not altogether acknowledged by the literary establishment. Just as in the 1920s and 1930s, only a limited number of exceptional women are fully canonized: Beauvoir and Duras now take their place alongside Rachilde, Colette, Noailles, Sarraute and Yourcenar. French school syllabuses today still do not reflect the wealth of female-authored works produced this century. Once, Noailles's politically conservative, lyric nature poetry was considered suitable teaching material; now, only Claire Etcherelli's *Elise, ou la vraie vie* (1967) is included, and this for reasons more related to its exploration of the French–Algerian question and its indictment of racism rather than for its feminist depiction of working-class women's social situation.

The similarities between current and Inter-war women writers extend beyond the literary environment into the actual nature of female literary creation. Modern women authors share a comparable range of thematic preoccupations converging around the construction of gender. It seems clear that Inter-war writers, in their attack on the representation of women as objects defined solely in relation to men, in their reconfiguration and ultimate rejection of the romantic hero, and in their refusal of the tenets and false promises of the romantic genre, have helped pave the way for later women writers. The popular romance and the ideal relationship it postulates between the sexes, for instance, continues to be a subject of some controversy, with many French female writers preferring to leave reactionary sentimental fiction to their Anglo-American counterparts, focusing instead on more realistic portrayals of romance. Here one might think of Annie Leclerc's critique of virile heroism and fraternity (which bears a strong resemblance to Némirovsky and de Vilmorin's). Or one might recall Christiane Rochefort who undermines the credo of pre-nuptial virginity, marital monogamy and resplendent fulfilment in maternity in her satirical anti-romances, which set dreams of sentimental love against a backdrop of alcohol abuse in *Le Repos du guerrier* (1958) and the poverty of the inner city in *Les Petits Enfants du siècle* (1961), culminating in a wife's rejection of her bourgeois husband in favour of sapphic embraces in *Les Stances à Sophie* (1963). More extensive links can be drawn between this general tendency to remodel our conception of the couple and the resurgent interest in virulent sapphism in the late 1960s and 1970s (best exemplified by Violette Leduc's *Thérèse et Isabelle* (1966) and Monique Wittig, whose innovative manifesto of radical feminism *Les Guérillères* reached an extensive readership in 1969) and the renewed interest in the relationship between mothers and daughters which characterizes much female-authored literature of the 1980s. This modern exploration of motherhood provokes a variety of quite different responses, just as it did in the Inter-war era. Audoux's portrayal of maternity as a restrictive, patriarchally imposed, often inimical social role may be seen to be reflected in the works of Christiane Rochefort, while the tensions in the mother–daughter bond as demonstrated by Némirovsky are reflected in realist works by Simone de Beauvoir and Annie Ernaux. In contrast, the representation of motherhood in Pozzi's fiction as a lost paradise of symbiotic bliss is repeated in quest narratives by Chantal Chawaf. Pozzi's emphasis on matriarchal inheritance also finds echoes in Hélène Cixous's and Marie Redonnet's exploration of female gift economies. Even Bibesco's glorification of motherhood as a uniquely female bodily experience is echoed and intensified by Annie Leclerc, Hélène Cixous and Marie Cardinal, who in the period following the legalization of abortion (1974) and female contraception (1977) are more free to exalt women's new-found empowerment in controlling reproduction.

A further similarity in Inter-war and present-day writers lies in their shared fascination with genre. The modern period has also seen a number of writers producing fascinating experimental works, which challenge and dismantle traditional categorizations, given the extent to which they cross genres, merging fiction with fantasy, and autobiographical, feminist testimonies with highly lyrical poetry. Specific links may be drawn between de Vilmorin's preoccupation with social satire, feminized myth, inheritance and fairy tale, and the fiction of Marie Redonnet, in particular *Rose Mélie Rose* (1987), the third volume of her trilogy. There are more general correspondences too. The current period, while seeing a sharp decline in popular French romances, has witnessed the emergence of numerous autobiographical works, aimed at interrogating personal experience in a more accessible way. These include Annie Ernaux's limpid portrayal of her mother's death in *Une Femme* (1987) – a work she herself describes as a fusion of literature, history and sociological testimony – Marie Cardinal's recording of the effects of her psychoanalytic treatment in *Les Mots pour le dire* (1975), Annie Leclerc's exploration of her relationship with writing in *Origines* (1988) and Marguerite Duras's compulsive re-telling of her adolescence in Indo-china, which in *L'Amant* (1984) in particular systematically dismantles the divisions between fiction and non-fiction, with its narrative omissions and inconsistencies and its constant oscillations between first- and third-person narration.

This said, it would be inaccurate to suggest that the relationship between Inter-war women writers and their modern-day counterparts is characterized solely by continuity. There are certain major differences. The primary contrast in the two periods lies in the fact that contemporary women not only reject patriarchal representations of womanhood and hierarchical generic classifications, but that they also refuse patriarchal linguistic models. Although Bibesco in *Catherine Paris* (1927) expressed the need for a specifically female means of self-expression to define and incarnate the body, responses to her cry for change were slow in coming. It is only in fairly recent years that women writers have endeavoured to write from within the female body, to represent its natural rhythms. This is evident in the avant-garde *écriture féminine* of Annie Leclerc, Hélène Cixous and Luce Irigaray. It is also present in Jeanne Hyvrard's spiralling invented words which subvert the heavily codified standard subject, verb and predicate sentence structure. It is evident in Marie Cardinal's scripted dialogues which seek to undercut the notion of authorial authority. It is also displayed in Chantal Chawaf's highly poetic, lyrical, mythic language.

A second related difference between writers of the two periods lies in the increased sway of psychoanalysis. Not only does the exploration of the unconscious mind and pre-Oedipal language colour the works of a number of present-day writers, in particular those involved in autobiographical genres, it also informs various branches of feminist literary theory. Here lies the most crucial difference between the two eras. Today, current women writers' works may be read against the backdrop of these literary theories. This has a certain advantage: it improves their chance of survival in the annals of literary history, because it promotes the study of these texts within higher and further education establishments – the establishments which have so much to do with canon formation. It is generally acknowledged that it is much easier to teach and to study works against a theoretical background. As modern works may be seen as part of a school or 'ism' they have a greater chance of survival than their antecedents, which are linked mainly by their temporal setting. Moreover, improved awareness amongst feminists of the marginalization experienced by previous generations of women writers should also help guarantee the renown of contemporary works.

Showalter's project of a female canon, then, despite its many worthwhile advantages, has certain inherent drawbacks. Not only might the construction of an alternative, exclusively female canon alienate a certain readership and further isolate women's literature, presenting it as a ghetto, a thing apart, in displaying minor writers as the missing links between different generations of great writers, one might risk presenting literature as a single monolithic scheme, an exclusively linear, continuous progression. Literature is much less ordered and

more diverse and rhizomatic than this scenario suggests. Works do not
necessarily follow on one from another in a logical or causal sequence.
Their relationships vary tremendously. Moreover, while period is of
paramount importance in moulding authors' concerns and attitudes,
as this study has demonstrated, it is crucial that critics come to recognize that women's literary production is not a homogeneous
entity, that there is not some universal female voice, for in any given
era there will always be diversity. As a consequence of this, a still more
fundamental change is required in the nature of canon construction.
It seems that anthologizers and literary historians' proper function
should be, to borrow a popular metaphor from women's literature
itself, like the role of a textile worker: Mme de Lafayette and Mme
de Graffigny's tier of knots, the *chanvreur* hemp dresser of George
Sand's pastoral novels, or, most appropriately, Louky Bersianik and
George Eliot's weaver.[8] They should work to illuminate a whole
gamut of possible links and bonds between disparate works, to suggest
diverse juxtapositions, to draw together the already canonized and
the popular, and to propose different ways of approaching texts.
Canon compilers ought to transfer their primary interest away from
categorizing, labelling and pinning down isolated literary works. They
should instead use their privileged position to help open up areas for
discovery, investigation and interpretation. Literary historians should
always be alert and responsive to the countless new possibilities which
suggest themselves, as many heterogeneous writers still await rediscovery, many threads still remain to be tied.

In the Middle Ages, François Villon, in his metaphorical refrain
'Where are the snows of yesteryear?' ('Où sont les neiges d'antan?')
in the 'Ballade des dames du temps jadis' of the *Testament* (1461–2)
reflects on the transient nature of reputation and renown. He notes
the ease with which women in particular – be they mythical, biblical,
literary or social characters – are erased from popular folk memory.
Five hundred years on, the problem still remains, as French women
writers of the Inter-war era, following severe critical neglect and
misunderstanding, already seem to resemble Villon's snows of yesteryear. In order to recover the Forgotten Generation of women writers
and help provide a more accurate and thorough picture of twentieth-
century literature as a whole, it is of vital importance that their
misrepresentation in canonical compilations *continue* to be redressed,
and that their works *continue* to be re-read and reassessed. It should
always be remembered that our literary heritage is neither fixed nor
static; it is a vibrant, ongoing, constantly evolving process ever open
to change and reappraisal.

Notes

1. Koppelman's private communication (1988) is quoted in D. Spender (1989), *The Writing or the Sex: or Why You Don't Have to Read Women's Writing to Know it's no Good*, New York, p. 51.
2. S. Benstock (1987), *Women of the Left Bank: Paris, 1900–1940*, London, p. 381.
3. Planté similarly suggests that in the previous century women were often placed on the periphery of established, recognized movements to which they did not completely adhere, which made their works seem strange or incoherent. C. Planté (1989), *La Petite Sœur de Balzac: essai sur la femme auteur*, Paris, p. 329.
4. Spender, *The Writing or the Sex*, p. 31.
5. This project is reminiscent of the medieval writer Christine de Pisan's *Livre de la cité des dames* (1404–5) and Renée Vivien's attempt at the turn of the century to create an alternative female canon.
6. A. Robbe-Grillet (1961), 'A quoi servent les théories?' in *Pour un nouveau roman*, Paris, pp. 7–13 (p. 10).
7. Jeanne Hyvrard, for example, presented herself quite inaccurately as a black Caribbean writer producing work from a psychiatric hospital to interest publishers in *Les Prunes de Cythère* (1975). For further details see E. Fallaize (1993), *French Women's Writing: Recent Fiction*, London, p. 109.
8. Mary Ann Evans's cryptic pseudonym 'Eliot', when reversed, gives the French term 'toile', or woven canvas, a leitmotif which both unites her work and serves as a metaphor for her aesthetic discipline.

Bibliography

Selected Primary Texts

Acrement, Germaine (1921), *Ces Dames aux chapeaux verts*, Paris: Plon.

——, (1927), *Gai? marions-nous*, Paris: Plon.

Andris, Colette (1939), *La Femme qui boit*, Paris: Gallimard (Les Livres de jour).

Auclair, Marcelle (1927), *Toya*, Paris: Gallimard.

Audoux, Marguerite (1910, reprint 1987), *Marie-Claire*, Paris: Grasset et Fasquelle (Les Cahiers rouges, no. 78).

——, (1920, reprint 1987), *L'Atelier de Marie-Claire*, Paris: Grasset et Fasquelle (Les Cahiers rouges, no. 79).

——, (1926), *De la ville au moulin*, Paris: Bibliothèque Charpentier.

——, (1931), *Douce Lumière*, Paris: Grasset et Fasquelle (Pour mon Plaisir, 8th series, no. 6).

Beaumont, Germaine (1930), *Piège*, Paris: Lemerre.

Bibesco, Princesse Marthe de (1924), *Le Perroquet vert*, Paris: Grasset (Les Cahiers verts, no. 40).

——, (1927), *Catherine Paris*, Paris: Grasset.

Charasson, Henriette (1926), *Les Heures du foyer*, Paris: Flammarion.

——, (1928), *Deux Petits Hommes et leur mère*, Paris: Flammarion.

Clairin, Lucy (1937), *Journal d'un mannequin: feuillets d'une année*, Paris: Fasquelle.

Clotis, Josette (1932), *Le Temps vert*, Paris: Gallimard.

——, (1934), *Une Mesure pour rien*, Paris: Gallimard.

——, (1946 posth.), *Le Vannier*, Paris: Gallimard.

Colette (1900), *Claudine à l'école*, Paris: Ollendorff.

——, (1901), *Claudine à Paris*, Paris: Ollendorff.

——, (1902), *Claudine en ménage*, Paris: Mercure de France.

——, (1903), *Claudine s'en va*, Paris: Ollendorff.

——, (1904), *Minne*, Paris: Ollendorff.

——, (1905), *Les Egarrements de Minne*, Paris: Ollendorff.

——, (1908), *Les Vrilles de la vigne*, Paris: Editions de la vie parisienne.

——, (1920), *Chéri*, Paris: Fayard.

——, (1923), *Le Blé en herbe*, Paris: Flammarion.

——, (1926), *La Fin de Chéri*, Paris: Flammarion.

——, (1928), *La Naissanace du jour*, Paris: Flammarion.

——, (1932), *Ces Plaisirs*, Paris: Ferenczi.

——, (1989), *Romans – Récits – Souvenirs (1920–1940)*, Paris: Robert Laffont.

Davet, Michel (1930), *Le Prince qui m'aimait*, Paris: Plon (La Palatine).

——, (1940), *Douce*, Paris: Plon.

Delarue-Mardrus, Lucie (1922), *L'Ex-voto*, Paris: Fasquelle.

——, (1924), *Le Roman de six petites filles*, Paris: Fasquelle.

——, (1926), *Embellissez-vous*, Paris: de France.

——, (1930), *L'Ange et les Pervers*, Paris: Ferenczi.

——, (1931), *L'Amour à la mer*, Paris: Lemerre (Les amours tragiques).

——, (1939), *La Girl*, Paris: Ferenczi (Le Livre moderne illustré).

Delly, (1916), *La Fin d'une Walkyrie*, 54th edn, Paris: Plon.

——, (1925), *Les Ombres*, Paris: Flammarion.

——, (1927), *Une Femme supérieure*, Paris: Gautier-Languereau (Bibliothèque de ma Fille).

Dunois, Dominiqe (1928), *Georgette Garou*, Paris: Calmann-Lévy.

Fauconnier, Geneviève (1933), *Claude*, Paris: Stock.

Galzy, Jeanne (1919), *La Femme chez les garçons*, Paris: Payot.

——, (1923), *Les Allongés*, Paris: Rieder.

——, (1925), *La Grand'rue*, Paris: Rieder.

——, (1926), *Le Retour dans la vie*, Paris: Rieder.

——, (1929), *L'Initiatrice aux mains vides*, Paris: Rieder.

——, (1934), *Jeunes Filles en serre chaude*, 19th edn, Paris: Gallimard.

Gérard, Rosemonde (1927), *La Vie amoureuse de Madame de Genlis*, Paris: Flammarion (Leurs Amours).

Gevers, Marie (1934), *Madame Orpha, ou la sérénade de mai*, Paris: V. Attinger.

Gramont, Elisabeth de (1932), *Mémoires: clair de lune et taxi-auto*, 3rd edn, Paris: Grasset.

Gyp (1894, reprint 1917), *Le Mariage de Chiffon*, Edinburgh: Collection Nelson.

——, (1928), *Le Chambard*, Paris: Flammarion.

——, (1931), *La Joyeuse enfance de la IIIème République*, 2 vols, Paris: Calmann-Lévy.

Harry, Myriam (1903), *Le Conquête de Jérusalem*, Paris: Calmann-Lévy.

——, (1914), *La Petite Fille de Jérusalem*, Paris: Fayard (Le Livre de demain).

——, (1918), *Siona chez les barbares*, Paris: Chabassol.

——, (1919), *Siona à Paris*, Paris: Fayard (Le Livre de demain).

——, (1922), *Le Tendre Cantique de Siona*, Paris: Fayard (Les Œuvres libres, no. 4).

——, (1926), *La Vie amoureuse de Cléopâtre*, Paris: Flammarion (Leurs amours).

——, (1927), *Siona à Berlin*, Paris: Fayard (Le Livre de demain).

Hervif, Louise (1936), *Sangs*, Paris: Denoël.

Houville, Gérard de (1903), *L'Inconstante*, Paris: Fayard.

——, (1905), *Esclave*, Paris: Calmann-Lévy.

——, (1908), *Le Temps d'aimer*, Paris: Calmann-Lévy (Les Romans du cœur).

——, (1925), *La Vie amoureuse de l'Impératrice Joséphine*, Paris: Flammarion (Leurs amours).

——, (1927), *Je crois que je vous aime*, Paris: Fayard.

——, (1928), *La Vie amoureuse de la Belle Hélène*, Paris: Flammarion (Leurs amours).

Leblanc, Georgette (1931), *Souvenirs*, Paris: Grasset (Pour mon plaisir, no. 9).

Le Franc, Marie (1927), *Grand Louis, l'innocent*, Paris: Rieder.

Machard, Raymonde (1927), *La Possession, roman de l'amour*, Paris: Flammarion.

Malraux, Clara (1945), *Le Portrait de Grisélidis*, Paris: Colbert.

Marx, Magdeleine (1919), *Femmes*, Paris: Flammarion.

Murat, Princesse Lucien (1927), *La Vie amoureuse de la Grande Catherine*, Paris: Flammarion (Leurs Amours).

Némirovsky, Irène (1926), *Le Malentendu*, Paris: Fayard (Les Œuvres libres, no. 56).

——, (1929, reprint 1986), *David Golder*, Paris: Grasset et Fasquelle (Les Cahiers rouges, no. 63).

——, (1930, reprint 1987), *Le Bal*, Paris: Grasset et Fasquelle (Les Cahiers rouges, no. 51).

——, (1932), *La Comédie bourgeoise*, Paris: Fayard (Les Œuvres libres, no. 132).

——, (1935, reprint 1988), *Le Vin de solitude*, Paris: Albin Michel.

——, (1936), *Jézabel*, Paris: Albin Michel.

——, (1938), *La Proie*, Paris: Albin Michel.

——, (1939), *Deux*, Paris: Albin Michel.

Noailles, Anna de (1903), *La Nouvelle Espérance*, Paris: Calmann-Lévy.

——, (1904), *Le Visage émerveillé*, Paris: Calmann-Lévy.

——, (1905), *La Domination*, Paris: Calmann-Lévy.

——, (1930), *Exactitudes*, Paris: Grasset

——, (1932, reprint 1976), *Le Livre de ma vie*, Paris: Mercure de France.

Noël, Marie (1959), *Notes intimes 1922–1940. . .*, Paris: Stock.

Normand, Suzanne (1926), *Cinq Femmes sur une galère*, Paris: Fayard (Collection de bibliothèque).

Pozzi, Catherine (1927, reprint 1988), *Agnès*, Paris: de la différence.

——, (1935 posth.), *Peau d'âme*, 7th edn, Paris: Corrêa.

——, (1987 posth.), *Journal 1913–1934*, Paris: Ramsay (Pour mémoire).

Rachilde (1884, reprint 1977), *Monsieur Vénus*, Paris: Flammarion.

——, (1887, reprint 1981), *La Marquise de Sade*, Paris: Mercure de France.

——, (1888), *Madame Adonis*, Paris: Monnier.

——, (1889, reprint 1980), *La Tour d'amour*, Paris: Le Tout sur le tout.

——, (1891), *Théâtre: Mme la Mort, Le Vendeur de soleil, La voix du sang*, Paris: Savine.

Bibliography

——, (1900, re-print 1982), *La Jongleuse*, Paris: des Femmes.

——, (1928), *Pourquoi je ne suis pas féministe*, Paris: de France (Leurs raisons).

——, (1934), *La Femme-Dieu*, Paris: Ferenczi.

——, (1947), *Quand j'étais jeune*, Paris: Mercure de France.

Rimbaud, Isabelle (1922, reprint 1978), *Reliques*, Paris: Mercure de France.

Saint-Hélier, Monique (1932, reprint 1985), *La Cage aux rêves*, Lausanne: de l'Aire.

Sainte-Soline, Claire (1937), *Les Sentiers détournés*, Paris: Rieder (Prosateurs français contemporains).

Sarraute, Nathalie (1939), *Tropismes*, Paris: Denoël.

Silve, Claude (1935), *Bénédiction*, Paris: Grasset.

Sorel, Cécile (1927), *La Vie amoureuse d'Adrienne Lecouvreur*, Paris: Flammarion (Leurs amours).

Tinayre, Marcelle (1899), *Hellé*, Paris: Mercure de France.

——, (1905), *La Rebelle*, Paris: Calmann-Lévy.

Triolet, Elsa (1938), *Bonsoir Thérèse*, Paris: Denoël.

——, (1944), *Le Premier Accroc coûte deux cent francs*, Paris: Denoël.

Vilmorin, Louise de (1934), *Sainte-Unefois*, Paris: Gallimard.

——, (1937), *La Fin des Villavide*, Paris: Gallimard.

——, (1970 posth.), *Carnets*, Paris: Gallimard.

Vincent, Raymonde (1937), *Campagne*, Paris: Stock.

Weiss, Louise (1938), *Souvenirs d'une enfance républicaine*, 11th edn, Paris: Denoël.

——, (1946), *Ce que Femme veut: souvenirs de la IIIème République*, 7th edn, Paris: Gallimard.

Yourcenar, Marguerite (1921), *Alexis ou le traité du vain combat*, Paris: Pareil.

——, (1921), *Le Jardin des Chimères*, Paris: Perrin.

——, (1922), *Les Dieux ne sont pas morts*, Paris: Sansot.

——, (1931), *La Nouvelle Eurydice*, Paris: Grasset.

——, (1932), *Pindare*, Paris: Grasset.

——, (1934), *Denier du rêve*, Paris: Grasset.

——, (1936), *Feux*, Paris: Grasset.

——, (1938), *Nouvelles orientales*, Paris: Gallimard.

——, (1939), *Le Coup de grâce*, Paris: Gallimard.

——, (1951), *Mémoires d'Hadrien suivi de Carnet de notes de Mémoires d'Hadrien*, Paris: Gallimard.

——, (1956), *Les Charités d'Alcippe*, Liège: Flûte enchantée.

——, (1968), *L'Œuvre au noir*, Paris: Gallimard.

——, (1977), *Archives du nord*, Paris: Gallimard.

——, (1981), *Anna, Soror. . .* in *Comme l'eau qui coule*, Paris: Gallimard.

Yver, Colette (1928), *Rose, Madame*, Paris: Fayard (Collection jeunes femmes et jeunes filles).

Secondary Texts

a) *Literary Histories, Bibliographies and Anthologies*

Abry, E., Crouzet, P. and Audic, C. (1942), *Histoire illustrée de la littérature française*, Paris: Didier.

Anthologie de la nouvelle prose française (1926), Paris: Sagittaire (chez Kra).

Baldensperger, F. (1943), *La Littérature française entre les deux guerres, 1919–1939*, Marseilles: Sagittaire.

Bethléem, Abbé L. (1932), *Romans à lire et romans à proscrire: essai de classification au point de vue moral des principaux romans et romanciers (1500–1932) avec notes et indications pratiques*, 11th edn, Paris: Editions de la revue des lectures.

Brée, G. (ed.), (1962), *Twentieth Century French Literature*, New York: Mac-Millan.

——, and Guiton M. (1962), *The French Novel from Gide to Camus*, New York: Harbinger Books.

Castex, P.-G. and Surer P. (1953), *Manuel des études littéraires françaises, XXème siècle*, Paris: Hachette.

Cazaiman, L. (1955), *A History of French Literature*, Oxford: Clarendon Press.

Chassang, A. and Senniger, Ch. (1970), *Recueil de textes littéraires français: XXème siècle*, Paris: Hachette.

Clouard, H. (1947), *Histoire de la littérature française du symbolisme à nos jours*, vol. 1 1885–1914, vol. 2 1915–1940, Paris: Albin Michel.

——, (1962), *Histoire de la littérature française du symbolisme à nos jours, de 1915 à 1960*, 2nd edn, Paris: Albin Michel.

Daspre, A. and Décaudin, M. (1982), *Manuel d'histoire littéraire de la France de 1913 à nos jours*, vol. 6, 1913–1976, Paris: Editions sociales.

Knowles, D. (1967), *French Drama of the Inter-war Years 1918–39*, London: Harrap.

Lagarde, A. and Michard, L. (1962), *XXème siècle*, Paris: Bordas.

Lalou, R. (1947), *Histoire de la littérature française contemporaine: de 1870 à nos jours*, 2 vols, Paris: Presses Universitaires de France.

Lanson, G. (1952), *Histoire de la littérature française (remaniée et complétée pour la périod 1850–1950 par Paul Tuffrau)*, Paris: Hachette.

Larnac, J. (1929), *Histoire de la littérature féminine en France*, 2nd edn, Paris: Kra (Les Documentaires).

Lemaître, H. (1985), *Dictionnaire Bordas de littérature française*, Paris: Bordas.

McMillan, D. and McMillan, G. (1950), *An Anthology of the Contemporary French Novel, 1919–1949*, London: J.M. Dent and sons.

Moulin, J. (1963), *La Poésie féminine de Marie de France à Marie Noël, époque moderne*, Paris: Seghers.

Peyre, H. (1955), *The Contemporary French Novel*, New York and Oxford: Oxford University Press.

Picon, G. (1949), *Panorama de la nouvelle littérature française*, 21st edn, Paris: Gallimard (le point du jour).

Bibliography

Raimond, M. (1976), *Le Roman contemporain: le signe des temps*, Paris: CDU et SEDES.

Simon, P.-H. (1963), *Histoire de la littérature française au XXème siècle, 1900–1950*, 2 vols, 7th edn, Paris: Armand Colin.

Talvart, H. and Place, J. (1928 onwards), *Bibliographie des auteurs modernes de langue française, 1801–1975*, Paris: de la Chronique des lettres française.

Thième, H. (1933), *Bibliographie de la littérature française de 1800 à 1930*, Paris: Droz.

Wilson, K.M. (1991), *An Encylopedia of Continental Women Writers*, 2 vols, Chicago and London: St James Press.

b) Biographical Studies

Barney, N. (1960), *Souvenirs indiscrets*, Paris: Flammarion.

Bartillat, C. de (1985), *Clara Malraux: le regard d'une femme sur son siècle, biographie – témoignage*, Paris: Perrin (Collection terre des femmes).

Beaumont, G. and Parinaud, A. (1951), *Colette par elle-même*, Paris: Le Seuil.

Borely, M. (1939), *L'Emouvante destinée d'Anna de Noailles*, Paris: Albert (La Renaissance du livre).

Broche, F. (1989), *Anna de Noailles: un mystère en pleine lumière*, Paris: Robert Laffont (Biographies sans masque).

Chalon, J. (1987), *Florence et Louise les magnifiques: Florence Jay-Gould et Louise de Vilmorin*, Monaco: du Rocher.

Chantal, S. (1976), *Le Cœur battant: Josette Clotis, André Malraux*, Paris: Grasset et Fasquelle.

Cocteau, J. (ed.), (1963), *La Comtesse de Noailles oui et non*, Paris: Librairie Académique Perrin.

Courtivron, I. de (1992), *Clara Malraux, une femme dans le siècle*, Paris: Editions de l'Olivier.

Dauphiné, C. (1985), *Rachilde, femme de lettres 1900*, Périgueux: Pierre Fanlac.

David, A. (1924), *Rachilde, 'homme' de lettres*, Paris: La Nouvelle Revue Critique.

Diesbach, G. de (1986), *La Princesse Bibesco: la dernière orchidée*, Paris: Perrin (Terres des Femmes).

Escholier, R. (1957), *La Neige qui brûle*, Paris: Fayard.

Fleury, R. (1990), *Marie de Régnier: l'inconstante*, Paris: Plon.

Gaubert, E. (1907), *Rachilde*, Paris: Sansot (Bibliothèque internationale, les Célébrités d'aujourd'hui).

Gille, E. (1992), *Le Mirador: mémoires rêvés*, Paris: Presses de la Renaissance.

Harry, M. (1946), *Mon amie Lucie Delarue-Mardrus*, Paris: Ariane.

Joseph, L. (1988), *Catherine Pozzi: une robe couleur du temps*, Paris: Editions de la Différence (Essais).

Larnac, J. (1931), *Comtesse de Noailles: sa vie, son œuvre*, Paris: Kra.

La Rochefoucauld, E. de (1956), *Anna de Noailles*, Paris: Universitaires (Classiques du XXè siècle).

Bibliography

Leroy, P. (1936), *Femmes d'aujourd'hui: Colette, Lucie Delarue-Mardrus*, Rouen: Maugard.

Lottman, H. (1991), *Colette: a Life*, London: Secker and Warburg.

Mackinnon, L. (1992), *The Lives of Elsa Triolet*, London: Chatto and Windus.

Madsen, A. (1989), *Silkroads: the Asian Adventures of Clara and André Malraux*, New York: Pharos Books.

Mignot-Ogliastri, C. (1986), *Anna de Noailles*, Paris: Meridiens Klincksieck.

Missoffe, M. (1932), *Gyp et ses amis*, Paris: Flammarion.

Perche, L. (1964), *Anna de Noailles*, Paris: Pierre Seghers.

Plat, H. (1994), *Lucie Delarue-Mardrus: une femme de lettres des années folles*, Paris: Grasset.

Reyer, G. (1942), *Marguerite Audoux: un cœur pur*, Paris: Grasset.

Rivière, A. (1989), *Isabelle Rivière: ou la passion d'aimer*, Paris: Fayard.

Sarde, M. (1978), *Colette, libre et entravée*, Paris: Stock.

Savigneau, J. (1990), *Marguerite Yourcenar: l'invitation d'une vie*, Paris: Gallimard.

Silverman, W.Z. (1995), *The Notorious life of Gyp: Right-wing Anarchist in Fin-de-siècle France*, New York and Oxford: Oxford University Press.

c) Historical Studies Covering the Inter-war Period

Albistur, M. and Armogathe, D. (1977), *Histoire du féminisme français du moyen âge à nos jours*, Paris: Editions des Femmes.

Auffret, M. (1972), *La France de l'entre deux guerres*, Paris: Culture, Arts, Loisirs.

Beddoe, D. (1989), *Back to Home and Duty*, London and San Francisco: Pandora.

Bensadon, N. (1980), *Les Droits de la femme des origines à nos jours*, Paris: Presses Universitaires de France (Que sais je?).

Bernier, O. (1993), *Fireworks at Dusk: Paris in the Thirties*, Boston and London: Little, Brown and Company.

Bock, G. and Thane, P. (eds), (1991), *Maternity and Gender Policies: Women and the Rise of the European Welfare States 1880s–1950s*, London and New York: Routledge.

Bonvoisin, S.-M. and Maignien, M. (1986), *La Presse féminine*, Paris: Presses Universitaires de France (Que sais je?).

Boxer, M.J. and Quataert, J.H. (1987), *Connecting Spheres: Women in the Western World, 1500 to the Present*, Oxford: Oxford University Press.

Brody, E. (1988), *Paris the Musical Kaleidoscope, 1870–1925*, 2nd edn, London: Robson Books.

Brassaï (1976), *The Secret Paris of the 30's*, trans. Miller, R., London: Chapman and Hall.

Brunhammer, Y. (1987), *The Nineteen Twenties Style*, London: Cassell.

Chapman, R. (ed.), (Autumn 1992), 'Culture and Class in France in the 1930s', *Nottingham French Studies*, vol. 31, no. 2.

Charrier, E. (1931), *L'Evolution intellectuelle féminine*, Geneva: Albert Mechelinck.

Bibliography

Cronin, V. (1994), *Paris: City of Light, 1919–1939*, London: Harper Collins.

Cruikshank, C.G. (1982), *Variations on a Catastrophe: Some French Responses to the Great War*, London and New York: Oxford University Press.

Desanti, D. (1984), *La Femme au temps des années folles*, Paris: Stock/Laurence Pernoud.

Faveton, P. (1982), *Les Années vingt*, Paris: Messidor.

Fitch, N.R. (1985), *Sylvia Beach and the Lost Generation: a History of Literary Paris in the Twenties and Thirties*, London and New York: Penguin (Literary Biographies).

Forbes, J. and Kelly M. (eds), (1995), *French Cultural Studies: an Introduction*, Oxford: Oxford University Press.

Goldman, D. (ed.), (1993), *Women and World War 1: the Written Response*, London: Macmillan.

Gouze, R. (1973), *Les Bêtes à Goncourt: un demi-siècle de batailles littéraires*, Paris: Hachette.

Guilleminault, G. (1958), *Les Années folles*, Paris: Denoël.

Hausse, S. and Kenney, A. (1984), *Women's Suffrage and Social Politics in the French Third Republic*, Princeton, NJ: Princeton University Press.

Holtby, W. (1978), *Women and a Changing Civilization*, Chicago and London: Cassandra Editions.

Joffroy, A. (1982), *La Vie réinvitée: l'explosion de années 20 à Paris*, Paris: Laffont.

Klejman L. and Rochefort, F. (1989), *L'Egalité en marche: le féminisme sous la Troisième République*, Paris: Editions des Femmes.

Koven, S. and Michel, S. (eds), (1993), *Mothers of a New World : Maternalist Politics and the Origins of Welfare States*, London and New York: Routledge.

McMillan, J.E. (1981), *Housewife or Harlot: the Place of Women in French Society, 1870–1940*, London and New York: Harvester Press.

Montreynaud, F. (1992), *Le XXème siècle des femmes*, Paris: Nathan.

Pugh, M. (1992), *Women and the Women's Movement in Britain 1914–1959*, London: Macmillan.

Roberts, M.L. (1994), *Civilization Without Sexes: Reconstructing Gender in Postwar France, 1917–1927*, Chicago and London: Chicago University Press.

Sachs, M. (1950), *La Décade de l'illusion*, Paris: Gallimard.

Sertillanges, A.D. (1908), *Féminisme et Christianisme*, Paris: J. Gabalda (Librairie Victor Lecoffre).

Woolf, V. (1979), *Three Guineas*, London and New York: Penguin.

Yver, C. (1922), *Dans le Jardin du féminisme*, Paris: Calmann-Lévy.

——, (1929), *Femmes d'aujourd'hui: enquête sur les nouvelles carrières féminines*, Paris: Calmann-Lévy.

Bibliography

d) General Works

Alexandrian, S. (1970), *Surrealist Art*, trans. Clough, G., London and New York: Thames and Hudson.

Allen, J.S. (1991), *In the Public Eye: a History of Reading in Modern France, 1800–1940*, Princeton, NJ: Princeton University Press.

Atack, M. and Powrie, P. (eds), (1990), *Contemporary French Fiction by Women: Feminist Perspectives*, Manchester: Manchester University Press.

Barrett, M. (ed.), (1979), *Virginia Woolf: Women and Writing*, London: The Women's Press.

Beauman, N. (1983), *A Very Great Profession: the Woman's Novel, 1914–39*, London: Virago.

Beauvoir, S. de (1949, reprint 1976), *Le Deuxième Sexe*, 2 vols, Paris: Gallimard (Folio).

Beizer, J. (1995), *Ventriloquized Bodies: Narratives of Hysteria in Nineteenth-century France*, Ithaca, NY and London: Cornell University Press.

Benstock, S. (1987), *Women of the Left Bank: Paris, 1900–1940*, 2nd edn, London: Virago Press.

Bernikow, L. (1980), *Among Women*, New York: Harmony Books.

Bertaut, J. [1909], *La Littérature féminine d'aujourd'hui*, Paris: Librairie des Annales.

Biolley-Godino, M. (1972), *L'Homme objet chez Colette*, Paris: Klincksieck.

Birkett, J. (1986), *The Sins of the Fathers: Decadence in France 1870–1914*, London: Quartet Books.

Birkett, J. and Harvey, E. (eds), (1991), *Determined Women: Studies in the Construction of the Female Subject, 1900–1990*, London: Macmillan.

Bonner, F., Goodman, L., Allen, R., James, L. and King, C. (eds), (1992), *Imagining Women: Culture, Representations and Gender*, Cambridge: Polity Press.

Brown, C.L. and Olson, K. (eds), (1978), *Feminist Criticism*, New York and London: Scarecrow Press.

Cardellichio, F. (1977), 'Intorno a Charles-Louis Philippe. Marguerite Audoux: Poesia e Semplicità', *Misure Critique*, no. 78–9, Naples, pp. 65–86.

Carr, H. (1993), *From My Guy to Sci-Fi: Genre and Women's Writing in the Postmodern World*, London: Pandora.

Chadwick, W. (1985), *Women Artists and the Surrealist Movement*, London and New York: Thames and Hudson.

Chaponnière, C. (1989), *Le Mystère féminin: ou vingt siècles de déni de sens*, Geneva: Olivier Orban.

Cixous, H. (1975), 'Le Rire de la Méduse', *L'Arc*, no. 61, pp. 39–54.

Coquillat, M. (1988), *Romans d'amour*, Paris: Odile Jacob.

Cranny-Francis, A. (1990), *Feminist Fiction: Feminist Uses of Generic Fiction*, Cambridge: Polity Press.

Dejean, J. (1989), *Fictions of Sappho, 1546–1937*, Chicago and London: Chicago University Press.

Bibliography

——, (1991), *Tender Geographies: Women and the Origins of the Novel in France*, New York: Columbia University Press.

——, and Miller, N.K. (eds), (1988), *The Politics of Tradition: Placing Women in French Literature*, New Haven, CT: Yale University Press (Yale French Studies, no. 75).

Didier, B. (1982), *L'Ecriture femme*, Paris: Presses Universitaires de France.

Dijkstra, B. (1986), *Idols of Perversity: Fantasies of Feminine Evil in Fin-de-siècle Culture*, Oxford: Oxford University Press.

Dudovitz, R.L. (1990), *The Myth of Superwoman: Women's Bestsellers in France and the United States*, London and New York: Routledge.

Duffy, J. (1989), *Colette: Le Blé en herbe*, Glasgow: University of Glasgow French and German Publications (Glasgow Introductory Guides to French Literature, no. 8).

Dumont, M. (1985), 'Les Modèles de culture chez Marguerite Audoux, Charles-Louis Philippe et Emile Guillaumin', unpublished Ph.D. thesis, Paris X.

——, (1986), 'La Main à plume – la main à charrue: Charles-Louis Philippe et ses amis Emile Guillaumin et Marguerite Audoux', *Les Amis de Charles-Louis Philippe*, no. 44, pp. 17–29.

Eagleton, M. (ed.), (1986), *Feminist Literary Theory*, Oxford: Oxford University Press.

Evans, M.N. (1987), *Masks of Tradition: Women and the Politics of Writing in Twentieth-century France*, Ithaca, NY and London: Cornell University Press.

Ezell, M.J.M. (1993), *Writing Women's Literary History*, Baltimore and London: Johns Hopkins University Press.

Fallaize, E. (1993), *French Women's Writing: Recent Fiction*, London: Macmillan (Women in Society).

Flat, P. (1909), *Nos Femmes de lettres*, Paris: Perrin (Librairie académique).

Flieger, J.A. (1992), *Colette and the Fantom Subject of Autobiography*, Ithaca, NY and London: Cornell University Press.

Fowler, B. (1991), *The Alienated Reader: Women and Popular Romantic Literature in the Twentieth Century*, London and New York: Harvester/Wheatsheaf.

Francelisse (26 October 1924), 'Figures féminines: Zénaïde Fleuriot', *Le Petit Echo de la mode*, no. 43.

Gilbert, S.M. and Gubar, S. (1988), *No Man's Land: The Place of the Woman Writer in the Twentieth Century*, vol. 1, London and New Haven, CT: Yale University Press.

Green, M.J. (1986), *Fiction in the Historical Present: French Writers and the Thirties*, Hanover, NJ: University Press of New England.

Griffiths, R. (1966), *The Reactionary Revolution: the Catholic Revival in French Literature, 1870–1914*, London: Constable.

Guide des Prix Littéraires (1955), 2nd edn, Paris: Cercle de la librairie.

Heilbrun, C.G. (1989), *Writing a Woman's Life*, London: The Woman's Press.

Hewitt, L.D. (1990), *Autobiographical Tightropes*, Lincoln and London: University of Nebraska Press.

Higonnet, M. (ed.), (1987), *Behind the Lines: Gender and the Two World Wars*, New Haven, CT: Yale University Press.

Hirsch, M. (1989), *The Mother–Daughter Plot: Narrative, Psychoanalysis, Feminism*, Bloomington and Indianapolis: Indiana University Press.

Holmes, D. (1977), 'The Image of Women in Selected French Fiction of the Inter-war Period: a Study of Literary Responses to the Changing Role of Women, 1918–1939', unpublished Ph.D. thesis, University of Sussex.

——, (1991), *Colette*, London: Macmillan (Women Writers).

Huffer, L. (1992), *Another Colette: the Question of Gendered Writing*, Michigan: University of Michigan Press.

Jelinek, E.C. (ed.), (1980), *Women's Autobiography*, Bloomington and Indianapolis: Indiana University Press.

Ketchum, A.A. (1968), *Colette ou la naissance du jour: étude d'un malentendu*, Paris: Minard (Bibliothèque des lettres modernes, no. 12).

King, A. (1989), *French Women Novelists: Defining a Female Style*, London: Macmillan.

Kramarae, C. (April/June 1977), 'Perceptions of Female and Male Speech', *Language and Speech*, vol. 20, no. 2, pp. 151–61.

Lanoizelée, L. (1954), 'Marguerite Audoux', *Les Amis de Charles-Louis Philippe*, no. 12, pp. 157–9.

La Rochefoucauld, E. de (1969), *Femmes d'hier et d'aujourd'hui*, Paris: Grasset.

Léautaud, P. (1929), *Journal littéraire*, 19 vols, Paris: Mercure de France.

Leavis, Q.D. (1979), *Fiction and the Reading Public*, Harmondsworth: Penguin.

Le Fort, G. von (1948), *La Femme éternelle: la femme dans le temps, la femme hors du temps*, trans. Boccon-Gibod, A., Paris: du Cerf.

Lejeune, P. (1975), *Le Pacte autobiographique*, Paris: Le Seuil.

Lombroso, G. (1922), *L'Ame de la femme*, trans. Le Hénaff, F., Paris: Payot.

Mann, M.A. (1989), *La Mère dans la littérature française, 1678–1831*, New York: Peter Lang.

Marks, E. (1960), *Colette*, New Brunswick: Rutgers University Press.

——, and Courtivron, I. de (eds), (1981), *New French Feminisms: an Anthology*, London and New York: Harvester Press.

Maroussia (21 September 1924), 'Mathilde Alanic', *Le Petit Echo de la mode*, no. 38.

Maurras, C. (1925), *Romantisme et révolution*, Paris: Nouvelle Librairie nationale (Les Ecrivains de la Renaissance française).

Mercier, M. (1976), *Le Roman féminin*, Paris: Presses Universitaires de France.

Miles, R. (1987), *The Female Form: Women Writers and the Conquest of the Novel*, London and New York: Routledge.

Miller, N.K. (ed.), (1986), *The Poetics of Gender*, New York: Columbia University Press.

——, (1988), *Subject to Change: Reading Feminist Writing*, New York: Columbia University Press.

Moers, E. (1978), *Literary Women*, London: Women's Press, 1978.

Moi, T. (1985), *Sexual/Textual Politics*, London and New York: Routledge.

Mylne, V. (Spring, 1991), 'Martin du Gard, the *Roman dialogué*, and Gyp', *French Studies Bulletin*, no. 38, pp. 3–5.

Nochlin, L. (1988), *Women, Art and Power and Other Essays*, London and New York: Thames and Hudson.

Olivier-Martin, Y. (1980), *Histoire du roman populaire en France de 1840–1980*, Paris: Albin Michel.

Paizis, G. (1986), 'The Contemporary Romantic Novel in France', unpublished Ph.D. thesis, University of London.

Parker, R. and Pollock, G. (1987), *Old Mistresses: Women, Art and Ideology*, London: Pandora.

Pasquier, M.-C. (ed.), (1984), *Stratégies des femmes*, Paris: Tierce (Collection femmes et sociétés).

Pigot, G. (ed.), (February 1924), 'Etudes et articles sur Madame de Noailles et sur Henry Marx', *Le Capitole*.

Pingaud, B. (ed.), (1960), *Ecrivains d'aujourd'hui, 1940–1960*, Paris: Grasset.

Planté, C. (1989), *La Petite Sœur de Balzac: essai sur la femme auteur*, Paris: Le Seuil.

Praz, M. (1970), *The Romantic Agony*, trans. Davidson, A., Oxford: Oxford University Press.

Le Prix Fémina: ancien Prix Vie heureuse, Album du cinquantenaire, 1904–1954, (1954), Paris: Georges Lang.

Rachilde (September 1898), 'La Mort d'Antinoüs', *Mercure de France*, vol. 27, no. 105, pp. 638–46.

——, (1 March 1907), 'Revue de la Quinzaine', *Mercure de France*, vol. 66, no. 233, pp. 112–17.

——, (16 February 1912), 'Revue de la Quinzaine', *Mercure de France*, vol. 95, no. 352, pp. 813–17.

——, (1 July 1917), 'Revue de la Quinzaine', *Mercure de France*, vol. 122, no. 457, pp. 127–31.

Radstone, S. (ed.), (1988), *Sweet Dreams: Sexuality, Gender and Popular Fiction*, London: Lawrence and Wishart.

Radway, J.A. (1987), *Reading the Romance: Women, Patriarchy, and Popular Literature*, 2nd edn, London: Verso (Questions for Feminism).

Rigney, B.H. (1982), *Lilith's Daughters: Women and Religion in Contemporary Fiction*, London and Madison: University of Wisconsin Press.

Robbe-Grillet, A. (1961), *Pour un nouveau roman*, Paris: de Minuit.

Robinson, C. (1995), *Scandal in the Ink: Male and Female Homosexuality in Twentieth-century French Literature*, London: Cassell.

Roe, D. (1983), 'Autour de Charles-Louis Philippe – Marguerite Audoux – Les premiers écrits de Marguerite Audoux', *Les Amis de Charles-Louis Philippe*, no. 41, pp. 48–58.

——, (1987), 'Marguerite Audoux – un récit retrouvé: *Le Suicide*, 1913', *Les Amis de Charles-Louis Philippe*, no. 45, pp. 55–62.

Rosbo, P. de (1972), *Entretiens radiophoniques avec Marguerite Yourcenar*, Paris: Mercure de France.

Sartori, E.M. and Zimmerman, D.W. (eds), (1994), *French Women Writers*, Lincoln and London: University of Nebraska Press.

Saunders, J. (1991), *The Craft of Writing Romance: A Practical Guide to Writing Contemporary and Historical Romantic Fiction*, London: Allison and Busby.

Sauvy, A. (1986), 'La Littérature et les femmes' in Martin, H.J., Chartier, R. and Vivets, J.P. (eds), *Histoire de l'édition française: le livre concurrencé, 1900–1950*, Paris: Promodis, vol. 4, pp. 242–55.

Schor, N. (1993), *George Sand and Idealism*, New York: Columbia University Press.

Showalter, E. (1982), *A Literature of Their Own*, London: Virago Press.

——, (ed.), (1986), *The New Feminist Criticism: Essays on Women, Literature and Theory*, 2nd edn, London: Virago Press.

Smith, S. (1993), *Subjectivity, Identity and the Body: Women's Autobiographical Practices in the Twentieth Century*, Bloomington and Indianapolis: Indiana University Press.

Spender, D. (1989), *The Writing or the Sex?: or Why you Don't Have to Read Women's Writing to Know it's no Good*, New York: Pergamon Press.

Stubbs, P. (1981), *Women and Fiction: Feminism and the Novel 1880–1920*, 2nd edn, London: Methuen.

Suleiman, S.R. (1990), *Subversive Intent: Gender, Politics, and the Avant-garde*, Cambridge, MA and London: Harvard University Press.

Talva, F. (1982), 'La Grandeur de Marguerite Audoux', *Les Amis de Charles-Louis Philippe*, no. 40, pp. 52–9.

Thiesse, A.-M. (1984), *Le Roman quotidien: lecteurs at lectures populaires à la Belle Epoque*, Paris: Le Chemin vert.

Todd, J. (1988), *Feminist Literary History: a Defence*, Cambridge: Polity Press.

Toute l'Edition, (13 January 1934), 'Les Prix littéraires en 1933'.

Waelti-Walters, J. (1990), *Feminist Novelists of the Belle Epoque: Love as a Lifestyle*, Bloomington and Indianapolis: Indiana University Press.

Warner, M. (1985), *Alone of all her Sex: the Myth and Cult of the Virgin Mary*, 2nd edn, London: Picador.

Wilwerth, E. (1986), *Visages de la littérature féminine*, Brussels: Pierre Mardaga.

Woolf, V. (1977), *A Room of One's Own*, London: Grafton.

Yourcenar, M. (1962), *Sous bénéfice d'inventaire*, Paris: Gallimard.

——, (1971), *Discours de réception à l'Académie royale belge de langue et de littérature française*, Paris: Gallimard.

——, (1980), *Les Yeux ouverts, entretiens avec Matthieu Galey*, Paris: Centurion.

——, (1981), *Discours de réception de Madame Marguerite Yourcenar à l'Académie française et réponse de Monsieur Jean d'Ormessom*, Paris: Gallimard.

Index

Lightning Source UK Ltd.
Milton Keynes UK
UKOW022359291111

182842UK00007B/27/P